Privatizing Pensions

Privatizing Pensions

THE TRANSNATIONAL CAMPAIGN FOR SOCIAL SECURITY REFORM

Mitchell A. Orenstein

PRINCETON UNIVERSITY PRESS

PRINCETON AND OXFORD

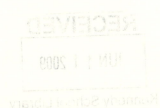

11575635

Copyright © 2008 by Princeton University Press

Requests for permission to reproduce material from this work
should be sent to Permissions, Princeton University Press

Published by Princeton University Press, 41 William Street,
Princeton, New Jersey 08540

In the United Kingdom: Princeton University Press, 6 Oxford Street,
Woodstock, Oxfordshire OX20 1TW

All Rights Reserved

Orenstein, Mitchell A. (Mitchell Alexander).
Privatizing pensions : the transnational campaign for
social security reform / Mitchell A. Orenstein.
p.   cm.
Includes bibliographical references and index.
ISBN: 978-0-691-13288-4 (hbk. : alk. paper) 978-0-691-13697-4 (pbk. : alk. paper)
1. Pensions—Government policy. 2. Social security—Government policy.
HD7091.O62   2008
331.25′22—dc22   2007048268

British Library Cataloging-in-Publication Data is available

This book has been composed in Sabon

Printed on acid-free paper. ∞

press.princeton.edu

Printed in the United States of America

10 9 8 7 6 5 4 3 2 1

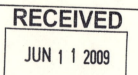

FOR MAX AND MAYA

Contents

Figures and Tables

Acknowledgments

I WISH TO THANK personally the numerous individuals and institutions who contributed in important ways to this project. The impetus for this book began with an invitation from Estelle James to join the Political Economy of Pension Reform Project in 1998. A research and writing grant from the John D. and Catherine T. MacArthur Foundation Program on Global Security and Sustainability in 2001–2002 enabled me to expand its scope. The Maxwell School of Syracuse University, the Belfer Center at Harvard's John F. Kennedy School of Government, and the Woodrow Wilson International Center for Scholars provided research leave and other support that facilitated the early stages of this project. Prom Peru provided funding and helped to organize a research trip to Peru that enabled me to learn more about Latin American reforms. I owe a special thanks to all of the above for sponsoring the initial phases of this work.

Over time, many scholars contributed to the realization of this project, and I deeply appreciate the time people have spent reading and providing comments on previous drafts, concepts, and ideas. The list of active scholars to whom I am deeply indebted includes Emily Andrews, Pablo Beramendi, Stephen Bloom, Michael Cain, Ilian Cashu, Jeffrey Checkel, Agnieszka Chłoń-Dominczak, Matthew Cleary, Linda Cook, Bob Deacon, Hilda Eitzen, Tracy Harbin, Petra Hejnova, Martin Hering, Richard Higgott, Robert Holzmann, Estelle James, Michael Lounsbury, Suzanne Mettler, Ramesh Mishra, Katharina Müller, Robert Palacios, J. David Richardson, Roberto Rocha, James Rosenau, Michał Rutkowski, Hans Peter Schmitz, Jeremy Shiffman, Diane Stone, David Strang, Brian Taylor, Hongying Wang, R. Kent Weaver, Mark Weiner, and Kurt Weyland, as well as participants in the Globalism and Social Policy Programme workshop at McMaster University in Hamilton, Ontario, in September 2004, a Syracuse University Department of Political Science manuscript seminar in October 2005, American Political Science Association annual meeting panels in Philadelphia and Washington, D.C., in 2003 and 2004, an ESPAnet conference in Bremen, Germany, in September 2006, and seminars at the Johns Hopkins School of Advanced International Studies, the University of Warwick Centre on Globalisation and Regionalisation, the University of Oxford Department of Social Policy and Social Work, and the Cornell University School of Industrial and Labor Relations in 2006 and 2007. I am grateful for these scholars' contributions and commentary.

I owe a particular debt to Kurt Weyland, Katharina Müller, and Sarah Brooks, distinguished scholars working on the political economy of pension reform. At numerous sessions at the American Political Science Association and other meetings over the years, I was able to learn from them about the spread of reform in Latin America and to exchange insights about emerging analytic approaches in the field. Working with my colleague Hans Peter Schmitz on our *Comparative Politics* article, "The New Transnationalism in Comparative Politics," helped me to think through ways to combine transnational and domestic politics explanations of an important global policy trend. Special thanks to Martine Haas for her love and support, her encouragement to finish this project, and for reading the manuscript multiple times. I also wish to acknowledge Syracuse University graduate students Ilian Cashu, Umut Ozkaleli, and Ruxandra Pond, Kelly Patterson of Cornell University, Elizabeth Isaman of Johns Hopkins University, and Viktoria Danics, who provided valuable research assistance at different stages of the project; I am very grateful for their energetic help. Any mistakes or misinterpretations in the text remain my own.

Finally, I would like to thank Chuck Myers for shepherding the book through the review process at Princeton University Press and the World Bank for granting me permission to publish revised versions of my earlier work as part of this book. A section of chapter 1 is based on Mitchell A. Orenstein, "Mapping the Diffusion of Pension Innovation," in Robert Holzmann, Mitchell A. Orenstein, and Michał Rutkowski, eds., *Pension Reform in Europe: Process and Progress* (Washington, D.C.: World Bank, 2003), including tables 1.1 and 1.2, and an earlier version of chapter 5 was previously published as "How Politics and Institutions Affect Pension Reform in Three Postcommunist Countries," World Bank Policy Research Working Paper 2310 (Washington, D.C.: World Bank, 2000).

Privatizing Pensions

Introduction

MOST AMERICANS KNOW of President George W. Bush's 2005 proposals for new pension reforms to privatize Social Security, but few are aware of a conversation that took place on September 11, 1997, between then Texas Governor Bush and José Piñera, a former Chilean Secretary of Labor and Social Security. Piñera is an internationally known advocate of private, individual pension savings accounts who led the effort to replace Chile's social security system with individual accounts in the late 1970s and early 1980s under the regime of General Augusto Pinochet. Pinochet's regime was highly controversial—as reviled by the left for its human rights abuses as it was lauded by the right for setting Chile on a course to strong economic growth and ultimately to democracy. After planning pension reform in Chile, Piñera made a career of spreading pension privatization throughout Latin America and worldwide. He met personally with numerous Latin American presidents as they contemplated reforms to their pension systems and advised organizations such as the World Bank and state officials in countries around the world (see Oravec 2006, 28–43, for a detailed account of his work in Slovakia). Piñera's meeting with President Bush took place at the governor's residence in Austin. Piñera portrayed pension privatization as a crucial element of an ownership society and helped to convince President Bush to embark on what now looks like a quixotic campaign to restructure Social Security and enact new pension reforms in the United States based on the Chilean model. Bush's campaign for pension privatization cost him a good portion of the political capital he gained in his 2004 re-election campaign and helped to send his popularity ratings plummeting in 2005. Given the high price he paid, it seems that President Bush acted out of conviction on this issue—a conviction that grew in part out of his meeting with Chile's pension reform guru.

This book analyzes the role of transnational policy actors in spreading pension privatization ideas and practices worldwide. Transnational policy actors are defined broadly as organizations (multilateral, state, or non-state) or individuals that seek to develop and advocate well-elaborated policy proposals in multiple national contexts. Through a detailed study of the privatization of state social security systems, this study seeks to answer several fundamental questions: Are national policy makers influenced by transnational policy actors who sell policy ideas from country to country? How much influence do transnational actors have on policies such as pension reform that have long been dominated by powerful domestic interest groups? If transnational actors are important, how are they important? What are the sources of their influence and when do they exert it?

This book addresses these questions by exploring the spread of pension privatization, which I also refer to as the new pension reforms, a set of policy reforms that have radically altered the post-war domestic social contract in more than thirty countries around the world. Pension privatization involves the partial or full replacement of social security type pension systems by ones based on private, individual pension savings accounts. Transnational policy actors, including the World Bank, the U.S. Agency for International Development (USAID), and other multilateral and bilateral aid agencies, transnational policy entrepreneurs, and expert networks, have been deeply involved in the development, diffusion, and implementation of these reforms. While pension privatization has affected mostly middle-income developing countries, these reforms also have been implemented in Sweden and the United Kingdom and proposed in the United States as well as in other developed countries.

Pension privatization represents an important example of the internationalization of public policy making in an area that I have had the opportunity to observe at close quarters over a number of years. In 1998, when I was invited to join a World Bank political economy research team investigating the politics of pension privatization in Europe, Central Asia, and Latin America, I found myself working among a core group of pension experts at the Bank who were advocating pension privatization in all corners of the earth. As a result of participating in a research project on the politics of pension reform worldwide, I had a unique opportunity to interview leading officials involved in pension reform processes in countries around the world. In 1999, I participated in a conference at the World Bank convened by then chief economist Joseph Stiglitz to critique and discuss the World Bank model for pension reform. This provided an opportunity to experience important debates within the Bank over pension privatization first hand. I later helped to edit a 2003 book, *Pension Reform in Europe: Process and Progress*, that brought together the results of a 2001 expert conference on the political economy of pension reform in Europe. This conference, sponsored by the World Bank, the International Institute for Applied Systems Analysis, and the government of Austria, was attended by scholars of the political economy of pension reform as well as pension officials from across the European Union 27 and a variety of international organizations. Between 1998 and 2004, I produced thorough case studies of pension reform in a number of Central and East European countries and Peru, conducting interviews with dozens of government officials, international advisers, and public interest group leaders. I also advised a Ph.D. dissertation by Ilian Cashu that undertook similar work in a different set of countries.

My close observation of the transnational campaign for pension privatization in the late 1990s and early 2000s seemed to contradict most of what I had been taught about the politics of welfare state development in graduate school. In political science, most accounts of welfare state development emphasize domestic political factors, such as labor mobilization and state political economic strategies. One school of thought suggests that domestic labor force mobilization encourages countries to develop welfare programs (Huber and Stephens 2001). Another emphasizes that welfare states represent national reactions to trends in the global economy. My own dissertation adviser at Yale, David R. Cameron, showed conclusively that smaller, trade-exposed states in Europe build larger welfare states to compensate workers for their greater vulnerability to external economic trends (Cameron 1978). This remains one of the classic statements in the literature and has been verified on a global scale by Rodrik (1998) and others. Pierson's (1994) work on path dependency suggests that national politics also determine the extent and nature of efforts to cut back or "retrench" welfare state institutions. This dovetails nicely with a prominent set of theories on "varieties of capitalism" that emphasizes that states choose a variety of different capitalist institutions and that these choices tend to constrain future behavior. Garrett (1998) and Swank (2002) further show that welfare state programs represent a state's reaction to international economic competition and that national, not international, politics drive their development and change.

Yet my observations of the campaign for pension privatization seemed to clash with this national perspective. I observed a core of pension reform advocates operating globally, advising top political leaders in dozens of countries around the world, and getting results. More than thirty countries around the world have implemented partial or full pension privatization, utterly changing preexisting systems and initiating a major path departure (Hering 2003) in welfare state structure for generations. In many cases, there appeared to be no domestic pressure or precedent for such changes; the ideas seemed to come from the outside, from these transnational actors. What was going on? Had the national perspective on welfare state development outlived its usefulness (Rodgers 1998; Clark and Whiteside 2003)? Had changes in the world system altered the politics of welfare state reform, making it more vulnerable to transnational influence? Was there a difference between the politics of reform in developed European countries, where most welfare state theories were hatched, and developing country welfare states that might be more vulnerable to transnational influences? Or was the transnational activity I observed simply a lot of sound and fury within international organizations that in the end signified nothing? How could one account for the new transnational politics of pension reform?

Transnationalization of Domestic Policy

In conducting further research for this project, I dug deeply into the growing literature on transnational public policy, a literature with roots in international relations theory and organizational sociology (DiMaggio and Powell 1983; Strang and Meyer 1993; Meyer et al. 1997; Strang and Soule 1998; Tolbert and Zucker 1983). In this literature, I found company with a group of scholars who argue that transnational and non-state actors are playing an increasing role in domestic policy development in countries around the world (Reinecke 1998). Pioneering works focused on transnational activist networks (Keck and Sikkink 1998), epistemic communities (Haas 1992), and a variety of other international actors that play a greater role than many scholars had previously thought in the making of domestic policy (Orenstein and Schmitz 2006).

National and transnational perspectives on policy are distinguished largely by their position on the autonomy of transnational actors. Transnationalist scholars believe that transnational actors and institutions play a fundamental and relatively autonomous role in policy making in multiple states (Reinecke 1998; Hewson and Sinclair 1999; Kaul et al. 1999; Stone 2003; Barnett and Finnemore 2004), while those working in a national politics or realist tradition see transnational actors as dependent on states that remain the final arbiters of policy decisions. Because the transnational actors that I observed seemed to have a great deal of control over their own agendas, I felt that it was important to integrate the transnational and national perspectives in order to explain the rise of pension privatization.

Ideas and Influence

If transnational actors are relatively independent, what is the source of their influence? One source is their normative and ideological influence. Transnational actors have become vessels for ideational influence on politics worldwide through the creation and diffusion of new policy ideas, norms, metrics, values, and technical expertise. Whereas many previous studies of transnational actors such as international organizations and multi-national companies have emphasized their ability to coerce countries into adopting certain policies, I emphasize their persuasive as well as coercive powers. It is often difficult to separate these two forms of influence, however. Following Jacoby (2004) and Epstein (2008), I question the usefulness of the "norms" versus "incentives" debate and instead focus on discerning specific mechanisms of influence that may combine both norms and incentives. Norms are defined here as principled ideas about how policies should be designed. Norms and ideas are said to be "new" to the extent they have not been previously adopted in a particular domestic context.

Studies that emphasize incentives and coercion, rather than norms and ideas, tend to start from a hard rational or materialist perspective on politics that assumes that the interests of policy actors are fixed. Therefore, actors must be coerced to change their positions. Ideational approaches to politics tend to start from the assumption that rational actors face considerable uncertainty about their interests or how to pursue them; their rationality is bounded by the limits of information and cognition (March and Simon 1993; Druckman 2004). Introducing new normative ideas or information can cause actors to reshape their policy preferences. As a result, interests are less stable than hard rationalists would predict (Druckman 2004). As U.S. Senator John Kerry famously said of a supplemental funding bill for the Iraq war, "I actually voted for the $87 billion before I voted against it." Likewise, in my study of pension privatization, I found many actors who initially opposed such reforms but later ended up supporting them because they gained new information or were persuaded of the normative case for these reforms by reform advocates. Some were also offered selective incentives to encourage compliance. As Juliet Johnson (2008) points out, some actors may be more influenced by norms, while others may only be influenced by material incentives. The most powerful transnational actors use a range of both ideational and material resources as circumstances permit. They apply all the tools they have in an effort to pursue their policy agendas to a successful conclusion.

In presenting an argument that combines both ideas and incentives, this work follows Blyth (2002), who argues that norms and ideas partly constitute actors' interests and policy preferences. Blyth suggests that ideas can help to reduce uncertainty in times of crisis by providing problem definitions that enable actors to understand the situation that they are in. Second, ideas can make collective action and coalition building possible by allowing agents to redefine their interests under conditions of uncertainty and to link up with other actors behind new programs. Third, ideas can be weapons in the struggle over existing institutions. They can help to delegitimize current institutions and the norms and ideas of opponents as well as justify policy preferences of reform advocates. Fourth, ideas can act as blueprints for new institutions, suggesting policies and methods of achieving stated goals. Finally, ideas can make institutional stability possible by providing justifications for institutions' existence and the policies that they transmit (Blyth 2002, 34–41).

Transnational actors, including international organizations, transnational non-governmental organizations (NGOs), expert networks, and individual policy entrepreneurs, have become leading sources of policy norms and ideas in countries worldwide in areas that often exceed their original mandate. Their ability to exercise normative influence depends on their organizational and institutional legitimacy. Barnett and Finnemore (2004) argue that transnational actors often have a unique authority to pursue their goals. International organizations often possess "delegated authority" explicitly granted by countries to pursue certain goals legitimately. Transnational actors may also have extraordinary "moral authority" by virtue of their mission to pursue legitimate and seemingly disinterested moral objectives, such as poverty alleviation or environmental protection. Finally, transnational actors often enjoy "expert authority" and are recognized as storehouses of global expertise in certain areas. Each of these sources of authority enables transnational actors to persuade other actors and organizations to accept their desired policy norms and ideas and join them in global campaigns.

RESHAPING PREFERENCES

In exerting their independent influence on policy, transnational actors use a variety of means to reshape the preferences of transnational and national policy makers. In the pension reform arena, transnational actors have successfully advocated new pension reforms that radically alter existing social contracts and affect the core material interests of numerous groups in society. Transnational actors have often been the first in a country to advocate pension privatization. By forging alliances with like-minded domestic partners (Jacoby 2008) and working with them to change the preferences of key veto players and other social groups, transnational actors have been highly successful in spreading pension privatization. Transnational actor interventions cannot explain all adoptions or non-adoptions of pension privatization. However, their role is crucial to explaining a very high proportion of existing cases. Transnational actors have been particularly influential in middle-income developing countries where domestic policy-making resources are relatively weak and the willingness to undertake risky reforms is relatively high. In such contexts, decision makers have been highly influenced by transnational actors, their normative policy ideas and campaigns, their legitimacy, and their resources.

THEORETICAL CONTRIBUTION

This book contributes to two literatures. On the one hand, it contributes to the literature on welfare state development and change by introducing a transnational dimension. It challenges the national perspective that has dominated the welfare state literature and argues that major changes in welfare state structure cannot be explained without reference to transnational actors and their policy campaigns. On the other hand, this work contributes to the growing literature on transnational policy and global governance by providing a detailed study of the transnationalization of domestic politics. It does so in a core area of "domestic" policy that is thought to be subject primarily to domestic pressures. This study is based on a conceptual model of transnational actor influence presented in chapter 3 that provides new insight into the interface between transnational and domestic policy and is supported by extensive case study research. It seeks to transcend the debate between rationalist and constructivist scholarship by exploring mechanisms of transnational influence that combine both material and ideational elements.

CONCEPTUAL AND METHODOLOGICAL ISSUES

Any study of the impact of transnational actors on policy faces serious conceptual and methodological challenges. While political science has refined methods for studying nation-state behavior over decades, methods for studying transnational actor influences on domestic policy remain in their infancy. One of the most fundamental problems in analyzing the role of transnational actors is that scholars often differ in their definitions of transnational actors. Many scholars tend to equate transnational influence with that of a single organization or type of transnational actor, such as international financial institutions, transnational activist networks, or policy entrepreneurs, while ignoring other transnational actors that may operate in the same policy domain or regime. Narrow definitions of transnational actors may obscure their influence. Similarly, scholars have a tendency to miscode organizations and individuals with deep transnational ties and activities as purely domestic. This suggests that identifying and distinguishing transnational and national actors can be a difficult analytical task. A second analytical difficulty is that since transnational actors necessarily act in partnership with domestic policy makers, it can be difficult to untangle the influence of transnational actors from that of the domestic actors they advise. This study provides evidence that transnational actors have not only been deeply involved in partnerships with domestic proponents of the new pension reforms, but they have been instrumental in putting these reforms on the policy agenda in country after country and providing the technical support to enable their domestic allies to push reform through. Finally, transnational actors tend to work together in global policy campaigns to advance policy reforms in multiple countries, often creating donor councils or meetings to divide responsibilities. This makes it difficult to analyze the impact of individual transnational actors.

Perhaps the best way to address these conceptual complications is to study the behavior of transnational actors in global policy campaigns through a case study method that allows close observation of the full range of transnational actors involved, their interventions in particular countries, and internal decision making. Such a method avoids making false or stylized assumptions about who transnational actors are and what they do. It allows for a more nuanced analysis of transnational actor behavior and its effects in particular countries and organizations. However, case study analysis also has its faults, creating the potential for observer bias and limited generalizability of findings. To remedy these problems, this study supplements case studies of organizations and country experiences with an analysis of the full range of transnational actor interventions in the pension reform arena. This is pursued through a comprehensive study of World Bank documents as well as through representative case studies of the full range of reform and non-reform cases. While most studies of the new pension reforms (Madrid 2003; Weyland 2005) and indeed of other transnational policy campaigns (Jacoby 2004; Kelley 2004) take either a regional approach or select a small number of representative cases for analysis, this study provides a comprehensive analysis of transnational actor involvement in the rise and spread of pension privatization worldwide. It studies their involvement over a broad scope of time, from agenda setting to implementation, and of space, from Central and Eastern Europe to Latin America to Asia to Africa. Taking such a comprehensive approach provides new perspective on the importance of transnational actors in setting domestic policy.

GENERALIZABILITY

How easy is it to generalize conclusions about pension privatization to other areas of transnational public policy? Every policy area is somewhat unique. Developments may vary according to the nature of policy issues, the types of organizations involved in them, their motivations, and the intensity of domestic politics (Jacoby 2004). Nelson (2004) has argued that the pension policy area is unusual in being dominated by a clear set of ideas promoted by a powerful international organization and its partners. Other policy areas may display greater fragmentation in transnational policy advice, less focused transnational campaigns, and more resistant domestic politics. No doubt, the campaign for pension privatization has been particularly well organized and successful.

Yet in some ways, the campaign for pension privatization is typical of transnational policy making in the world today. Pension privatization typifies the spread of a vision of economic "best practice" by transnational actors. These reforms provide a technocratic fix to the problem of population aging and are part of a broader set of neoliberal economic policies that have spread worldwide (Biersteker 1990; Graham 1998; Campbell and Pedersen 2001; Fourcade-Gourinchas and Babb 2002). In nearly every public policy sphere, a variety of types of organizations—state, non-state, and intergovernmental—are active in global policy campaigns advocating economic reform solutions. They interact with domestic partners in broadly similar ways and seek to have similar impacts on national policy in multiple jurisdictions. While specific features of the pension privatization process are no doubt distinctive, the general model of the transnational policy process presented here should be relevant to other areas.

Pension privatization provides an appropriate and extremely useful venue in which to test the influence of transnational actors on national policy. Previous studies have attempted to evaluate transnational actor influence in areas where one would expect to find it. Environmental policies, for instance, often have externalities that invite transnational actor interventions (Young 1999). Human rights policies similarly carry strong rationales for transnational intervention, such as the potential for civil conflict that may spill over into international conflict (Risse et al. 1999). By contrast, pension policies of states rarely create problems that require outside actor interventions. Transnational actors do not need to get involved in national pension reforms because of their interests. They do so rather because of their normative beliefs and organizational priorities.

Pension privatization does not provide an open and shut case for demonstrating the impact of transnational policy actors. Quite the opposite, pension policy provides a particularly challenging venue for testing the influence of transnational actors, where most previous literature has emphasized domestic causes. To demonstrate that transnational actors have had a significant influence on the spread of the new pension reforms is to show that transnational actors have a far greater influence than is commonly understood on many areas of "domestic" politics. If transnational actors are important in shaping national pension policies, the domestic models of the policy process that are commonly employed to explain policy in a wide range of areas require substantial revisions. The findings of this study thus hold important implications for public policy research more generally.

METHODS AND CHAPTER PLAN

This book employs detailed case study and process-tracing methods to provide a comprehensive analysis of transnational actor influence on the development, transfer, and implementation of new pension reform ideas in more than thirty countries around the world. It draws on a wealth of primary data from original documents and more than seventy interviews with key transnational and national policy makers to investigate the nature of transnational actors' role and the extent of their influence in spreading pension privatization. It analyzes the transnational campaign for the new pension reforms across a wide scope of time and space, from the development of new pension reform ideas in Chile and the United States to the implementation of these reforms in places as diverse as Sweden, Kazakhstan, Nigeria, and Taiwan.

I provide a particularly in-depth look at the activities of the World Bank and USAID in spreading pension privatization worldwide. The internal decision making of these organizations has an important influence on policy in multiple countries. Therefore, I aim to provide a careful analysis of their activities, the sources, mechanisms, and modes of their influence, and how their agendas change over time. I analyze the interactions between international and domestic actors in the new pension reforms through three detailed case studies of reform as well as shorter critical case studies of reform processes around the globe. I also take special care to analyze any negative cases, scouring the globe for instances of reform without transnational actor involvement and transnational actor campaigns that have failed to produce reform. By following these diverse lines of analysis, providing a wealth of new data, and taking a comprehensive approach across time and space, this study provides new insights into the extent and limits of transnational actor influence.

Chapter 1 explores the global spread of pension privatization and compares this to the spread of first pension systems worldwide in the period 1889–1994. This analysis suggests that pension privatization has spread more rapidly, particularly between regions of the world. The spread of pension privatization follows typical diffusion patterns and does not occur only in countries with similar demographic structures, economic conditions, or politics. Instead, pension privatization occurs in countries with very young and very old populations, with relatively small and very large shares of GDP spent on state pensions, and diverse political histories and institutional legacies. This analysis sets the stage for questioning the national approach to welfare state development and investigating the role of transnational actors.

Chapter 2 examines the methodological problems facing studies of the impact of transnational actors on policy reform and uses a study of World Bank project documents and USAID records to show that the impact of these transnational actors may be greater than previously recognized. This chapter presents the results of a comprehensive study of World Bank project documents that shows that most current measures of World Bank influence are insufficiently precise. Because the World Bank does not advise adoption of pension privatization in all countries in which it works, studies that assume the Bank provides consistent advice tend to underestimate World Bank influence. The World Bank may be influential in determining which countries do not reform, as well as those that do. This chapter suggests a research approach based on closer attention to the internal dynamics of transnational policy actors themselves, their policy objectives, and the specific mechanisms of their influence.

Chapter 3 presents a general model of the influence of transnational actors on domestic policy processes. This chapter explores the internal decision-making process of transnational actors involved in pension privatization, particularly the World Bank and USAID. It shows how internal processes have influenced the policies of these organizations and cooperation among them in the global campaign for pension privatization. Building on the bureaucratic approach to international organizations (IOs) (Barnett and Finnemore 2004), this chapter emphasizes that transnational actors use different modes and mechanisms of influence that vary across time, according to the phase of the policy process. It provides an explanation of why domestic policy actors seek out transnational partners and provides an analytic framework for explaining the distinctive influence of domestic and transnational actors on policy.

Chapter 4 provides a narrative account of the global campaign for pension privatization, a "campaign coalition" (Tarrow 2005), led by a loose network of transnational policy actors. It documents the launch of pension privatization in Chile in the early 1980s and the subsequent campaign by Chilean advisers to spread these reform ideas to Latin America and beyond. It shows how in 1994, the World Bank took a leadership role in the emerging transnational coalition for pension privatization with the publication of *Averting the Old Age Crisis*, which created a cadre of reform advocates at the Bank. Other organizations joined in the advocacy coalition for pension privatization, including USAID, the Organization for Economic Cooperation and Development (OECD), and the regional development banks. Typically, multiple transnational actors were involved in pension privatization advocacy work in each adopting country.

Chapter 5 analyzes the influence of transnational actors on domestic pension privatization policy through detailed case studies of reform in three postcommunist countries, Hungary, Poland, and Kazakhstan. Drawing on the veto players approach developed by Tsebelis (2002), this chapter explores the interactions of transnational "proposal actors" and domestic "veto" and proposal actors, providing a clear analytical approach to understanding the nexus of transnational and domestic political decision making. The chapter shows that transnational policy actors form strategic partnerships with domestic veto and proposal actors and seek to alter their political capabilities and preferences. It finds that transnational policy actors have used five main mechanisms of influence: conferences and seminars that teach officials about pension privatization, grants and loans to fund the activities of reform teams led by domestic partners, pre-reform technical assistance, technical assistance in reform implementation, and career path incentives for reform officials.

Chapter 6 tests the influence of transnational actors using a global sample of reforming and non-reforming countries. This chapter presents data on international policy actor involvement in pension privatization worldwide. It creates a typology of different levels and forms of transnational policy actor influence and presents case studies that explore examples of each type. These case studies show that transnational policy actor influence has been ubiquitous in the spread of pension privatization. Despite numerous claims, it finds only a handful of cases where transnational policy actor efforts to facilitate adoption of the new pension reforms have clearly failed (Korea, Slovenia, and Venezuela). Several OECD countries have implemented partial pension privatization without substantial transnational policy actor involvement. However, transnational policy actors have been directly involved in policy transfer and implementation in most reforming countries. This suggests that transnational policy actors are necessary to explaining the global spread of pension privatization, particularly in the middle-income and poorer developing countries where the World Bank and USAID focus their activity. Chapter 7 draws conclusions and implications from this research. The Appendix provides a primer on new pension reform issues and definitions.

CONCLUSION: THREE PUZZLES

The spread of pension privatization in a diverse group of countries and the seemingly ubiquitous involvement of transnational actors in this process raises three important analytical puzzles. First, what role do transnational actors play in the diffusion of policy trends from country to country? Second, how do we understand the influence of transnational actors when they necessarily interact with national actors in policy development? And third, when and under what conditions do transnational actors influence policy areas like pension reforms that are subject to strong domestic interests? In posing and answering these questions in a comprehensive study, this book highlights the growing transnationalization of domestic politics through an analysis of the global campaign for pension privatization, one of the most significant economic policy trends of our time that reshapes the intergenerational social contract in countries worldwide.

Chapter One

The Rise of Pension Privatization

Pension privatization, involving the creation of state-mandated systems based on individual, private pension savings accounts, is not just a revolution in the postwar social contract. Its adoption in more than thirty countries worldwide provides a leading example of the transnationalization of domestic policy. This chapter charts the rise of pension privatization and shows that standard explanations based on economic conditions and domestic politics cannot fully explain the rapid diffusion of these new pension reforms. Comparing the spread of pension privatization to the spread of first pension systems in countries worldwide shows that the diffusion of pension privatization has been faster, particularly between regions of the world. This chapter begins by providing a brief explanation of the content of pension privatization, which I also will refer to as the new pension reforms, for reasons discussed below, indicating that they constitute a revolution in welfare state provision by upending the social security contract. Subsequent chapters show transnational actors to be deeply implicated in this global policy trend and seek to evaluate their impact and modes of influence.

Because pension systems often constitute a major part of the total economy, between 10 and 15 percent of gross national income in most OECD countries (though less in many developing countries; see Table 1.4 below), the design of pension systems has a major impact on growth, wages, redistribution, and the economy as a whole. As used in this book, the term "pension privatization" is defined as the partial or full replacement of social security pension systems with ones based on private, individual, pension savings accounts. More broadly, the term "pension privatization" or "the new pension reforms" refers to a range of policy changes that apply neoliberal principles of individualism over collectivism and reliance on private markets over public management in pension provision. Mandatory systems of private, individual pension savings accounts are the centerpiece of this effort, but the new pension reform trend also includes (1) notional defined contribution (NDC) pension systems that create individual accounts without private management or prefunding, (2) reforms that emphasize reliance on more private and less public sources of pension provision, and (3) reforms that limit state-managed social security systems to a poverty-reduction role. Definitions of these terms are provided in a separate appendix that provides a guide to the highly technical terminology and debates of pension economics. The key variable analyzed in this book is the implementation of pension systems based on private pension savings accounts, similar to the reforms President Bush proposed for the United States in 2005. Pension privatization revolutionizes the organization of pension systems worldwide and radically alters the cost-benefit calculation for individuals in every country where it has been introduced, with enormous distributive consequences.

Assessing the Impact of Pension Privatization

In any country considering pension privatization, one of the key questions is, who stands to lose and who to gain? How do we assess the impact of these reforms? In all countries of the world, pension privatization is controversial because it has distributive consequences. Social security pension systems redistribute income from one age group to another, from one income group to another, and from one time of life to another. Therefore, participants and beneficiaries may be highly attuned to the economic consequences of these systems. What are the distributive consequences of pension privatization?

Assessing the impact of a transition from a social security pension system to one based on individual private accounts requires evaluating general features of both systems and specific features of a country's pension system and economy. This section provides a general comparison of both systems. In the most general terms, pension privatization is based on a neoliberal philosophy that emphasizes individual rights, economic growth, and private property. Pension privatization individualizes risk and returns in pension systems, relies on private rather than public management, and depends on pre-funding rather than the "pay-as-you-go" (PAYG) financing that is characteristic of social security systems. Social security systems tend to redistribute income with a view toward poverty relief and risk pooling, rather than strictly individual income-related benefits, though they often combine both elements, and some social security type systems redistribute less than others. The following paragraphs compare the method of financing of the two systems, their administration, and their benefit structure to provide a clear framework for explaining their relative advantages and disadvantages. Note that many reforming countries do not completely replace their social security system, but only reduce it while introducing a private pension system. Because mixed systems share characteristics of both, differences are somewhat less stark than a side-by-side comparison would suggest (see the Appendix for further elaboration).

The most fundamental difference between privatized and social security pension systems concerns the method of financing. Pension privatization creates "funded," "defined contribution" pension systems to fully or partially replace social security and other "defined benefit" systems (such as those provided in the past by many U.S. and European employers). Under pension privatization, individuals save for retirement in pension savings accounts, putting aside a proportion of their income in a personal investment account. This money earns a return on investment; retirement income is determined by lifetime earnings, lifetime savings, and investment return. Systems that rely on such accounts are called "funded" systems because the funds to sponsor retirement are actually on hand at the outset of retirement. They are called "defined contribution" systems because the rate of contribution to the funds is often set by law, but the benefit level is not. By contrast, social security systems are "defined benefit" systems funded on a "pay-as-you-go" basis. They pay a benefit that is defined in advance and often calculated to replace a certain proportion of a person's income. Such systems are typically financed on a rolling basis, such that retirement benefits in a particular year are paid (mostly) by workers' payroll taxes in that year. Money to pay benefits comes in on a "pay-as-you-go" or rolling basis, rather than up front, as in a "funded" system. While "pay-as-you-go" financing is typical for defined benefit systems, some social security type systems also rely to a greater or lesser extent on general tax revenue and partial funding, such as the U.S. Social Security Trust Fund. Differences between "pay-as-you-go" and "funded" financing mechanisms are portrayed in figure 1.1.

A second key difference displayed in the figure is that privatized pension systems rely on private management of retirement investments, rather than state management. Social security systems are usually managed by a social security administration that collects revenues and disburses retirement income. In developed countries, administrative costs of such a system are very low, due to administrative centralization and economies of scale. However, advocates of pension privatization argue that the returns on investment in a publicly managed system often are also low, because state agencies lose out on better returns available in private markets and tend to use social security funds to achieve state objectives, rather than maximizing the returns for retirees (Iglesias and Palacios 2001). For instance, excess social security revenues may be used to finance a budget deficit or to support construction of low- and middle-income housing, earning returns that do not match those available in private markets. Advocates of social security systems point out that the higher returns in private investments often are offset by high administra-

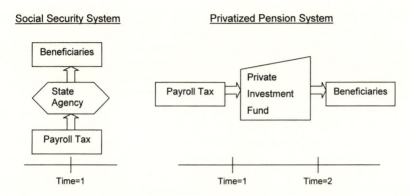

Fig. 1.1. Financing of social security and privatized pension systems.

tive fees charged by private management companies (Fultz 2004). Indeed, many of the first countries to implement pension privatization have come under extensive criticism for the exorbitantly high fees charged for pension fund management (Gill et al. 2005). In at least some countries, there is evidence that income from private accounts has been negative initially when corrected for fees and inflation (Fultz 2005). Another important aspect of private management of pension funds is that pension savings become available for investment. Advocates of the new pension reforms emphasize that these reforms create a pool of domestic capital that can be used to finance economic growth, increasing incomes of all citizens, including retirees.

Finally, pension privatization tends to individualize risks and returns in contrast to social security systems that rely on a more collective ethos and a variety of forms of redistribution. Basically, an individual account under pension privatization is individually owned and controlled. Amounts deposited come from a person's income; investment returns are guided by an individual's lifetime investment decisions. In such a system, returns are individualized, rather than based on a formula that tends to redistribute funds from one person to another. Those that have longer work histories, higher incomes, greater savings rates, and/or better investment decisions have more prosperous retirements. Individuals with shorter work histories, lower pay levels, lower savings rates, and/or poorer investment strategies do worse. Risks are also individualized. If you suffer an incapacitating illness or injury, your investment account stops growing. On average, those who benefit from individual pension savings accounts tend to be younger workers (with longer periods of investment return), more highly paid workers, and people with less interrupted work histories. Critics of pension privatization argue that these reforms tend to favor those who need protection the least. Proponents argue that some component of pension savings needs to be earnings-related and that individual accounts are the most efficient form of earnings-related pension benefits. Redistributive and minimum guarantee pensions can be provided by the state in other ways, in combination with a system of individual, private accounts. In fact, systems of individual, private pension savings accounts are often combined with a state commitment to a minimum, flat, or redistributive social security system that provides a safety net for the poor. Thus, pension benefits move toward a liberal model (Esping-Andersen 1990), where the state provides only a basic pension and the funded system provides more individualized, earnings-related benefits.

Who benefits from pension privatization and who loses? The answer depends on the nature of the previous system and the parameters of the reform, such as changes to the retirement age, the level of complementary state benefits, or the impact of the pension system on economic growth. It is difficult to make a blanket statement about reform beneficiaries without analyzing the particular elements of a reform proposal in a particular context. For instance, in a country with a well-managed public pension system, private management may seem risky and expensive, whereas in a country that has suffered from corruption and poor administration in its social security system, private management may seem more transparent and fair. In the absence of detailed information about domestic context and exact reform proposals, debate over pension privatization has tended to revolve around its purported benefits in theory.

In theory, advocates of pension privatization argue that everyone benefits. Retirees benefit from higher returns on their pension investments than those paid in state-managed systems. The whole economy benefits from the creation of vast pools of pension savings, which can be used for productive domestic investment. This increases economic growth and raises incomes of employees and retirees alike. Private management of benefits provides more reliable administration with greater choice for individuals. Detractors argue that the rich benefit more than the poor from pension privatization. Poor and middle-income people may lose benefits available in the social security system, while pension privatization disproportionately benefits those with consistent, well-paying jobs. Meanwhile, investment companies make tremendous returns from the fees on individual, private accounts, reducing pension benefits proportionately.

Analysis of costs and benefits, however, ultimately depends on specific features of system design that are difficult to generalize. In the United States, for instance, President George W. Bush's reforms were perceived by opponents as an attempt to dismantle the social security system and impoverish those relying on it, while providing only a limited private benefit that is already accessible to most people through 401(k) plans and other vehicles. In Sweden, trade unions and the social democratic party supported privatizing a small part of their heavily income-related benefit system (Palme 2003; Anderson and Immergut 2007). In Chile, many people believe that pension privatization benefited the whole economy by providing a pool of investment capital, despite high administrative fees. Others believe that public sector workers, who previously benefited from special pension provisions, however, lost benefits overall (Mesa-Lago 2002). That pension privatization can be implemented in such diverse countries as Chile and Sweden, albeit to different extents and in different ways, suggests that it is a highly contextual judgment whether and how pension privatization benefits or harms different groups in society. What is clear, however, is that such a radical reorganization of pension provision is bound to have a substantial redistributive impact on society and therefore to be highly controversial under any circumstances.

DIFFUSION OF PENSION PRIVATIZATION

What makes the new pension reforms remarkable is not only their revolutionary character, but also the speed with which they have spread from country to country, being implemented in more than thirty countries around the world with diverse histories, economies, pension systems, and levels of economic development. This speed and the inherently international nature of this policy trend is most evident when we compare the spread of pension privatization to another event: the spread of first pension systems worldwide, starting with Germany in 1889. This section analyzes the spread of pension privatization in the context of the literature on the diffusion of innovations. It allows us to better understand what is unique about the spread of pension privatization.

Diffusion of First Pension Systems (1889–1994)

Table 1.1 charts the first adoption of a pension system in the 152 countries listed in the U.S. Social Security Administration's publication *Social Security Programs throughout the World* (SSPTTW), 2001 Web edition. Each country is coded according to the International Standards Organization's (ISO 3166) two-letter country codes, also available on the Web. This provides a standard plot size for each country on the chart, enabling

TABLE 1.1
Global Spread of First Pension System Adoption, 1889–1994

	Europe/ Antipodes/ US/CA	Latin America/ Carribean	Africa/ Middle East	Asia
1880s	*DE*			
1890s	*DK, NZ*			
1900s	*AU, AT, BE, IS, UK,* CS, IE			
1910s	*FR, IT, NL, SE,* ES, RO, *LU*			
1920s	*CA,* BG, EE, HU, LV, LT, PL, RU, YU, GC	CL, EC	ZA	
1930s	*FI, NO, US,* GR, PT	BR, PE, TT UY, BB		
1940s	AL, CH, TR, MC	AR, CO, CR, DO, GY, MX, PA, PY, VE	DZ, GQ	*JP*
1950s	CY, JE, LI, MT, SM	BO, HN, JM, NI, SV, BS	BI, EG, IQ, GN, IR, IL, LY, MU, MA, RW, SY, ZR, CV	CN, ID, IN, MY, PH, SG, LK, TW
1960s	AD	CU, HT, GT, BM, GD	BF, CM, CF, CG, CI, ET, GA, GH, KE, LB, MG, ML, MR, NE, NG, SA, TG, TN, TZ, UG, ZM	NP, VN, FJ, FM, MH, PW
1970s		AG, BZ, DM, LC, VC, VG	BJ, TD, JO, KW, LR, OM,	
1980s		GM, YE	PG, VU	
1990s		ZW, BW	TH	

TABLE 1.1 (*cont'd*)
Global Spread of First Pension System Adoption, 1889–1994

Source: SSPTW.

Bold indicates country with over 1m population in 2000. Italics indicate high-income OECD country. Countries listed alphabetically by category.

ISO 3166 country codes: AD = Andorra, AG = Antigua, AL = Albania, AR = Argentina, AT = Austria, AU = Australia, BB = Barbados, BE = Belgium, BF = Burkina Faso, BG = Bulgaria, BH = Bahrain, BI = Burundi, BJ = Benin, BM = Bermuda, BO = Bolivia, BR = Brazil, BS = Bahamas, BW = Botswana, BZ = Belize, CA = Canada, CF = Central African Republic, CG = Congo, CH = Switzerland, CI = Ivory Coast, CL = Chile, CM = Cameroon, CN = China, CO = Colombia, CR = Costa Rica, CS = Czechoslovakia, CU = Cuba, CV = Cape Verde, CY = Cyprus, DE = Germany, DK = Denmark, DM = Dominica, DO = Dominican Republic, DZ = Algeria, EC = Ecuador, EE = Estonia, EG = Egypt, ES = Spain, ET = Ethiopia, FI = Finland, FJ = Fiji, FM = Micronesia, FR = France, GA = Gabon, GC = Guernsey (my abbr.), GD = Grenada, GH = Ghana, GM = Gambia, GN = Guinea, GR = Greece, GT = Guatemala, GQ = Equatorial Guinea, GY = Guyana, HK = Hong Kong, HN = Honduras, HT = Haiti, HU = Hungary, ID = Indonesia, IE = Ireland, IL = Israel, IN = India, IQ = Iraq, IR = Iran, IS = Iceland, IT = Italy, JE = Jersey (my abbr.), JM = Jamaica, JO = Jordan, JP = Japan, KE = Kenya, KI = Kiribati, KR = South Korea, KW = Kuwait, LB = Lebanon, LC = St. Lucia, LI = Liechtenstein, LK = Sri Lanka, LR = Liberia, LT = Lithuania, LU = Luxembourg, LV = Latvia, LY = Libya, MA = Morocco, MC = Monaco, MG = Madagascar, MH = Marshall Islands, ML = Mali, MR = Mauritania, MT = Malta, MU = Mauritius, MX = Mexico, MY = Malaysia, NE = Niger, NG = Nigeria, NI = Nicaragua, NL = Netherlands, NO = Norway, NP = Nepal, NZ = New Zealand, OM = Oman, PA = Panama, PE = Peru, PG = Papua New Guinea, PH = Philippines, PK = Pakistan, PL = Poland, PT = Portugal, PW = Palau, PY = Paraguay, RO = Romania, RU = Russia, RW = Rwanda, SA = Saudi Arabia, SB = Solomon Islands, SC = Seychelles, SD = Sudan, SE = Sweden, SG = Singapore, SM = San Marino, SN = Senegal, ST = St. Tome & Principe, SV = El Salvador, SY = Syria, SZ = Swaziland, TD = Chad, TG = Togo, TH = Thailand, TN = Tunisia, TR = Turkey, TT = Trinidad and Tobago, TW = Taiwan, TZ = Tanzania, UG = Uganda, UK = United Kingdom, US = United States, UY = Uruguay, VC = St. Vincent, VE = Venezuela, VG = Virgin Islands, VN = Vietnam, VU = Vanuatu, WS = Samoa, YE = Yemen, YU = Yugoslavia, ZA = South Africa, ZM = Zambia, ZR = Zaire, ZW = Zimbabwe.

visual quantitative comparisons.[1] Countries are listed alphabetically by decade of adoption and region. Three of these regions are purely geographical, while the first one, "Europe/Antipodes/US/CA" is more cultural and economic in nature. It represents the high-income OECD nations minus Japan, including the developed countries that have long been governed by settlers of European origin. These countries can be considered a single cultural/economic region for purposes of policy innovation and dissemination.

Note that by focusing on the first establishment of national pension systems, table 1.1 aggregates pension systems of three distinct types. Scholars of European welfare states have identified two ideal types of first pension systems in Europe (Bonoli 2000, 10–11). First, Bismarckian social insurance systems emphasized providing workers a pension that reflected a proportion of their income while in work. Second, the Danish (1891) or later Beveridgean (U.K.) model was essentially an extension of the poor laws and emphasized poverty relief and the maintenance of basic minimum living standards. Financing of these two types of systems differed in accordance with these goals. While the Bismarckian system relied on contributions from employers, employees, and the state, Denmark's 1891 system was general tax–financed. Italy, France, the United States, and Switzerland initially followed the social insurance model, while New Zealand, the United Kingdom, Sweden, and Norway initially followed the Danish poverty prevention tradition. These two pension system types were quite different at first, but most national systems tended to adopt elements of both over time (Bonoli 2000, 12). The result is that now "the guarantee of a minimum income combined with a partial replacement of earnings is a common feature to almost all pension systems," though Germany and Denmark remain exceptions to this rule (Bonoli 2000, 13). A third distinct type of pension system was the national provident fund, a central savings fund administered by the government that generally provided a lump-sum benefit at retirement. These were popular in Asian and some African countries under British colonial influence (Gillion et al. 2000, 501). As this brief discussion suggests, a more detailed analysis of the spread of each of these types of systems internationally might yield an even more nuanced view of patterns of cultural and regional patterns of

---

[1] I use the date of adoption of pension systems reported in SSPTTW, which is usually the date of first pension legislation, rather than the date of reform implementation. These dates are used advisedly, because in several countries legislation was adopted well before pension systems were actually created. Other anomalies may exist. However, I did not attempt to correct the SSPTTW data, but instead chose to use a single, standardized source to avoid errors of bias, as has long been the standard in the field (Collier and Messick 1975, 1302).

pension system diffusion. However, the aggregate analysis presented here focuses on arguably the main event in this first phase of reform, the establishment of a broad, national pension system where none existed before.

What can we learn about the diffusion of pension systems from an analysis of the spread of first pension systems? First, that pension systems have spread globally in ways that are consistent with previous studies of the diffusion of policy innovations. Studies of the diffusion of innovations (Walker 1969; Mintrom 1997; Berry and Berry 1999; True and Mintrom 2001) have focused on four explanatory variables—state wealth, size, industrialization, and geographic region—to explain the spread of policy reforms, all of which seem to be confirmed in table 1.1. First, the level of economic development is highly correlated with the timing of adoption of pension systems (Walker 1969; Collier and Messick 1975). The average high-income OECD country established a pension system approximately forty years before the average non-OECD country. Collier and Messick (1975), however, note that later adopters tend to adopt at much lower absolute levels of economic development. Second, country size is also an important factor. In each region of the world, large countries innovated before very small countries (countries with a population of less than one million in 2000 are in lightface type in table 1.1). Also, the regional variable is a strong influence. Pension reform diffused for thirty years in Europe and the high-income OECD countries before being adopted in Latin America. African and Asian countries innovated approximately twenty years later than their counterparts in Latin America, creating a regional cascade effect. One reason for this, of course, is the earlier history of statehood in Latin America.

The international diffusion of pension systems follows the usual distribution pattern for adoption of innovations, in which a few countries are pioneers, followed by a steep increase in the rate of adoption, with a few laggards filling in at the end. When charted cumulatively, this results in an S-curve. The curve resembles similar curves for policy diffusion among the fifty United States, which have been explained by the confluence of a large number of inter-related factors that determine policy adoption and the learning and interaction effects between adopting states (Gray 1973, 1175–1176).

Finally, an intra-regional cascade effect is visible, particularly through the graphic analytical approach in table 1.1. In Europe, it is notable that the first countries to innovate were mainly Anglo-Saxon, with Germany the policy creator. Denmark and New Zealand came next, followed by Australia, Austria, Belgium, Iceland, United Kingdom, Ireland, and Czechoslovakia, which was at that time part of the Austro-Hungarian Empire. Next came the Mediterranean and Romance countries, France, Italy, Spain, Luxembourg, and Romania, along with the Netherlands and Sweden, during the 1910s. This suggests that reform ideas travel by some type of social learning process in regard to regional examples (Dolowitz and Marsh 1996; 2000). Pension innovation spread to Eastern Europe only in the 1920s, after thirty years of gestation in the West (see also Collier and Messick 1975, 1312, for a graphic display), coinciding with the creation of the International Labour Organization (ILO), which pressed for social reforms to combat socialism.[2]

At the same time, the innovation jumped to the leading Latin American countries, including Chile and Brazil, in the 1920s and 1930s. Most large, industrialized Latin American countries adopted it by the end of the 1940s, while the smaller and Caribbean countries followed in the 1950s and 1960s. Only small island nations were left in the 1970s. In Africa, too, the first innovator was South Africa, while the first in Asia was Japan in the 1940s. In both continents, most of the major countries followed within twenty to thirty years, then the smaller and more peripheral states. This intra-regional cascade strengthens the finding that wealth, size, and region are key factors determining policy innovation, with the larger, wealthier, more industrialized countries in each region innovating first, and reform then spreading out concentrically from core to periphery. This underlines the global importance of a relatively stable set of regional policy innovation leaders, just as Walker (1969) found in the United States. In sum, an analysis of the spread of first pension systems suggests

---

[2] Note that cross-regional diffusion of pension reform accelerated after the Second World War. Why? It bears noting that this coincided with a major push by the International Labour Organization (ILO) to make social security systems part of the post-war peace (Craig and Tomeš 1969; Collier and Messick 1975, 1305). After the Second World War, the ILO set international norms for social protection, generated reform templates, provided consultants and consulting advice, and used high-level regional meetings to popularize its ideas and approach. Most crucially, the ILO's 1944 Declaration of Philadelphia won the endorsement of the major victorious powers as the template for a new, peaceful, post-war social order. It makes for impressive reading, and was clearly highly inspirational at the time. The Declaration of Philadelphia was significant not only for its high-level political support (ILO 1944; 1945), but for the way it set strong, highly idealistic, yet widely agreed and specific norms for full employment and social protection after the war (ILO 1944), though it should be noted that pension provision was only one element in this vision. The ILO energetically distributed information about its program through high-profile regional meetings that brought top political leaders together to discuss specific social policy challenges (ILO 1948a; 1948b). The ILO provided legislative reform templates, in the form of detailed information about reform programs in leading states (Schoenbaum 1945), regular updates about the progress of reform in different countries (Acosta 1944), and reports by regional leader countries about their activities in spreading reform in their region (Altmeyer 1944). The ILO also provided expert advice to reforming countries (Acosta 1944, 46), including actuarial support. All in all, it played a major role in the establishment of social welfare states, articulating a global vision for social reform and creating momentum behind the first phase of pension system adoption in countries around the world.

TABLE 1.2
Global Spread of Pension Privatization, 1981–2004

	Europe/ Antipodes/US/CA	Latin America/ Carribean	Africa/ Middle East	Asia
1980s	UK	CL		
1990s	SE, HU, PL	AR, CO, PE, UY, BO, MX, SV		KZ, CN
2000s	BG, HV, LV, EE, LT, MK, RU, SK, RO	CR, DO, NI	NG	HK, UZ, TW

Sources: Palacios and Pallarès-Miralles 2000 and own data.
Notes: Bold indicates country with over 1 million population in 2000. Italics indicates high-income OECD country. Countries listed alphabetically by category.
For ISO 3166 country codes, see table 1.1.

that pension policies have typically spread globally in a manner consistent with the theories of the diffusion of policy innovations.

Diffusion of Pension Privatization (1981–2041)

Has the spread of pension privatization mirrored the adoption of first pension systems? Or are there differences in innovation patterns? A key difference between the spread of first pension systems and pension privatization is the speed of diffusion, particularly inter-regional diffusion. In the case of first pension systems, it took more than thirty years before pension reform spread out of Europe. In the case of pension privatization, mandatory funded pension systems spread from Chile to Central and Eastern Europe in the following decade, before most capitalist core countries had adopted the innovation. This suggests that policy ideas travel faster now, perhaps due to global communications channels and, I hypothesize, the increasingly powerful role transnational actors play in spreading policy ideas across regional boundaries. Current trends indicate that this second phase innovation is spreading at approximately double the rate of the first wave. If this trend continues, it will take approximately sixty years for pension privatization to sweep the globe (1981–2041), with the peak occurring somewhere in the 2000s and 2010s.

Factors explaining the spread of pension privatization are explored later in this chapter. However, table 1.2 is suggestive of a few observations. First, regional example appears to be an important predictor of pension reform adoption (Brooks 2002; 2005; Weyland 2004; 2005).

Latin America, which had the initial example of Chile, experienced the most rapid spread of pension privatization during the second decade of reform. Factors such as language and perceived social similarities probably facilitated this. Similarly, it is notable that the first two decades of pension privatization were concentrated in Latin America and post-communist Europe. Asia's reform wave began with Kazakhstan and Hong Kong in 1998 and 2000. Nigeria adopted pension privatization in 2004 (and South Africa was in the process of doing so in 2007), signaling the start of a reform wave in Africa. Diffusion effects appear far more likely to occur within regions, while inter-regional diffusion remains more difficult. Other regional effects are also evident. One particularly striking feature is that the first reforming regions in the first phase were the same as the first reforming regions in the second phase—Europe/Antipodes/US/CA and Latin America—although in a somewhat different order. In addition, it is interesting that Chile was not only the first country to adopt the new pension reforms, but also the first Latin American country to adopt a pension system in 1924. This suggests that there may be enduring reasons that particular regions and countries are more innovative in social policy (Walker 1969).

Types of Pension Privatization

While diffusion studies focus on the formal adoption of policy reforms in different countries, it is important to explain not only the adoption but the type of reforms adopted in each country and the ways they have been adapted to local circumstances (Hall 1989; Jacoby 2004). There are a number of ways to distinguish between new pension reform types; however, a primary one is whether the system completely replaces the former social security system or not. Pension privatization comes in three basic forms: substitutive, mixed, and parallel (Mesa-Lago 1998). Substitutive reforms phase out traditional social security systems and replace them with systems based on private individual accounts. Mixed reforms reduce the size of social security systems, while adding complementary systems of private, individual accounts. Parallel reforms introduce systems based on private, individual accounts but give participants a choice of which system to contribute to and benefit from. Countries have adopted pension privatization on each of these three models (see table 1.3).

Countries have also differed in the size of contributions to the mandatory, private system, as well as in their administration, coverage, and other variables (see appendix table A1.1). Therefore, studies of the political economy of pension reform have tended to address two dependent variables: whether or not countries adopt pension privatization and the form

TABLE 1.3
Types of Pension Privatization

Substitutive	Mixed	Parallel
Chile 1981	Sweden 1994	UK 1986
Bolivia 1997	China 1997[a]	Peru 1993
Mexico 1997	Hungary 1998	Argentina 1994
El Salvador 1998	Poland 1999	Colombia 1994
Kazakhstan 1998	Costa Rica 2001	Uruguay 1996
Dom. Rep. 2001	Latvia 2001	Estonia 2001
Nicaragua 2001	Bulgaria 2002	Lithuania 2002
Kosovo 2001	Croatia 2002	
Nigeria 2004	Macedonia 2002	
Taiwan 2004	Russia 2002	
	Slovakia 2003	
	Romania 2004	
	Uzbekistan 2004	

Sources: Orenstein 2000; Madrid 2003; Müller 2003; Palacios 2003; Fultz 2004; Holzmann and Hinz 2005; Becker et al. 2005; Orifowomo 2006; and Web resources from the World Bank, IDB, and USAID. Note that reforms sometimes characterized as "mixed" in the literature are coded here as "parallel," particularly Argentina and Estonia. In mixed systems, participation in both private pension accounts and the social security system is mandatory for new entrants to the labor force, while in parallel systems, participants continue to have the choice to participate solely in the former pay-as-you-go system. Uruguay is a borderline case, because private pensions are mandatory for the top 10 percent of earners, those who earn six times the minimum wage, but voluntary for those below this income threshold. Ecuador's legislated but not yet implemented system is similar (Gill et al. 2005, 22–28). One could include in this chart countries that have converted optional, funded, occupational pension systems to mandatory ones, including the Netherlands, Switzerland, Denmark, and Iceland; however, this process differs from the partial or full replacement of social security pension systems, so these countries are left out of the narrow definition of pension privatization applied here, though they are part of the broader new pension reform trend. Australia, which implemented mandatory private pensions without a prior history of social security, also is a special case.

[a] China began to legislate a mixed system in 1997, but it had not been fully implemented as of 2007 (Piggott and Bei 2007, 7–10).

or extent of their adoption. Both are important to any careful analysis of the spread of these revolutionary social programs. This book focuses on the decision to adopt or not to adopt pension privatization, while also considering the ways countries adapt these new pension reforms to domestic circumstances.

EXPLAINING THE SPREAD OF PENSION PRIVATIZATION

What causal factors lie behind the spread of pension privatization? As Huntington (1991) points out, there may be many explanations for why countries adopt a policy or practice at the same time. First, there could be a *single cause*, such as some important external factor or event. Second, it could be a case of *parallel development*, such that all countries experience similar changes in key independent variables around the same time. Third, they could be affected by *snowballing* or demonstration effects, meaning that countries are affected by policy adoption in neighboring or peer countries. Finally, the effect could be caused by a *prevailing nostrum*, such that despite different trends in different countries, they all adopt the same response that reflects prevailing views. Huntington's discussion is useful in suggesting multiple possible explanations. However, Huntington's general discussion has little to say about the exact sorts of reasons for choosing the new pension reforms.

Analysts of the political economy of pension reform have identified three types of explanations for the spread of pension privatization: (1) economic, demographic, and fiscal factors, (2) domestic political factors, and (3) social learning between countries as well as from transnational actors. Explanations based on economic factors and domestic politics support the notion of "parallel" development of pension privatization in different countries, whereas explanations based on social learning emphasize the existence of a "prevailing nostrum" or "snowballing" effects between countries. In the following section, I show that the spread of pension privatization cannot be fully explained by explanations that rely on "parallel development" alone and that transnational actors play a major role in facilitating social learning between countries.

Economic and Demographic Factors

Most analysts agree that economic and demographic factors provide one set of reasons why countries choose to implement pension privatization. As advocates of pension privatization have pointed out (World Bank 1994), these reforms respond to a worldwide trend toward demographic aging that is present to a greater or lesser extent in most countries. Social security–type systems face particular difficulties coping with the increased proportion of retirees in country populations. Why? Because social security systems rely on the contributions of current workers to fund current retirees, when the proportion of retirees to workers increases, the system faces fiscal stress. Ultimately, benefit levels become more difficult to sustain, forcing governments to increase social security taxes or to reduce benefits. Pension privatization offers a way out of this dilemma by linking retirement income to individual earnings and savings. This insulates an individual's pension income from the impact of demographic trends that may be favorable or unfavorable at different points in time. Demographic change thus helps to explain why countries opt for pension privatization to solve long-term fiscal problems generated by population aging. Without demographic aging and the fiscal difficulties aging imposes on social security–type systems, pension privatization would be unlikely if not unimaginable.

However, demographic aging provides an incomplete explanation of the pension privatization trend. If countries adopted pension privatization solely to address demographic aging, one might expect the pressure for pension privatization to be highest in countries where demographic aging is most advanced and where fiscal crises of pension systems are most proximate and severe (Brooks 2005, 281–282). However, that has not always been the case. Table 1.4 shows that pension privatization has not been adopted by countries with the oldest populations nor by those countries with the largest pension burden as a proportion of GDP. Instead, pension privatization has been adopted by a wide range of countries with very different economic circumstances, some with large pension systems that pose a major burden on national budgets, some with very small pension systems, some with old populations, and some with relatively young populations. While statistical analyses have shown that age and economic circumstances do play a role in pension decisions, the wide variety of economic circumstances in countries that have adopted these reforms suggests that economic factors alone do not tell the whole story (Bonoli 2000; Weaver 2003, 21).

One reason is that the same economic factors that dictate a response to demographic change also make it difficult to implement pension privatization. Brooks (2002), for instance, found that countries with a high public debt to GDP ratio are less likely to privatize their pension systems because they cannot afford the transition costs associated with the reform. Wealthy countries with aging populations and large pension systems may have greater incentives to change systems, but less ability to do so, while younger, poorer countries have smaller incentives, but greater ability to change. Another reason is that objective pressures to reform do not always result in reform. Countries appear to adopt pension privatization for a variety of different reasons, although at a similar point in time, suggesting that the mechanism of adoption may be Huntington's "prevailing nostrum," whereby a certain policy fix tends to be adopted to address a wide range of domestic conditions.

TABLE 1.4
Public Pension Expenditures as a Percentage of GDP (OECD, Latin America, Central and Eastern Europe, and former Soviet Union)

Country	Year	Pension expenditures	Proportion of population age 60+ (2000)
Italy	1997	17.6	24.1
Uruguay	1996	15.0	17.2
Austria	1997	14.4	20.7
Poland	1995	14.4	16.6
Slovenia	1996	13.6	19.2
Switzerland	1997	13.4	21.3
France	1997	13.4	20.5
Belgium	1997	12.9	22.1
Cuba	1992	12.6	13.7
Germany	1997	12.1	23.2
Finland	1997	12.1	19.9
Greece	1997	11.9	23.4
Luxembourg	1997	11.9	19.4
Croatia	1997	11.6	20.2
Sweden	1997	11.1	22.4
Netherlands	1997	11.1	18.3
Spain	1997	10.9	21.8
United Kingdom	1997	10.3	20.6
Latvia	1995	10.2	20.9
Portugal	1997	10.0	20.8
Brazil	1997	9.8	7.8
Czech Republic	1999	9.8	18.4
Hungary	1996	9.7	19.7
Slovakia	1994	9.1	15.4
Denmark	1997	8.8	20.0
Macedonia	1998	8.7	14.4
Ukraine	1996	8.6	20.5
Norway	1997	8.2	19.6
Belarus	1997	7.7	18.9
Moldova	1996	7.5	13.7
United States	1997	7.5	16.1
Bulgaria	1996	7.3	21.7
Lithuania	1998	7.3	18.6
Estonia	1995	7.0	20.2
Japan	1997	6.9	23.2
New Zealand	1997	6.5	15.6

TABLE 1.4 (*cont'd*)
Public Pension Expenditures as a Percentage of GDP (OECD, Latin America, Central and Eastern Europe, and former Soviet Union)

Country	Year	Pension expenditures	Proportion of population age 60+ (2000)
Kyrgyz Republic	1997	6.4	9.0
Argentina	**1994**	**6.2**	**13.3**
Australia	**1997**	**5.8**	**16.3**
Chile	**1993**	**5.8**	**10.2**
Iceland	1997	5.7	15.1
Russia Fed.	**1996**	**5.7**	**18.5**
Canada	1997	5.4	16.7
Uzbekistan	**1995**	**5.3**	**7.1**
Romania	**1996**	**5.1**	**18.8**
Albania	1995	5.1	9.0
Kazakhstan	**1997**	**5.0**	**11.2**
Ireland	1997	4.6	15.2
Panama	1996	4.3	8.1
Costa Rica	**1997**	**4.2**	**7.5**
Armenia	1996	3.1	13.2
Tajikistan	1996	3.0	6.8
Georgia	2000	2.7	18.7
Venezuela	2001	2.7	6.6
Azerbaijan	1996	2.5	10.5
Bolivia	**1995**	**2.5**	**6.2**
Nicaragua	**1996**	**2.5**	**4.6**
Turkmenistan	1996	2.3	6.5
El Salvador	**1996**	**1.3**	**7.2**
Peru	**1996**	**1.2**	**7.2**
Colombia	**1994**	**1.1**	**6.9**
Ecuador	1997	1.0	6.9
Guyana	1996	0.9	6.9
Dominican Republic	**2000**	**0.8**	**6.6**
Guatemala	1995	0.7	5.3
Honduras	1994	0.6	5.1
Belize	1992	0.2	6.0
Mexico	**2000**	**n.a.**	**6.9**

Source: Palacios and Pallarès-Miralles 2000, with updates from World Bank Pensions Web site, www.worldbank.org/pensions (accessed June 20, 2005), and United Nations (2002).

Bold type indicates countries adopting pension privatization.

Domestic Politics

An alternative set of theories emphasizes that pension reform decisions can be explained by domestic politics. Indeed, pension systems have often been seen as an essential element of modern political economy and state-craft. German Chancellor Otto von Bismarck designed the first national pension system in the 1880s in order to counter the rise of socialist parties and to tie workers' allegiances to the nation-state. His idea was "to bribe the working classes, or, if you like, to win them over, to regard the state as a social institution existing for their sake and interested in their welfare" (quoted in Dawson 1912, 11). Since the time of Bismarck, scholars of the welfare state have argued that welfare state policies represent a national response to problems of industrialization, the growing power resources of the working class (Huber and Stephens 2001), openness to international trade (Cameron 1978), or previous domestic policies (Pierson 1994; Bonoli 2000). This long literature on welfare state development and retrenchment suggests that pension and other welfare state systems rise and fall for reasons of national, not international, politics. Similarities among countries are evidence of "parallel development," resulting from similar domestic political and economic circumstances.

Scholars have sought to apply these domestic politics frameworks to explain the spread of pension privatization . Brooks has hypothesized that because pension privatization is expected to be highly controversial, more inclusive democracies may have a more difficult time passing such reforms. Conversely, authoritarian regimes with more concentrated authority may enact more radical change. This hypothesis is supported by the observation that pension privatization was first enacted under the authoritarian regime of General Augusto Pinochet in Chile. If true, countries with a smaller number of veto actors and lower civil rights may enact reforms more readily (Brooks 2005, 283). This would be consistent with theories of path dependency that suggest that policies tend to empower interest groups that may have an interest in perpetuating existing policies. To the extent that these interest groups are stronger, they would be more influential in fighting pension privatization. Explanations based on the domestic politics of path dependency suggest that the likelihood of a country adopting a policy depends greatly on the constellation of internal political forces (Myles and Pierson 2001). Again, the logic of domestic politics explanations suggests that if countries adopt similar reform, it is because of similar domestic political circumstances, an instance of "parallel development."

While domestic political factors surely influence the adoption of the new pension reforms, they cannot tell the whole story. First, there is the wide diversity of countries that have adopted pension privatization. It would be hard to argue that domestic political factors are the main determinants of reform when countries as different as Taiwan, Nigeria, Peru, and Sweden have adopted them. Second, domestic political explanations must contend with considerable evidence that reform decisions are linked closely with neighboring countries' decisions. As shown above, in both the waves of first pension system adoption and adoption of pension privatization, substantial regional effects are visible. Countries appear to observe and learn from one another, adopting pension reforms, to some extent, according to a "snowball" type pattern. They adopt pension privatization at a similar time to their neighbors, regardless of substantial political and economic differences. To the extent that domestic policy makers rely on neighboring country experiences or "prevailing nostrums" rather than simply obeying the influence of domestic interest groups, sources other than domestic politics must be identified. This does not mean that domestic political factors (and economic factors) are not important. The case studies in chapter 5 below show a variety of domestic political and economic forces to be co-determinants of reform. Rather, the argument is that we must investigate other, less traditional reform dynamics to explain the similar outcomes in more than thirty diverse countries that have adopted pension privatization thus far.

Social Learning

While economic, demographic, and domestic politics explanations of pension reforms emphasize a model of "parallel development," patterns of policy diffusion have raised questions about social learning and the highly visible activities of international actors in the pension privatization debate in country after country. The fact that countries with such widely disparate circumstances have adopted pension privatization suggests that any explanation based on "parallel development" alone should be suspect. However, while most scholars agree about the influence of economic, demographic, and domestic political explanations, they disagree on the role of social learning and the influence of transnational actors in facilitating social learning.

Essentially, there are two distinct social learning perspectives. One might label the first "non-hierarchical" social learning. This perspective suggests that while international organizations have had a moderate influence on pension reform processes, the major factor explaining the spread of the new pension reforms is non-hierarchical social observation of neighboring country reform experiences. Much of this literature emphasizes the processes by which other Latin American countries learned from the Chilean reform model (Brooks 2005; Weyland 2005). A second perspective is the "hierarchical" social learning model, which suggests that transnational actors play a major role in persuading or empowering like-minded domestic interest groups to enact pension privatization (Orenstein 2000; Madrid 2003; Hasselman 2006).

Scholars who emphasize non-hierarchical social learning emphasize the importance of domestic reformers and their choices. Weyland (2005; 2007), in the most sophisticated statement of this position, focuses on the cognitive heuristics of domestic leaders in choosing pension reform designs. He argues that when faced with the need for reform, domestic leaders begin to search for solutions to their problems. Rather than searching for policy options rationally and systematically, policy makers tend to use shortcuts based on the availability of reform models and their perceived effectiveness in peer countries. Policy makers' use of heuristics of availability, anchoring, and representativeness helps to explain why geographically clustered sets of countries tend to adopt relatively similar reforms. They learn from their neighbors. In this non-hierarchical social learning perspective, transnational policy actors are perceived to have some impact on domestic reform processes, but more weight is placed on the influence of neighboring countries, such as Chile.

By contrast, Madrid (2003, 46) suggests that "the international financial institutions, especially the World Bank, have played a particularly important role in promoting pension privatization; as a result pension privatization has been more common in those countries where the World Bank has more influence." This perspective can be labeled "hierarchical" social learning. Countries and country officials learn not only from peer countries, but also from international organizations and transnational actors that exert influence in a variety of domestic settings. Such learning is "hierarchical" insofar as it operates through various forms of incentives and influence, rather than free borrowing.

Most scholars of the political economy of pension reform argue for the influence of a combination of variables, and few would suggest that only one variable matters. For instance, Madrid (2003) finds support for economic crisis factors and domestic politics as well as for the role of transnational actors in spreading reform ideas (45–58).

However, most scholars working in this area argue for the primacy of domestic over international factors in explaining the spread of pension privatization. Brooks (2005, 273) argues that "pension reform decisions remain subject to domestic political and economic considerations, including demographic pressures, financial costs and incentives to reform, and constraints delimited by the political institutions in each nation." Müller (1999; 2000) finds international financial institutions (IFIs) to play a role in spreading pension privatization, but only to the extent that countries' economic circumstances make them dependent on IFIs. She argues that the leverage of the IFIs is greater when a country's "general level of external indebtedness" is higher (Müller 2003, 8). Yang (2004) shows that transnational policy actors were unable to force pension privatization on Korea in the midst of the global financial crisis of 1997–1998. Yang concludes that domestic reformers are necessary to reform, while transnational policy actors are not. Tavits (2003) argues that Estonia adopted pension privatization without transnational policy actor advice. This brief review shows that although analysts tend to incorporate the role of transnational policy actors to some extent, there is considerable disagreement on when, how, and how much effect they have. Among these scholars, there is widespread agreement about the ubiquity of transnational policy actors' involvement in pension reform processes worldwide, but disagreement about their importance.

Conclusions

Pension privatization has spread to more than thirty countries around the world following a diffusion pattern that differs substantially from the diffusion of first pension systems. Differences concern the speed of diffusion and particularly the speed of cross-regional diffusion. Most scholars emphasize economic conditions and domestic political factors to explain the adoption and development of pension reforms. Yet it is impossible to ignore the role of transnational actors in the spread of pension privatization. A new wave of literature has grown to address it, with scholars reaching divergent conclusions. The following chapters suggest that current research methods have tended to underestimate the influence of transnational actors (chapter 2) and provide a new model of their influence in the spread of pension privatization (chapter 3).

CHAPTER TWO

Evaluating the Impact of Transnational Actors

TRANSNATIONAL ACTORS have been directly involved in the enactment of pension privatization in countries around the world, but have they been important or only tangentially involved? How does one evaluate their impact and limits? This chapter evaluates the existing literature on pension privatization and finds substantial conceptual and methodological problems with the way transnational actor influence is assessed. It presents the results of a comprehensive study of World Bank project documents that suggests that transnational actors may have a greater impact than previously assumed. This study goes beyond previously published works by showing that the World Bank has not advocated pension privatization in every country in which it worked. Analyzing World Bank advice in a new way and looking at cases of non-reform as well as reform, this chapter contributes to a better understanding of transnational actor roles and policy impacts. It suggests a need to improve our conceptualization and method of study of transnational actors, what they do, and their interventions in domestic political contexts.

While many previous studies have been regional or selective in scope, assessing the importance of transnational actors in the diffusion of pension privatization requires taking a global perspective and considering the full range of cases, including (1) any cases where transnational policy actors were involved and pension privatization was implemented, (2) any cases where transnational policy actors were involved but pension privatization was not implemented, and (3) any cases where transnational policy actors were not involved but pension privatization was implemented. Up to the present time, however, most analyses of the impact of transnational policy actors on pension reform have had a country or regional focus (Orenstein 2000; Ney 2003; Weyland 2004; 2005; Hasselman 2006). Only a few studies have used a cross-regional (Müller 2003) or global (Madrid 2003; Brooks 2005) sample. This chapter looks at the complete universe of cases and addresses a central issue of debate: how to assess the impact of transnational policy actors? It suggests that a first step is to develop a clearer model of what transnational actors do.

Problems of Conceptualization and Measurement

Despite considerable disagreement about the role and influence of transnational policy actors in the new pension reforms, data and methods for studying transnational policy actor involvement have been surprisingly weak and biased against findings of transnational actor influence. The approaches adopted by many studies tend to underestimate the impact of transnational actors in three ways. First, scholars have differed in their identification of transnational actors. Some actors, such as Chilean economists and reform advocates, have been defined as domestic or regional actors in some studies and as transnational reform advocates in others. Second, scholars have often made simplistic assumptions about what transnational actors want, rather than studying the complex decision-making processes of transnational actors and their differentiated advice in different countries. Third, most studies focus on the World Bank and ignore the ways that transnational actors cooperate in campaign coalitions, sometimes magnifying their influence beyond that exerted by any one organization. This chapter illustrates these issues and presents empirical evidence to support more extensive findings of transnational actor influence on pension choices in developing countries than has been recognized to date. After reviewing the theoretical issues surrounding who transnational actors are, what they want, and how they cooperate with other organizations to achieve their goals, this chapter defends a broad definition of transnational actors and presents research results that emphasize the importance of systematic attention to these factors.

Who Transnational Actors Are

One of the most surprising issues of the current literature on the political economy of pension reform has been the difficulty of coding policy actors as "transnational" or "domestic." Some studies that have found a low influence for transnational actors have simply coded them as local when they may be more appropriately seen as transnational. For instance, Tavits's (2003) work on policy learning in Latvia and Estonia argues that Latvia reproduced international models in its pension reforms under the influence of the World Bank, while Estonia designed its program independently. Estonia reportedly rejected resources from the World Bank "because of the reluctance to create any kind of dependency on international organizations" (2003, 655). Both countries adopted similar new pension reforms around the same point in time. Lindemann (2004, 12), a prominent international adviser on pension reform, likewise reports that Estonia's pension reforms were "home grown."

Other sources contradict the view that Estonia designed its reforms independently of transnational influence. The Republic of Estonia's (2000) Memorandum of Economic Policies to the International Monetary Fund (IMF) shows that Estonia promised the IMF to implement pension privatization quickly, while receiving technical advice from the World Bank. World Bank evaluations also show deep involvement of World Bank advisers in Estonia (World Bank 2005, 30). Estonian researchers Kulu and Reiljan (2004, 32) report that "an international seminar was organized in Estonia in 1999 including World Bank staff and other pension experts, where specific design issues of the Estonian pension system were discussed." Toots (2002) points out that Estonia not only benefited from international financial institutions' support for its pension privatization process, but also that the "independent" policymakers whom Tavits (2003) suggests were carefully insulated from World Bank influence in fact had close ties to the World Bank. Of the five Estonian members of the Commission on Social Security Reform that designed the Estonian reforms, one (A. Hansson) had worked as an expert of the World Bank, and a second (M. Jesse) had been a local counselor to the World Bank and later coordinator of the World Bank/Estonian Health Policy Project (Toots 2002, 2–3).

Weyland's (2005) study on pension reforms in Latin America raises similar definitional quandaries. While Weyland argues that international financial institution (IFI) influence has been limited, he places a great deal of explanatory weight on the role of Chilean policy advisers in Latin American reforms. Yet Chilean advisers may also be regarded as transnational policy entrepreneurs. After pension privatization in Chile in the early 1980s, Chilean Secretary of Labor and Social Policy José Piñera began a long career advising countries that were considering replacing their social security systems with private, individual pension savings accounts. According to Piñera, he has worked in twenty-three countries that adopted pension privatization (interview, January 2006) in Latin America and Europe. Piñera has also worked closely with the World Bank and USAID in the provision of pension policy advice. While not an IFI, Piñera can undoubtedly be seen as a transnational policy entrepreneur with a global policy agenda. Thus, constraining the definition of transnational actors to IFIs alone excludes consideration of transnational actors that have been important in spreading reform in Latin America, such as Chilean policy entrepreneurs.

Such disparities indicate the difficulties comparative politics scholars face in coding "domestic" versus "transnational" actors. In part, differences stem from the mental model of the reform process that researchers apply. To a researcher attuned to the study of domestic politics, it may appear that Estonian reformers are domestic actors, while a student of transnational politics and policy may be sensitized to the ways that Estonian reformers are connected to transnational networks. Such networks can be difficult for scholars to recognize, because they depend on consulting and other relationships that may not be immediately visible. For instance, IFIs may co-opt local actors as one mode of influence, offering national officials a high-paying career route to policy advisory capacities in other countries, a lucrative stint in Washington, or speaking engagements at instructional conferences (Hunter and Brown 2000, 119). IFI incentives, which are often studied at the country level, may operate more effectively at the individual level. IFI officials may also appoint their own employees to high positions in reforming country policy teams. This has occurred in Poland, Hungary, and Croatia, where top-ranking IFI bureaucrats took leading positions in national teams dedicated to pension privatization (see table 6.1, below). In some cases, these officials were citizens of the reforming country; in other cases not. Thus, for a variety of reasons, it becomes difficult to ascertain the localism or transnationalism of policy reform teams. Is a reform team with all Estonian members "local" if two of the members have run World Bank projects in the past? Or are they better understood as local members of a transnational policy network?

What Transnational Actors Want

A second key problem in analyzing transnational influence is the difficulty in defining what transnational actors want. Studies of the influence of transnational actors often begin from stylized assumptions about what transnational actors are trying to achieve. Such assumptions are usually made in the spirit of theoretical and empirical parsimony, but they are sometimes inaccurate. Ascertaining the goals of transnational actors often requires careful attention to the complex internal decision making of actors with diverse centers of power and multiple stakeholders. By ignoring the internal politics of transnational actors, studies often make overly broad assumptions that cannot be backed up by systematic evidence.

For instance, in quantitative studies, it has become standard in the political economy of pension reform literature to use total World Bank lending to a country as a proxy measure for transnational influence (Madrid 2003; Brooks 2005). Doing so requires making a number of assumptions. First, it assumes that the World Bank wants the same outcome and therefore gives the same advice in each country. However, Holzmann and Hinz (2005) and World Bank (2006) show that this is not the case. Transnational actors do not treat all countries equally. Some countries are more strategic than others; transnational actors may make internal decisions to focus on implementing reform in one country or region over another.

Further, transnational actors may have a most preferred reform outcome and a second-choice outcome (Müller 1999, 28). The only way to understand the priorities of transnational actors is to learn more about their internal policy decisions. Madrid (2003) begins to unpack this complexity by using two measures of World Bank influence: the existence of a World Bank pension mission and total loans as a share of GDP. He finds, like Brooks (2005), no effect for total loans, but a strong and significant relationship between the World Bank sending a pension reform mission and enactment of pension privatization.

However, observing the dispatch of a World Bank mission does not imply knowing what advice it gives. Holzmann and Hinz (2005) find that the Bank has dispensed a wide variety of advice on pension issues, depending on country circumstances. Studies that assume that the World Bank offers standard advice and that use a simple proxy measure for World Bank influence or involvement without looking into the content of the advice offered may underestimate the extent of its influence. Advice may vary based on organizational characteristics. In some organizations, individual consultants may determine the nature of advice, while other organizations are more centralized and consistent. Such consistency cannot be assumed.

Finally, total World Bank lending to a country may not be an accurate predictor of the amount of pressure the Bank is able to bring to bear on pension reform issues. Pension lending is typically a small part of total lending to a country (Holzmann and Hinz 2005; World Bank 2006), and countries with high total lending may not be under pressure to adopt pension privatization. For instance, the World Bank may judge a poor, highly indebted country to have insufficient administrative capacity to implement pension privatization. A better measure of influence may be total World Bank pension lending to a country. However, such data is difficult to obtain. A recent World Bank internal evaluation found that most pension lending took place in the context of broader social sector or structural adjustment loans (World Bank 2006). Determining the amounts spent on pensions proved difficult even for World Bank personnel with full access to this data, and the data have not been made fully available to other analysts. Data availability can be a problem, despite the increasing transparency of transnational organizations.

In summary, standard methods for evaluating the impact of transnational actors tend to make strong assumptions about what transnational actors want that are not always backed up by empirical evidence. Yet the study of what transnational actors want and how they behave is complex and requires careful examination of their internal decision making and behavior.

Campaign Coalitions

A third issue for the literature on pension privatization is the difficulty of studying the coalitions of transnational policy actors that appear to have influenced these reforms. Most studies of global governance focus on a single actor, such as the IMF (Stone 2002), or one type of actor, such as transnational advocacy networks (Keck and Sikkink 1998), international organizations (Barnett and Finnemore 2004), or transgovernmental networks (Slaughter 2004). Such approaches offer analytic clarity, particularly for international relations theory. However, if policies are being spread by voluntary, temporary, but intensively involved "campaign coalitions" (Tarrow 2005) of actors that rally around particular issues, creating informal coalitions to pressure states, then the influence of these informally organized networks must be taken into account.

Tarrow (2005, 179) argues that transnational campaign coalitions are the most efficacious form of transnational activist cooperation. Campaign coalitions are issue-focused, not venue-focused, so they have the opportunity to switch venues when necessary and to work at multiple levels of the policy process. They are flexible, not highly institutionalized, and thus depend on voluntary compliance by their members, but their goals and activities are long-term and highly involved. Tarrow contrasts campaign coalitions to event-driven campaigns, which are more short-term, and instrumental coalitions and federations, which involve lower levels of engagement.

Similarly, transnational actors within campaign coalitions may coordinate by dividing responsibility for certain countries and elements of reform. Mechanisms of coordination are often informal, with no public access and no paper trail. While the World Bank has played a central role in spreading pension privatization, it is important to remember that USAID and other organizations such as the Asian Development Bank, Inter-American Development Bank, Organization for Economic Cooperation and Development, Cato Institute, and many other organizations and individual policy entrepreneurs have also played an important role. Therefore, measuring World Bank influence alone may underestimate overall transnational policy actor influence on reform processes.

This section has laid out three issues scholars have faced in analyzing the influence of transnational actors on pension privatization. It has argued for a better understanding of who transnational actors are, what they want, and how they cooperate with a range of organizations to pursue their objectives in multiple national policy arenas. The following sections respond to this agenda by presenting a more inclusive definition of who transnational actors are, conducting a more precise analysis of what transnational actors want, and showing that considering the cooperation of transnational actors in campaign-oriented coalitions also provides a more accurate picture of their involvement in the spread of pension privatization. The first section is definitional; the second and third present the results of the research study.

Defining Transnational Actors

It is crucial to start any analysis of the impact of transnational actors on policy with a definition of what is meant by transnational actors. Whereas many studies adopt a rather narrow definition, focusing only on international financial institutions, or even on a single organization, the World Bank, there are strong reasons to employ a more encompassing definition. As noted above, one of the central theoretical issues in the welfare states literature at present is the importance of international factors in the determination of welfare state policy. Most of the welfare state literature has tended to ignore transnational actors and instead has focused on analyzing the impact of economic globalization, defined as increased trade and financial flows. If we are interested in the issue of transnational influences on policy, it makes sense to consider the full range of transnational actors involved in policy. Only such an encompassing approach will allow us to answer the key question: are international influences important or not?

This study adopts a broad definition of transnational actors, considering an actor to be transnational if it is engaged in the development, transfer, or implementation of policy in multiple nation states. Such a definition includes intergovernmental organizations such as the World Bank, IMF, OECD, and ILO. It includes transnational policy entrepreneurs who advise on pension reform in multiple countries, such as Chilean economists and policy makers (Pinheiro 2004; Weyland 2005). It also includes state agencies, particularly bilateral aid agencies such as USAID, involved in the promotion of policies in multiple states. While such a definition may seem overly broad to those interested in distinguishing different types of international actors from one another (Risse-Kappen 1994), it makes sense if one is interested in distinguishing international from domestic political influences on welfare state development and change.

Agendas of Transnational Actors

In addition to knowing who transnational actors are, we need to understand what they want if we are to judge their effectiveness. This section provides evidence from a comprehensive analysis of World Bank project documents in all countries where the World Bank provided assistance on pensions between 1994, the year in which it began advocating pension privatization, and 2004. It shows that an analysis of what the World Bank wants helps us to better understand its rate of success. World Bank project documents are made publicly available on the World Bank Web site, and the data presented here reflect the full findings of a search of project documents related to "pensions" conducted by the author in July 2004. World Bank project documents on the public Web site include primarily loan documents, technical assistance agreements between the World Bank and country governments, and country assistance strategies. The category of "project documents" does not include policy research working papers and other research documents that may also advocate pension privatization. However, such research publications sometimes reflect the views of individuals and do not have the same status as official Bank recommendations. While there is reason to believe that project documents posted on the public Web page are chosen systematically, they do not represent the full range of project documents, many of which are included on an internal World Bank Web site. I chose to use the publicly available documents so that the findings of this study can be easily replicated by other researchers. Research on World Bank project activities was supplemented by extensive interviews with leading members of the World Bank social protection team, to fill any gaps in the data that might not have been published in publicly available accounts. This research was conducted as part of a larger research project that included in-depth studies of three countries where the World Bank was deeply involved in policy making. These studies involved dozens of interviews with World Bank officials as well as country officials in various ministries, members of the pension reform team, and interest group leaders (see the list of interviews at end of the References section). The full set of reforming countries has been compiled from multiple sources and verified through interviews as well. These data cover the complete set of countries where the World Bank was involved, but also countries where it was not, as well as reforming and non-reforming countries.

World Bank project documents show that fifty-two countries received pension assistance from the World Bank between 1994 and 2004. This differs from figures reported by the World Bank (2006, 12) and Holzmann and Hinz (2005), which show sixty-eight countries receiving pension assistance over the period 1984–2004—a difference that can be accounted for by the longer period of the World Bank (2006) study. The question addressed in this study is whether World Bank advice was in fact consistent and similar in all countries it advised. World Bank (2006) attests that the World Bank did not always advise countries to adopt pension privatization during the period 1984–2004. My own study of World Bank project documents between 1994 and 2004 verifies this result for the period after the publication of *Averting the Old Age Crisis* in 1994, the World Bank publication that became the blueprint for the World Bank approach to pension reform and is discussed in detail in chapter 4 below.

Analysis of these data shows that during the period 1994–2004, World Bank policy makers clearly sorted countries into promising reform prospects and others, in a manner consistent with policy statements from the Director of Social Protection, Robert Holzmann (Holzmann 1999; Holzmann and Hinz 2005). In particular, the World Bank appears to have advised pension privatization primarily in middle-income developing countries, while advising poorer countries, lacking sufficient administrative capacity, to get their administrative house in order before attempting pension reforms. Of the fifty-two countries receiving pension reform assistance, fourteen were poor countries where the World Bank provided technical assistance for administrative improvements of existing systems with no immediate plans for reforming the pension system. In some cases, programs were directed toward enabling reform "in the long run." These countries were located in Sub-Saharan Africa (6), Southeast Europe (3), Central Asia (2), Southeast Asia (1), North Africa (1), and Latin America (1). The median gross national income (GNI) per capita (in purchasing power parity terms) of these countries was $3665 (World Bank 2003). By contrast, the thirty-eight countries where the World Bank advised some type of pension reform had a median gross national income per capita (in purchasing power parity terms) of $6410 (World Bank 2003).

These data show that transnational actors do not behave the same in every context. They often distinguish between countries, using various criteria to determine their preferred roles and behaviors. The fact that they do so complicates statistical and other analyses of impact. Using a proxy measure of transnational actor influence, such as total indebtedness, tends to obscure differences in what transnational actors propose in particular countries. In this particular instance, simply excluding the countries where the World Bank has not advised adoption of pension privatization from the sample dramatically increases its observed rate of success.

Of the thirty-eight countries where the World Bank advocated structural reform of the pension system since 1994, twenty-three listed in the first column of table 2.1 (61 percent of the total) have initiated a reform that includes the establishment of a system of private, individual pension savings accounts. They are located in Latin America (10), Central and Eastern Europe (11), and Asia (2). The reform category includes China, which adopted pension privatization in 1998, although implementation has been spotty and the system covers only urban workers (Frazier 2004; China Economic Research and Advisory Programme 2005; Piggot and Bei 2007). In addition, four countries where the World Bank has advised pension reform since 1994 have adopted reforms that are consistent with the new pension reforms, but do not include mandatory, private accounts (Brazil, Kyrgyz Republic, Panama, and Turkey) (Fultz 2004; Castel and Fox, n.d.). Several of these countries adopted so-called notional defined contribution (NDC) pension reforms that create "notional" individual accounts receiving annual "interest rates" from governments, but are not real individual savings accounts (Brazil, Kyzgyz Republic). Instead, they reflect an individualized way of accounting for benefits under social security–type pension systems. The World Bank has often seen NDC systems as a second-best reform option to pension privatization and has supported such reforms in place of and in addition to individual pension savings accounts in many countries (Holzmann and Palmer 2006). Two countries have partially implemented private, individual accounts at the time of publication (Ecuador and Ukraine). Taking these partial success cases into account, the total success rate of World Bank projects in producing reform consistent with pension privatization is nearly 76 percent. This should be seen as a very high instance of success, considering that pension reform is a highly contentious and difficult issue in most countries. While the World Bank may tend to work with countries that have already decided to reform, inflating these numbers, the case studies in chapters 5 and 6 show that in many, if not most cases, transnational actors recruit country officials to initiate reform rather than vice versa. Even in countries where officials wish to initiate reform, they often require the support of transnational actors to achieve it.

The World Bank has been unsuccessful so far in producing pension privatization in nine countries where it has conducted pension reform projects, including either loans, technical assistance, or both. Most of these are poorer countries in Africa (3), Asia (2), Caucasus (2), Latin America (1), and the Middle East (1), as shown in table 2.1. One of these countries, Korea, is a relatively wealthy, middle-income country that appears to have resisted World Bank pressures to adopt pension privatization. It provides an interesting case of a national government that successfully opposed reform efforts being actively pushed by the international financial organizations. Korea rejected World Bank–led efforts to promote pension privatization after the 1997 Asian financial crisis apparently because the government of Kim Dae-Jung viewed these reforms as another example of the technocratic neoliberalism embraced by previous authoritarian governments (Yang 2004). However, the Korean case is exceptional. Most other cases where the World Bank has been unsuccessful in getting its advice adopted are poorer developing countries.

The fact that it is largely poor countries with relatively undeveloped pension systems that reject World Bank advice to implement pension privatization shows a major limitation in Myles and Pierson's (2001) finding

TABLE 2.1
World Bank Advice on Pension Privatization, 1994–2004

World Bank advises restructuring of pension system[a]	*World Bank supports improvement of social security system*
1. Argentina	39. Albania
2. Bolivia	40. Azerbaijan
3. Bulgaria	41. Bosnia and Herzegovina
4. China	42. Cape Verde
5. Colombia	43. Gabon
6. Costa Rica	44. Ghana
7. Croatia	45. Laos
8. Dominican Republic	46. Moldova
9. El Salvador	47. Morocco
10. Estonia	48. Niger
11. Hungary	49. Senegal
12. Kazakhstan	50. Serbia and Montenegro
13. Kosovo	51. Turkmenistan
14. Latvia	52. Uganda
15. Macedonia	
16. Mexico	
17. Nicaragua	
18. Peru	
19. Poland	
20. Romania	
21. Russia	
22. Slovakia	
23. Uruguay	
24. *Brazil*	
25. *Kyrgyz Republic*	
26. *Panama*	
27. *Turkey*	
28. *Ecuador*	
29. *Ukraine*	
30. *Armenia*	
31. Cameroon	
32. Djibouti	
33. Georgia	
34. Honduras	
35. Korea	
36. Sri Lanka	
37. West Bank and Gaza	
38. Zambia	

Source: World Bank Project Documents, 2004, author search.

[a] Countries 1–23: adopted pension privatization with funded individual accounts.
Countries 24–27: adopted NDC and other new pension reforms.
Countries 28–29: Mid-reform.

that countries with less developed earnings-related pension systems are more likely to adopt such reforms. The World Bank has had greater difficulties in pursuing its agenda not in countries with large pension systems, but rather in countries with low state capacity.

Table 2.1 shows a strong correlation between World Bank assistance and pension privatization. Likewise, only three countries have implemented the new pension reforms without advice from the World Bank: Chile, the United Kingdom, and Sweden.

This analysis of project document data offers several insights into the objectives and impact of one transnational policy actor, the World Bank, on adoptions of pension privatization. First, the World Bank modulates its policy advice based on the perceived administrative capacity of a country. This often correlates with country wealth, measured in gross domestic product (GDP) or gross national income (GNI) per capita. In poor countries with troubled social security systems, the World Bank often advises first to improve and reform the administration of the existing pension system, rather than embarking on structural reforms. This occurred in 27 percent of the cases where evidence was found of World Bank technical assistance for pension reform, as listed in the second column of Table 2.1. In some countries, the World Bank has supported NDC reforms as an alternative or in addition to private pension savings accounts. What the World Bank wants varies from country to country and depends on its assessment of country conditions (World Bank 2006, 14).

Second, since 1994, where the World Bank does advocate structural reforms, it has been highly consistent in advocating pension privatization, though with some flexibility depending on country circumstances. In all thirty-eight cases studied where the World Bank advised structural pension reform, it advised the introduction of mandatory or voluntary individual private accounts or notional defined contribution reforms to the first pillar, or all of the above, as in the case of Poland. In most cases, it advised mandatory, individual pension savings accounts, but in countries with weaker administrative capacity or financial markets or lacking other preconditions, it advised only voluntary accounts or notional defined contribution reforms to the first pillar, as in Kyrgyzstan (Becker et al. 2005). These findings are consistent with those of an internal World Bank evaluation (World Bank 2006) that found the Bank to be committed to advancing pension privatization worldwide. Yet the range of country reform projects supported by the World Bank also suggests that the Bank responds to country conditions and preferences. The World Bank does not advocate a cookie-cutter solution, but rather a ranked order preference list of reforms that are consistent with the new pension reform trend and philosophy. Where the World Bank advocates structural reforms, its overriding objective is implementation of reforms consistent with pension privatization. None of its advice between 1994 and 2004 has deviated from this goal.

Third, looking at actual pension advice rather than total World Bank lending suggests that the World Bank has been highly successful in working with countries to implement pension privatization. Most adopting countries do so with World Bank advice; few have done so without it. World Bank assistance comes in a variety of forms, making it difficult to distinguish which elements are most influential. The World Bank has played a role in formulating basic ideas about pension privatization. It has sponsored publications and conferences, training policy makers and technicians from around the world in the theory and administration of privatized pension systems. It has provided loans for system transition and long-term support for reform implementation, including training in forecasting software, creation of databases, public relations campaigns, and many other forms of assistance. The World Bank aims for the implementation of privatized pension systems, but is flexible about the exact parameters and allows for a fair degree of country variation (World Bank 1994; Holzmann 1999). This approach is consistent with the broad-based activities of the World Bank, which include providing general information about pension privatization, discussing reform options, training country officials in the use of modeling software, as well as the provision of specific policy advice and support for policy implementation.

At the same time, the data indicate important limitations of World Bank influence. In particular, the World Bank is constrained by domestic politics and political leadership. In cases like Korea, the World Bank cannot foist new pension reforms on unwilling governments. It is forced to convince political leaders of the benefits of pension privatization and to work only with countries where the government already wishes or is convinced to enact structural pension reform. The World Bank has numerous tools that it may use to influence domestic reformers and policy makers, from norms to economic incentives. However, its ability to establish pension privatization in a country is dependent on its ability to secure powerful local partners (Jacoby 2004; Epstein 2008).

This raises an important chicken-or-egg question that is critical to evaluating the influence of transnational actors. Do countries decide to implement reform and then request assistance from the World Bank? Or does the World Bank promote reform and then sell it to countries? Only detailed case study evidence can help to untangle the causal mechanisms at work here. As mentioned above, existent case studies provide plenty of reason to suggest that the World Bank is driving demand for reform, rather than merely responding to it. First, most countries adopted pension privatization after the World Bank began to promote it starting in 1994. No countries aside from Chile and the United Kingdom implemented such reforms before that date, although several Latin American countries had begun to adopt a version of the Chilean model before the World Bank began its advocacy campaign (Weyland 2005). Second, the 1994 World Bank publication *Averting the Old Age Crisis* created a vision of pension privatization that went well beyond the Chilean model. In particular, it advocated "mixed" model reforms that would maintain a reduced social security pension system alongside one based on private, individual accounts. Most countries have adopted this compromise model, attesting to the influence of World Bank policy development. Third, the World Bank and other transnational actors have often been instrumental in putting pension privatization on the policy agenda and empowering domestic allies to prepare comprehensive reform proposals relying on the best international expert advice. While motivated reformers may well seek out Bank assistance, evidence from many countries suggests that the Bank has recruited and trained reformers in an effort to stimulate demand for its services.

The Bank appears to have been successful in promoting its vision of reform around the world. Many countries it advises have adopted the World Bank's first best reform option: pension privatization including a system of individual, private pension savings accounts. Others have adopted second- and third-best solutions proposed by the World Bank either because particular countries do not meet reform prerequisites or because current domestic political and economic conditions do not allow for the first-best reform option. In this study, I define adoption of pension privatization as a success and adoption of reforms consistent with the new pension reforms, but not including private, funded, individual accounts as partial success cases (see the Appendix for a discussion of the full range of "consistent" reforms).

How Transnational Actors Cooperate in Campaign Coalitions

While the World Bank has been a central player in policy development and transfer of pension privatization, it has not acted alone. Instead, the World Bank has cooperated with a "campaign coalition" (Tarrow 2005) of transnational organizations and policy entrepreneurs in advancing this agenda. This coalition draws together organizations with different capabilities and specialties and has developed mechanisms of consultation and modes of collaboration that facilitate a division of labor. Coordination is achieved through donor meetings, informal contacts, and internal procedures of individual organizations. USAID, for instance, always evaluates what other organizations are doing when developing its own work plan for a country and tries not to duplicate other organizations' activities (interview with Denise Lamaute, Senior Pension Advisor, USAID, April 2006). The transnational coalition for pension privatization has been opposed by a second coalition that includes the International Labour Organization (ILO) and International Social Security Association (ISSA) (Queisser 2000; Charlton and McKinnon 2002). However, the World Bank–centered coalition has had greater resources and fits with a dominant neoliberal policy agenda worldwide; perhaps not surprisingly, it has had greater success. While the World Bank focuses on policy development, creation of modeling software, research publications, and broad policy advice, other organizations have developed different niches, such as setting up administrative systems, training regulators, and running public relations campaigns. In many countries, regional development banks and USAID may provide the on-the-ground presence that the World Bank cannot offer. Chilean reformer José Piñera often helps to inspire and convince skeptical policy makers of the benefits of pension privatization. Some consultants specialize in advising government ministries on reform design, others in drafting reform laws. It is impossible to gauge the full impact of the transnational campaign for pension privatization without analyzing the impact of this extensive network of actors.

To demonstrate how focusing on the World Bank alone tends to ignore important contributions that a range of actors make to the transnational campaign for the new pension reforms, this section provides further detail on one organization, USAID, that has been particularly active in reform in postcommunist Europe and Eurasia. It shows that ignoring USAID's work in this area may cause one to underestimate the influence of transnational actors.

USAID's substantial activities in spreading pension privatization have often been downplayed because, in contrast to the World Bank, USAID engages in little or no norms creation activities and creates no publications or reports detailing its own activities. USAID tends to work in a decentralized fashion, meaning that few in the organization have a good overview of the full extent of its activities. However, USAID often offers far more sustained day-to-day involvement with the officials and institutions involved in setting up and running privatized pension systems (Lamute interview, April 2006). USAID has had a particularly strong influence in the postcommunist countries of Central and Eastern Europe and Central Asia, through provision of technical assistance in the formulation of reform projects, public relations campaigns in support of pension privatization, and long-term technical assistance to government agencies charged with implementing pension privatization (see table 2.2). USAID cooperates closely with the World Bank and other organizations in the promotion of pension privatization. It trains its own employees and country officials with whom it is working at World Bank seminars, for instance. The World Bank likewise relies on USAID to implement long-term programs of technical assistance that the Bank does not have the staff resources to pursue.

USAID has enjoyed a remarkable success rate in the promotion of pension privatization, in part because of its exhaustive, long-term approach. In contrast to the World Bank, USAID will stay involved in the promotion of pension privatization in a country for a decade or more, through various ups and downs, until reform legislation is passed and implemented. USAID has played a role in designing privatized pension systems in ten countries (and jurisdictions): Bosnia and Hercegovina, Bulgaria, Kazakhstan, Kosovo,[1] Macedonia, Montenegro, Romania, Russia, Serbia, and Ukraine. As shown in table 2.2, assistance has included training for reform officials, funding for reform teams, assistance with legislative drafting, hiring of consultants on all aspects of reform, and public relations campaigns. All but Bosnia have implemented or plan to implement individual, private pension savings accounts. In addition, USAID has played a critical role in supporting reform implementation in these countries as well as several additional countries where the World Bank led the pension privatization effort: Croatia, Hungary, Lithuania, Poland, and Slovakia.

USAID-sponsored implementation assistance has lasted from three to eight years and has focused on establishment of pension fund regulators, public relations campaigns, and other technical assistance. USAID has also funded an OECD-led effort to create a network of pension fund supervisors that can act as an avenue for further training in pension privatization. USAID has also funded many domestic policy makers to attend World Bank Institute training courses on pension privatization. USAID officials have attended these trainings too (interview with Estelle James, lead author, *Averting the Old Age Crisis*, June 28, 2005). Countries where pension privatization most likely would not have been implemented without USAID assistance include Kazakhstan and Kosovo, and possibly in the future Montenegro, Serbia, and Ukraine, where reforms are in the planning stages. USAID has almost never worked on pension reform in a country that has not adopted individual, private accounts, with the exception of Bosnia. This would suggest that excluding USAID from analyses of the impact of transnational actors could underestimate the influence of such actors. Similarly, ignoring the division of labor, breadth of resources, and full range of organizations involved in these campaigns may downplay the extent of transnational influence.

[1] See Cocozzelli 2007 for a brief description of the reform process in Kosovo.

TABLE 2.2
USAID Pension Reform Assistance in Europe, 1994–2005

Bosnia	Assistance in improving existing pay-as-you-go institutions.
Bulgaria	Technical assistance to reform team, drafting of laws and regulations, public relations campaign, technical assistance to implement a payroll contribution, registration, and tracking system.
Croatia	Public relations campaign, technical assistance for implementation of pension fund auditing and supervisory training and information technology systems design for collection and record keeping.
Hungary	Implementation technical assistance for regulatory body overseeing private pension funds.
Kazakhstan	Technical assistance to reform team, provision of modeling software and training, legislative drafting, and implementation assistance to pension fund regulatory body.
Kosovo	Technical assistance to reform team, provision of modeling software and training, and legislative drafting. Implementation technical assistance to pension fund regulatory body and new administrative bodies.
Lithuania	Supportive technical assistance to reform team.
Macedonia	Technical assistance to reform team, implementation technical assistance for creation and training of pension fund regulatory body.
Montenegro	Technical assistance to reform team for reform and improving efficiency of current system.
Poland	Implementation technical assistance and public relations campaign.
Romania	Technical assistance to government reform teams over the course of several governments.
Russia	Technical assistance to reform team and legislative drafting.
Serbia	Technical assistance to reform team for reform and improving efficiency of current system.
Slovakia	Supported training for senior government officials with the Public Employees Retirement System in Idaho.
Ukraine	Technical assistance to reform team, provision of modeling software and training, and legislative drafting. Public relations campaign.
OECD	Helped to establish the International Network of Pension Regulators and Supervisors and to fund its activities.

Source: Snelbecker 2005. Based on information provided by Denise Lamaute, Senior Pension Reform Adviser, USAID.

Other transnational actors have also played a substantial role in the campaign for pension privatization. The IMF has supported World Bank pensions work by conducting fiscal projections for countries contemplating these reforms and integrating them into broader fiscal plans. The OECD has organized an independent association of pension fund regulators that exchanges knowledge and best practices from around the world. Regional development banks, such as Asian Development Bank and Inter-American Development Bank, have often taken the lead on pensions policy advice and loans to countries within their spheres of influence and sponsored the transfer of regional best practices.

Conclusion

This chapter has evaluated the growing literature on the political economy of pension reform and suggested three ways to improve our understanding of the influence of transnational actors on the spread of pension privatization. First, we need a better sense of who transnational actors are. This study has argued for adopting a broad definition of transnational actors that includes all actors active in the development, transfer, and implementation of pension privatization policies in multiple national contexts. A central theoretical question in the welfare states literature is whether transnational influences are important. Addressing this question effectively requires that we move beyond a focus on a single transnational actor or type of actor (such as IFIs) to consider the full range of actors involved. Second, we need to know more about what transnational actors want. Studies often make crude assumptions about the impact of transnational actors, assuming, for instance, that the World Bank wants to achieve reform in every country where it works or that it wants to achieve certain specific features of reform rather than reforms consistent with its broader vision. This can prevent accurate measurement of transnational actor effectiveness. A comprehensive analysis of World Bank project documents shows that the World Bank does not advocate pension privatization in every country. Instead, it makes a determination about whether reform will succeed, and sets its advice accordingly. Third, we need to know more about how transnational actors cooperate in campaign coalitions to advance their reform agendas worldwide. Transnational actors have limited resources, and cooperation with other organizations provides a means of magnifying their impact. Transnational actors have detailed protocols for managing cooperation with other organizations in their field and they do this effectively, agreeing on a division of labor within specific countries, for instance, or more broadly within a campaign coalition. This study has explored the impact of USAID within the transnational coalition for pension privatization and argued that the influence of these coalitions needs to be taken into account when debating the impact of transnational actors. An approach that focuses on a single organization runs the risk of underestimating the impact of transnational actors overall. A first step in responding to these concerns is to develop a model of transnational actor behavior, a task that is addressed in the following chapter.

CHAPTER THREE

A Model of Transnational Actor Influence

THE PREVIOUS CHAPTER showed that many studies underestimate the influence of transnational actors by adopting restrictive definitions of who they are, stylized understandings of what they want, and a narrow focus on a single organization or type of organization. This chapter provides an enhanced framework for analyzing the activities and influence of transnational actors on domestic policy. This framework builds on the veto players model of Tsebelis (2002) and the bureaucratic approach to the study of international organizations proposed by Barnett and Finnemore (2004). It suggests that transnational actors can best be understood as proposal actors—defined as individual or collective actors that develop and advocate well-elaborated policy proposals and work with domestic veto players to affect policy in multiple states.

The great puzzle of transnational actor influence is how actors with no formal veto power can play an important role in setting domestic welfare state policy. This lack of formal veto power has often led analysts to conclude that transnational actors are not important determinants of policy. Because many scholars believe that political power derives primarily from formal veto rights (Tsebelis 2002), actors without such powers are necessarily considered secondary. Scholars searching for the sources of power of transnational actors have often focused on their use of conditionalities. Loan or membership conditionalities appear to give transnational actors quasi-veto powers. If developing state borrowers or aspirant members do not adhere to certain conditions, their access to resources or membership is effectively vetoed. This veto power can give transnational actors informal influence over policy where they do not have formal veto power. However, this emphasis on conditionalities and their veto-like properties is problematic. Loan and membership conditionalities are often not obeyed; adherence to loan and membership conditions remains voluntary and contingent in most cases (Woods 2006, 6). This has caused many scholars to investigate other modes of transnational actor influence, especially ideational ones. Those who emphasize ideational or normative influence focus on mechanisms such as persuasion and socialization, whereby transnational actors use communicative action to influence others and rely more on legitimate authority than coercive means to ensure compliance (Checkel 2005; Blyth et al. forthcoming).

This book contributes to efforts to combine rationalist and constructivist approaches to international political economy by acknowledging the influence of norms and resources and the ways these are often linked (Blyth 2002; Jacoby 2004; Kelley 2004; Brooks 2005; Herrera 2006; Epstein 2008; Johnson 2008). The proposal actors and veto players framework proposed here seeks to combine rational and ideational influences on policy. This framework incorporates material influences on policy, but also suggests that proposal actors can reshape veto player perceptions of interest and exert a pervasive, if sometimes diffuse, influence on policy. Transnational actors have the legitimacy and resources to establish policy agendas in a transnational space and to shape the ideas, information, and norms of domestic veto players.

PROPOSAL ACTORS

Since the pioneering work of Tsebelis (2002), domestic policy processes have often been seen as dependent on the preferences, strategies, and influence of domestic "veto players." Veto players are those actors that exercise a formal veto over the policy process (Tsebelis 2002). This veto right could be generated by virtue of constitutional powers, or the power of parties that make up a coalition government. While there are several important benefits of a veto actor perspective, there are also deficiencies. One benefit is simplicity. While previous debates about the impact of institutions on policy revolved around comparisons of presidential versus parliamentary democracy, majoritarian versus consensus democracy, democracy versus authoritarianism, and a host of other institutional differences, Tsebelis showed that these overlapping institutional constraints could be modeled as endowing a greater or lesser number of actors with veto power, thus simplifying comparative analysis. A second benefit is measurement. While previous institutional variables were often hard to measure, the number of veto players usually is more straightforward. A third benefit is that the number of veto players has proven to have a significant effect on policy outcomes in numerous circumstances.

However, the veto players framework also has its weaknesses. For one, Tsebelis's model assumes that veto actors have preferences on all policy issues. Veto players develop these preferences with regard to their own actions and interactions with competitors. However, observation of real policy processes shows that veto actors sometimes do not have well-formed or solid preferences, while other policy actors may be agenda setters without having a veto in the political process. NGOs, social movements, and transnational policy advocates are good examples (Risse et al.

1999). The veto players framework is incomplete without an account of how non-veto actors influence the preference formation of veto actors.

Second, the veto players framework ignores the existence of stages and time in the policy process. Growing out of a literature on parliamentary voting behavior, the veto players framework tends to assume that policy bargains are struck at a single point in time, such as the time of legislation. However, this perspective underemphasizes the agenda-setting stage as well as policy implementation, when different veto players and proposal actors may come into play. For instance, James Scott (1985) showed in a classic study that peasants who were excluded from formal policy processes often had the ability to exercise a veto over policy implementation. Analyzing a policy process in stages shows different actors and bargaining venues to be relevant at each stage (Soule and King 2006).

This chapter argues that policy processes need to be analyzed with attention to two sets of actors, veto players and proposal actors. Veto players are defined in a manner consistent with Tsebelis (2002) as actors with a formal veto over the policy process. Proposal actors are defined as those actors that develop fully elaborated reform proposals and advocate them in the course of domestic policy debate. Proposal actors may achieve their goals by influencing the preferences of veto players or by strengthening the resources of one veto player over another and thus helping to develop stronger coalitions for reform.

Transnational policy actors often operate as proposal actors in domestic politics. While lacking veto rights, they have the power to formulate legitimate and well-elaborated policy proposals. Proposal actors orient their activity toward convincing domestic veto players to adopt their problem definitions, norms, and proposed solutions.

Because of their lack of formal, concentrated veto power, transnational actors are forced to use a variety of channels of influence to co-opt, cajole, inspire, and recruit domestic veto players to their cause. Membership and loan conditionalities are one set of tools. Others include the deployment of expertise to develop new problem definitions and policy proposals, workshops, publications, and conferences that spread information about proposed policy solutions, strategic use of resources to encourage states and domestic actors to adopt proposed policies, and technical assistance in reform implementation. Sections below show that transnational actors often attempt to influence policy development as well as policy transfer and implementation. In domestic politics, they often work with government veto players to formulate reform programs, with parliaments and other public deliberative bodies to promote reform and to engineer compromises, and with administrative agencies and interest groups to smooth policy implementation.

Transnational proposal actor interventions are often pervasive, taking place in a variety of deliberative forums across time. This presents one of the key methodological problems in assessing transnational actor influence, because there is rarely a single moment or event that encapsulates the full range of transnational actor influence. Instead, transnational actors behave like nervous parents hovering over domestic reform processes, bemoaning their own lack of control, yet exerting subtle influence at all stages. Determining the extent to which outcomes are due to nature or nurture may well be impossible. The claim made here is more limited: that nurture explains a significant proportion of the variance.

Finally, because transnational proposal actors influence domestic policy in partnership with domestic veto players, transnational actor influence must be studied at two levels of analysis—transnational and domestic. This study seeks to incorporate insights from both comparative politics and international relations to provide a detailed understanding of the involvement of transnational actors at the transnational and national levels of the policy processes. In the next section, I begin to develop a model of transnational actor influence that emphasizes the interaction of transnational and national actors across time. This model provides a framework for the case study analysis in chapters 4 and 5 below.

A MODEL OF TRANSNATIONAL ACTOR INFLUENCE

As a first step in presenting this model, I emphasize the temporal dimension and justify the division of the policy process into distinct stages. The transnational policy process for the development of pension privatization or any other policy reforms can be divided into three phases: policy development, policy transfer, and implementation. Policy development has sometimes been referred to in the literature as "norms creation" (Barnett and Finnemore 2004; Brooks 2005). It encompasses the creation of new problem definitions, metrics, and policy programs. The second phase is policy transfer, sometimes called "norms teaching." It consists of the dissemination of problem definitions and policy solutions to other organizations and states, using a wide variety of methods. The third phase, implementation, often occurs within a particular nation state or jurisdiction. While these three phases are not always clearly delineated across time, they tend to be arrayed in a sequence with policy development coming first. Policy development, however, may be an ongoing process, while policy transfer and implementation may occur simultaneously in different states and regions.

Because transnational proposal actors typically do not have the formal power to enact reform on their own, they must involve themselves in domestic politics. The key to transnational actor influence in areas like pension privatization is to influence the information, interests, values, and policy preferences of domestic veto players in order to achieve preferred policies. While domestic policy actors hold formal veto power, transnational actors can provide the legitimate, well-elaborated policy proposals that domestic actors often lack along with the resources to win domestic support for reform. To shape the views, information, and preferences of domestic veto players, transnational actors often exert ideological or normative influence across three phases of the domestic policy process: commitment building, coalition building, and implementation. Each phase involves distinct policy actors and deliberative forums. In commitment building, transnational actors seek to win governmental commitment to reforms. In coalition building, emphasis shifts to public deliberation in order to win the support of a broader coalition of actors and to secure parliamentary approval for reforms. In implementation, transnational actors work with domestic actors to build the bureaucracy, administration, and regulatory framework for reform.

As opposed to many models of transnational actor behavior, I do not suppose that transnational actors are monolithic or unchanging. Rather, I suggest that analysts must incorporate attention to transnational actors' internal organizational behavior. Transnational actors' behavior is dictated by their own ideas, resources, and internal decision and learning processes, which often change over time. They change in relation to transnational actors' own internal circumstances and lessons they draw from experience. Careful analysis must avoid stylized assumptions that impute stability of preferences, information, resources, personnel, and behavior to transnational actors. This complicates evaluation of transnational actor influence and suggests the utility of a case study method in studying actor preferences over time.

A further element of this model is that transnational actors often work in campaign coalitions (Tarrow 2005) for the adoption of particular policies. These campaign coalitions can magnify the influence of transnational actors by creating a division of labor. Some organizations focus on a particular set of countries or on functional specializations. One part of a transnational advocacy network may focus on policy research and development, while another specializes in policy implementation. One organization may have a special ability or mandate to work with governments, while another sponsors public relations campaigns. Transnational actors also compete for influence, advocating different policy approaches. Often, opposing networks compete for influence in a given policy sphere. It is

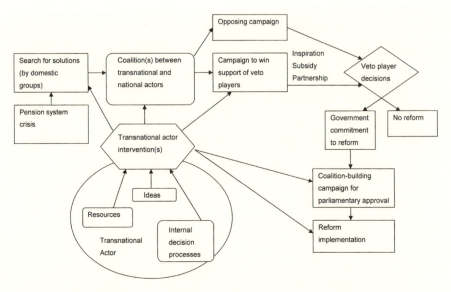

Fig. 3.1. A model of transnational actor influence on pension system reform.

important to analyze both cooperation and competition of transnational policy advocates within a sphere of governance.

In sum, this model advances a perspective on transnational actors that is based on five main observations. (1) Transnational actor strategies are based on their lack of veto power over domestic political decisions, which forces them to behave as proposal actors. (2) The influence and operations of transnational actors must be analyzed at two levels of analysis: transnational and national. (3) Lacking formal veto power, transnational actors attempt to use a wide variety of indirect modes of influence to set agendas and encourage compliance. (4) The internal processes of transnational actors are not stable across time; their ideas, resources, and decisions may change within a single policy intervention or between policy interventions. (5) The influence of transnational actors often depends on patterns of cooperation and competition between transnational actors within particular policy spheres.

A general model of transnational actor intervention based on these observations is presented in figure 3.1. This model is developed in subsequent sections and then used to analyze the campaign for pension privatization in chapter 4 and the nature of specific country interventions in chapter 5.

POLICY CRISES AND THE SEARCH FOR SOLUTIONS

The model presented in figure 3.1 incorporates the influence of policy crises. It is widely accepted in the literature on the political economy of development that crises stimulate a search for policy solutions and new policy norms (Müller 2003, 14–15). Some scholars have pointed out that crises may be manufactured by creating new problem definitions or frames around issues not previously understood as crises. Others have emphasized that policy networks continually advance new policy proposals, irrespective of crisis (Sabatier and Jenkins-Smith 1999). While recognizing these objections, the conclusion that crises stimulate policy responses still seems valid. In perceived crises, policy makers tend to accelerate their search for policy solutions and use various shortcuts (Weyland 2005) to achieve results more quickly.

One such shortcut is to seek available, ready-made policy options rather than to spend the time and resources to conduct an exhaustive analysis. In crises, policy makers do not use the techniques of rational learning, but rather rely on heuristics of availability, anchoring, and representativeness (Weyland 2005). Policy makers often rely on numerous and competing policy proposals advanced by different policy advocacy networks. Many of these networks are transnational. Advocacy coalition proposals can have a major impact on domestic political actors. For instance, policy preferences of domestic veto players can be shaped by proposals advocated by networks of transnational policy actors, in particular when domestic veto players do not have well-formed preferences on an issue or when their preferences are disrupted by new information or problem definitions. In such circumstances, the ideas promoted by transnational policy advocates can suggest the creation of new institutions and new political coalitions to support reform (Blyth 2002).

INTERNAL PROCESSES OF TRANSNATIONAL ACTORS

Transnational actors are often guided by their own institutional procedures and priorities and by epistemic communities (Haas 1992) that rise to power within these institutions. Following Barnett and Finnemore (2004), I propose that transnational proposal actors are relatively autonomous with substantial control over their own functions and decisions. While they may operate under constraints imposed by various stakeholders, they retain substantial organizational freedom to maneuver. This can be seen in the way in which transnational actors seek new mandates and provide themselves with new roles and legitimacy. Transnational actors often pursue these roles with a view to enhancing their moral, expert, and legal legitimacy. This leads to substantial shifts in organizational mission. For instance, Kapur, Lewis, and Webb (1997) document the World Bank's shift from being a multilateral lending institution for postwar reconstruction into a development bank seeking to prevent poverty. It has been widely observed that international organizations rarely die in part because of their ability to shift mandates and provide such new or renewed rationales for their existence.

Transnational actors' reform interventions tend to be driven by three factors: their ideas, resources, and decision-making processes. Every transnational actor has a distinct manner of developing policy ideas. Some organizations devote substantial resources to policy research and development in an attempt to come up with innovative and effective policy proposals. Others borrow their ideas from other organizations. Organizations often choose from a number of ideational frames that compete to define a policy area (Lindstrom 2008). These ideational frames tend to dictate policy approaches, for instance, defining problem definitions and desired outcomes, differentiating among countries, and ordering organizational priorities. Transnational actor ideas are influenced both by their original mandates and by epistemic communities that hold sway within an organization.

Transnational actor behavior is also heavily constrained by resources. Resources help to determine the ability of a transnational actor to advance its proposals effectively. Resources are important for norms teaching as well as for resource-leveraging activities. The World Bank, for instance, has one of the largest budgets globally for norms creation and norms teaching (Stone and Wright 2007). These resources allow it to be a world leader in norms production and promotion. Organizations with fewer resources can also create and diffuse norms, but they are unlikely to have as great an impact across such a wide range of areas.

Resources create or restrict opportunities to use various policy tools. For instance, a small organization without substantial resources may not be able to use a resource leveraging strategy effectively. However, it may be able to mount a small publication series and recruit other organizations with larger resources to support its policy goals. Large organizations with substantial resources may have greater choice over the use of policy instruments and may employ all or only a few selectively. Both large and small organizations continuously try to recruit other organizations as partners in their advocacy campaigns, providing an important multiplier effect for their influence and adding capabilities that they do not necessarily have in house.

Finally, transnational actors' activities tend to be constrained by their internal decision-making procedures. Some organizations answer to powerful masters, such as states. Others do not. All organizations have distinctive methods for reaching decisions and setting policy priorities that can shape the course of an intervention. In many cases, transnational actors attempt to learn from experience in an ongoing process of policy feedback (Haas and Haas 1995; Pierson 1994). Other organizations may be resistant to learning and simply seek to pursue reforms without corrections (Haas 1990). Such differences in decision making can have a material impact on domestic reforms.

TRANSNATIONAL POLICY PROCESS

This discussion of transnational actor influence takes place at two levels of analysis: the transnational and national policy-making processes. At the transnational level, the policy process can be divided into three phases: policy development, policy transfer, and implementation. Transnational proposal actors tend to be active across all three phases, because they lack the formal veto powers that might concentrate their influence at a single stage. This analysis shows that different transnational actors tend to use different modes and mechanisms of influence at distinct stages in the policy process.

Policy Development

Policy development encompasses the process of creating new policy proposals and enacting them in a first, innovating state. Two major elements of a definition stand out: first the process of devising new policy ideas and, second, the process of formulating a policy change in a particular locale. The drawing board part of policy development is akin to what many authors have called "agenda-setting" or "policy formulation" (Heclo 1974; Baumgartner and Jones 1993; Kingdon 1997; Lukes 2005). Some scholars have expressed skepticism about the possibility of tracing the development of policy ideas. In particular, Kingdon (1997) speaks of the "primeval soup" of policy discourse and suggests that policy ideas tend to evolve spontaneously in policy discussions between networks of experts that are difficult to trace. However, this skepticism seems overdrawn; the development of ideas can be traced. Many contemporary accounts emphasize the role of "policy networks," "epistemic communities," or "advocacy coalitions" on policy formulation (Fischer 2003, 31–35). Transnational policy actors are sometimes highly active in these networks or coalitions.

Advocacy coalitions are epistemic communities of like-minded policy actors that seek to develop policies that reflect their core beliefs, which do

TABLE 3.1
Modes and Mechanisms of Influence at Different Policy Stages

Stage	Policy development	Policy transfer	Implementation
Modes of influence	Norms creation	Norms teaching Coercion	Norms teaching Coercion
Mechanisms	Publications Working groups Conferences	Training seminars Reform team funds Technical assistance Loans	Agency funds Employee training Public relations
Organizations (Pension privatization)	World Bank Policy entrepreneurs	World Bank USAID Policy entrepreneurs	World Bank USAID

not readily change (Sabatier and Jenkins-Smith 1999). From these beliefs, policy actors develop a problem definition in a particular area, a broad strategy that is generative of more specific policy ideas. For instance, the neoliberal reform agenda was rooted in trends in academic economics, new ideas and observations about economic policy, and networks of individuals trained in this tradition who went on to revise economic policy in numerous areas. These individuals brought new problem definitions and strategic responses to the fore. This process has been analyzed by sociologists (Bockman and Eyal 2002), who look at the development and spread of neoliberal ideas within the professional networks of the economics profession. Other scholars have worked on the development and spread of neoliberal-inspired economic policies (Campbell and Pedersen 2001) focusing on state enterprise privatization (Kogut and Spicer 2003; Kogut and MacPherson 2004), deregulation, central bank independence (Johnson 2008), and monetary policies (Simmons and Elkins 2004) that have swept the world since the early 1980s. Much of this work finds ways to trace the development of new policy ideas.

Much norms creation work takes place within the first adopting country. Every policy reform must happen somewhere first, and the first instance provides a critical "laboratory" for experiments in policy reform (Bockman and Eyal 2002). The literature on diffusion of innovations (Rogers 1995), which often focuses on technical innovations, places significant emphasis on first innovators and how their decision processes may differ from those of later innovators. Just as Louis Brandeis spoke of the fifty United States as national laboratories for the development of U.S. federal policy, today laboratory countries play that role for the entire world. And just as in the United States, certain states (such as California, New Jersey, and New York) are known as innovator states, so in the world certain countries are seen as policy leaders. The greatest impact of a laboratory country is felt among its "peer" states in a particular region or among states with similar characteristics or aspirations.

In conclusion, the notion of "policy development" advanced here draws on standard accounts of agenda setting and policy formulation, but seeks to "stretch" this category to encompass policy networks, advocacy coalitions, epistemic communities, and the like that are transnational in scope, rather than confined to a particular national setting. Policy development is a distinct activity that some transnational actors may be active in and some may not. It requires resources, expertise, and moral authority to pursue successfully. For norms created by transnational actors require legitimacy if they are to be successfully spread and pursued. Policy development is necessarily prior to policy transfer and implementation, but may also take place on a continuous basis through transfer and implementation. This may complicate analysis of the impact of transnational actors, because their policy objectives evolve over time.

The power of transnational proposal actors in developing policy ideas can be hard to capture in quantitative or qualitative analysis, though this influence is fundamental. If an idea were not invented, it would not be implemented anywhere. However, it is often difficult to know this for certain, because one can always argue the materialist point made by Marx that ideas always arise to justify the material interests of powerful social groups. Because of this ever-present counter-factual, it is always difficult to determine the influence that an organization has had by simply generating or creating a popular policy idea.

Policy Transfer

A second phase of transnational proposal actor involvement in global policy making involves the transfer of a policy innovation beyond the "laboratory" country or innovating agency to other jurisdictions around the world. This process sometimes is labeled policy diffusion. A process of diffusion is one in which a newly invented norm or policy is adopted by other individuals, organizations, or states through a communication mechanism such as social learning rather than independent invention.

There is nothing necessary about policy diffusion. Some policies may not diffuse at all. Veto players in various countries and agencies may choose to adopt a policy or not; there may be substantial differences among adoptions of nominally similar policies (such as central bank independence); and the diffusion process may take a longer or shorter period of time.

Transnational proposal actors have a variety of mechanisms to encourage policy transfer. These are often grouped into the categories of norms teaching and resource leveraging, sometimes also called "coercion" (Brooks 2004; Kelley 2004; Henisz et al. 2005). One could also think of the distinction as one between "soft" (norms) versus "hard" (resources) power (Brooks 2005). *Norms teaching* encompasses activities intended to spread awareness of and compliance with norms, values, epistemic communities, or policy ideas of transnational actors. These can include seminars at which reform ideas are discussed, book publications, promotional conferences, study trips, and the like. Normative influence can also be exerted by organizations through monitoring and reporting activities. *Resource leveraging* or *coercion* involves the use of monetary, membership, or other resources to force countries to comply with a certain norm or policy idea advocated by a transnational organization. One example is the use of IMF loan conditionalities to encourage countries to comply with policy reforms or risk losing out on large amounts of money. Another is the use of membership conditionality by the EU to force countries to adopt elements of the *acquis communautaire* (Vachudova 2005).

Jacoby (2008) develops a useful typology of transnational actor mechanisms that combines norms teaching and resource leveraging perspectives, focusing on four modes of external influence (see also Tarrow 2005). The first is "inspiration," whereby external actors influence state bodies through the development and promotion of ideas. The second mode is "subsidy," whereby external actors offer support conditional on the enactment of reform. The third mode is "partnership," whereby an external actor supports the political fortunes of domestic political allies. The fourth mode is "substitution," whereby external actors seek to enforce their preferred solution without cooperation from domestic actors. Jacoby's typology analytically distinguishes between norms teaching and resource leveraging roles but also acknowledges that the two functions are often combined in particular modes of behavior.

In the pension area, policy transfer has been achieved through a combination of "inspiration," "subsidy," and "partnership." Specific tools of influence include the use of loans and technical assistance to offer conditional support for reform, to forge partnerships with domestic political allies, and to inspire cooperation from potential new allies. The toolbox of transnational actors includes organizing and running informational conferences and seminars, providing expertise and funding for reform teams, promising loans or other support for the implementation of reforms, organizing study trips to countries that have already implemented the reforms, and developing public relations campaigns to win public support for reform.

Policy Implementation

While scholars have emphasized the role of transnational actors in policy transfer, less attention has been given to their policy implementation activities. Yet policy implementation assistance has been central to the transnational campaign for pension privatization. Policy implementation may be extremely important both for transnational and domestic actors. For transnational proposal actors, policy implementation can make the difference between a major success story and a dramatic policy failure. Both can influence further cases of policy transfer. A dramatic success story can help to convince neighboring countries and other peer countries to adopt a reform through social learning, while a policy failure can persuade countries not to adopt. Therefore, transnational proposal actors may be extremely sensitive to the possibility of policy failure and have a strong incentive to be actively involved in policy implementation to avoid it. For domestic actors, difficulties with implementation of a complex reform can create an incentive to avoid reform. Even if it seems good in theory, fears about problems with implementation may cause domestic actors to avoid reform. Conversely, the knowledge that a leading transnational actor will remain involved over a multi-year period in setting up the technical and regulatory infrastructure, providing loans and advice to government officials, and the like, can help to tip the balance in favor of reform.

Some organizations may specialize in reform implementation, just as others specialize in policy development. For instance, USAID has played this role in postcommunist pension reforms. While the World Bank has provided "inspiration," policy ideas, and advice, USAID has committed technical missions to make pension reform work across the postcommunist countries at the ground level for periods of three to eight years. The World Bank has also provided loans and intermittent policy advice, but often the day-to-day technical implementation issues have been left to USAID. OECD has crafted an international network of private pension system regulators whose purpose is to trade expertise and to spread norms and ideas. It is funded in part by USAID. Transnational actors' influence over policy implementation relies on modes similar to those for policy transfer. Norms teaching and resource leveraging remain critical, encompassing such activities as creating new agencies and laws, training personnel, fostering regulatory norms of fairness, accuracy, and transparency among pension funds, and creating incentives for governments to reach certain administrative targets or risk losing funds. Pension privatization typically involves the creation of new laws, government agencies, products, financial industries, and expert groups, taking place over a period of five to ten years. Policy adoption is only the first step in the implementation.

STRATEGIC BEHAVIOR OF TRANSNATIONAL PROPOSAL ACTORS

As can be seen from this review of transnational actor interventions, transnational proposal actors often exert a pervasive influence across multiple stages of the policy process. Transnational actors develop new problem definitions and policy solutions and seek to advance new information and norms through expert publications, workshops, and seminars. They seek to identify and recruit potential partners, ascertaining their political will and training them in reform ideas and methods. Transnational actors typically provide resources to partners with "political will" to help them to prevail in domestic reform battles. They help to engineer campaigns and forge compromises in an effort to win additional domestic allies. Transnational actors often assist with the implementation of reforms in order to guarantee that reforms succeed and become a more influential example for peer countries. Transnational actors also specialize and coordinate with other actors in a policy sphere in order to maximize their contribution to the joint effort. Transnational actors also sponsor non-hierarchical social learning, by creating opportunities for neighboring countries to learn from regional reform leaders through conferences, study trips, and journalist training, for example. The essence of the strategic behavior of transnational actors' is to influence the preferences of key veto players in order to win support for reform. Transnational actors often promote their agendas prior to any serious crisis, but they are particularly important when a crisis situation takes hold of a country's pension system and policy makers are forced to consider policy solutions. Their chances of forming partnerships and affecting behavior through subsidies increase.

Transnational actors' methods of influence often depend on the phase of the domestic policy process for reform and change over time. Domestically, the reform process can be divided into three phases. In the first phase, commitment building, transnational actors seek to win governmental approval for their program. Techniques include high-profile conferences and advisory activities. In the second phase, coalition building, transnational actors seek to win broader public support and parliamentary approval for reform legislation. Here methods include public relations campaigns and technical assistance to negotiators. In the third phase, implementation, transnational actors support reform implementation with an eye to avoiding reform disasters and ensuring long-term continuation of reform institutions. These domestic policy phases are discussed in greater depth in chapter 5 below.

Transnational Advocacy Coalitions and Conflict

So far, this chapter has described the activities of a single transnational advocacy coalition. Yet in most policy areas, multiple transnational advocacy coalitions compete for influence. Competing coalitions often seek to inspire and partner with domestic veto players in a single country at the same point in time. In the pension area, the World Bank/USAID coalition has been opposed by a coalition led by the International Labour Organization (ILO) and International Social Security Association (ISSA) (Charlton and McKinnon 2002, 1178–1179; Quiesser 2000), described in greater depth in chapter 4 below. The success of transnational advocacy coalitions thus depends not only on their own resources, ideas, legitimacy, and organizational behavior, but also on their relative standing. In the case of pension privatization, it is quite clear that the World Bank–led coalition has enjoyed much greater access to resources than the ILO-led coalition. The reasons for this are institutional and situational. The World Bank is both wealthier and more in tune with the reigning neoliberalism of Western development policy. Nonetheless, the ILO-led coalition has had significant impacts on countries where it has worked. It appears to have had greater influence in some poorer developing countries where the World Bank has chosen not to work. Interestingly, because both the World Bank and ILO are part of the U.N. system, they have been forced to coordinate their activities to some extent through policy dialogues and consultation, even if they remain opposed on policy programs. Transnational actors thus often operate in conflict and loose coordination with other organizations active in their field.

Transnational Actor Effectiveness

What are the implications of this model for transnational actor effectiveness? First, this model suggests that transnational actors will be more effective when they are relatively unified around a set of policy ideas. This may occur because an epistemic community, for instance, has taken power within a transnational actor or actors and gained control over agendas in a particular area of policy. Second, transnational actors are more likely to be successful when they have sufficient resources at their disposal to exert a pervasive influence on all phases of the policy process, from policy development to implementation. Such resources and pervasive influence make up for transnational actors' lack of formal veto power. Third, transnational actors are more likely to be effective if they are relatively adaptable (Huntington 1968) and their internal decision-making processes enable them to respond to changing circumstances. Fourth, transnational actors are more likely to be effective when they recruit other organizations to join a campaign coalition around a set of policy ideas. Fifth, transnational actors are more likely to be effective when opposing transnational advocacy coalitions are not sufficiently mobilized or lack the resources to pursue a plausible counter-offensive. Finally, transnational actors are more likely to be effective when crisis conditions exist. This helps to render the problem definitions and institutional solutions proposed by transnational actors more legitimate and desirable in the eyes of national officials.

Conclusion

This chapter has developed a general model of transnational actor influence on domestic policy processes. This model is presented graphically in figure 3.1. It shows that transnational advocacy coalitions exert influence across different phases of the policy process by behaving as proposal actors rather than veto players. It suggests that transnational actor interventions are determined by the ideas, resources, and decision-making processes of transnational actors themselves and that these organizational factors change over time. The model follows Jacoby (2008) in suggesting that transnational actors work with domestic actors through different modes of influence including "inspiration," "subsidy," and "partnership." It elaborates these coalition interactions between transnational and domestic actors across time and policy phases. This model also provides some clear hypotheses about the conditions for transnational actor effectiveness, outlined in the previous section. The following chapters flesh out this model at the transnational (chapter 4) and domestic (chapter 5) levels of analysis. They explore the hypotheses presented above and provide a nuanced analysis of transnational actor influence on the enactment of pension privatization in countries around the world.

CHAPTER FOUR

The Transnational Campaign
for Pension Privatization

SINCE 1994, transnational actors have organized and coordinated a campaign to promote pension privatization in countries around the world. This chapter provides a narrative account of the development of this campaign and the transnational actors involved in it. It illustrates the model of transnational actor influence developed in chapter 3 above. First, it shows how a transnational epistemic community supporting pension privatization was established and took up positions of power within leading international organizations, including the World Bank. Second, it shows that these organizations have enjoyed sufficient resources to exert a pervasive influence on domestic pensions policy in multiple countries. Third, it demonstrates that the World Bank in particular has adopted a relatively flexible reform template and learned from experience and internal debates in the course of its campaign. Fourth, it shows that a wide variety of transnational policy actors have joined the global campaign for pension privatization, including independent policy entrepreneurs, major international organizations, and professional networks. Finally, it provides evidence that an opposing transnational advocacy coalition led by the ILO has not had the resources to counter the World Bank–led campaign effectively. The campaign for pension privatization shares many of the features of what Tarrow (2005) calls a "campaign coalition," a joint venture among different activist organizations characterized by long-term coordination and a high intensity of collaboration toward the achievement of a principled policy goal.

DEVELOPING A TRANSNATIONAL CAMPAIGN

Pension privatization often is portrayed as a Chilean innovation that was copied elsewhere, but this interpretation obscures the reforms' transnational roots. While pension privatization was launched first in Chile in the late 1970s and early 1980s, it was inspired, planned, and implemented by economists embedded in a transnational movement determined to initiate a neoliberal economic revolution in Latin America. This movement was assisted by the U.S. Agency for International Development, which supported the university training of many of Chile's so-called Chicago boys and the economics department of the Catholic University of Santiago, which became their academic and spiritual home (Valdes 1995). Chile quickly became a model for other neoliberal economists in Latin America, and Chilean economists contributed greatly to a transnational campaign to advance the neoliberal economic model. Several Chileans subsequently became prominent international policy entrepreneurs in their own right (Brooks 2005; Weyland 2005).

The transnational campaign for pension privatization gained substantially in power and influence in 1994 with the publication of a major World Bank report that heralded full support of the Bank for pension privatization. Since 1994, transnational actors have been deeply involved in each subsequent instance of pension privatization. Although the World Bank, with its unparalleled resources and legitimacy, became the core actor in the campaign for pension privatization, many other organizations joined in support. There is evidence of coordination as well as conflict within this coalition, which includes USAID, the Inter-American Development Bank (IDB), the Asian Development Bank (ADB), and OECD, among others.

The transnational coalition for pension privatization has been opposed by a second coalition that has continued to support the social security pensions model, and was led by the ILO and the ISSA (Queisser 2000, 35). Interestingly, the European Union largely stayed out of the pension reform debate, though it issued several communications in the late 1990s that gave a subtle green light to pension privatization experiments in Central and Eastern Europe and the rest of the EU (European Union 1997).

Over time, the types of reforms advocated by the transnational coalition supporting pension privatization have changed somewhat, particularly within the World Bank (2005, 2). Internal debates within transnational actors and between them have had a substantial effect on the policy advice given in different countries. For instance, the World Bank has been stung by allegations of high fees in Latin America's new private pension systems and has altered its advice to countries as a result. The ILO has showed some responsiveness to World Bank agendas in the hope of moving beyond an outright confrontation (Charlton and McKinnon 2002, 1182).

Pension privatization has been advocated by a transnational coalition that spread these reforms as part of a well-organized campaign. This campaign began when members of a neoliberal epistemic community took positions of power in leading state and transnational organizations and worked to formulate a coherent global agenda to guide their activity. Ultimately, the campaign for pension privatization encompassed a variety of transnational actors working in cooperation and conflict, whose actions have been driven by their own ideas, resources, and internal decisions that have changed over time. This chapter explores the nature of the campaign (and counter-campaign) they developed and how it has sought to influence countries' pension reform choices.

POLICY DEVELOPMENT: THE CHILEAN MODEL

The story of pension privatization begins in Chile in the early 1980s, a dramatic setting that has shaped debates on pension privatization ever since. After the U.S.-supported overthrow of the democratically elected government of Salvador Allende by General Augusto Pinochet in 1973, Pinochet's government began a series of radical economic reforms inspired by "Chicago school" neoliberal economics. Indeed, a central part of this story are the "Chicago boys" (Mesa-Lago 1994; Valdes 1995; Kay 1998; Kurtz 1999; Madrid 2003), a group of young Chilean economists trained at U.S. universities, sometimes with U.S. government support. The story of the Chicago boys has been told many times. To those on the left, it represents the violence of the regime and the defeat of more humane leftist economic policies in conjunction with U.S. domination in Latin America. To the right, it represents an unusual and successful effort to impose right-thinking economic policy in the face of leftist revolution—an effort that is now bearing fruit in economic growth and progress toward democracy. The Pinochet regime, and the pension reforms that came with it, was one of the most dramatic episodes in twentieth-century political economy. It became a critical policy laboratory for later reforms in countries in Latin America and around the world.

The Chilean reforms of 1980–1981 have often been viewed in a purely domestic context, but they actually represented a transnational collaboration among reformers, external advisers, and "local" economists who were educated in the United States and formed part of a growing transnational network or epistemic community (Haas 1992) of neoliberal economists carefully cultivated by economists in leading U.S. universities. After implementing pension privatization in Chile, this transnational network further refined and debated these ideas and eventually was able to persuade many transnational policy actors, notably the World Bank, to join an advocacy coalition for advancing pension privatization in countries around the world.

The Chilean reforms of the 1970s and 1980s represented the vanguard of a transnational movement that had advocated monetarist economics and market-oriented policies as a counterweight to the Keynesianism that dominated economic policy in most of the world since the Second World

War. A leading center for this new monetarist economics was the University of Chicago, whose economics department and graduate school of business entered into a U.S. government–sponsored aid program to Chile in the 1950s (Valdes 1995, 126). The purpose of the program was to train a group of elite economists to return to teach at the Catholic University of Santiago to counter the leftist economics that were dominant in Latin America at the time and produce local economists who could assist further aid efforts. This program proved remarkably successful. Chicago graduates, trained by Milton Friedman and other ultra-conservative economists, returned to Chile to build up the Catholic University economics department. Despite some early resistance from students there, they introduced monetarist economics into the academic debate in Chile and later, under the Pinochet regime, were gradually called into government service to provide a radical new direction for Chilean economic policy. The Chicago boys, then, were the outgrowth of a successful long-term plan to alter the balance of Chilean economic policy by one branch of the U.S. government, USAID. They went on to implement a complex series of reforms, including monetarist inflation stabilization, labor market reforms, enterprise reforms, and pension privatization, among many others. Recent analysts of Chile's neoliberal experiment have emphasized that these reforms occurred in stages (Kurtz 1999), starting with more radical monetarist approaches that were later tempered by social and political concerns, reflecting a process of political and policy learning.

The Chilean Chicago boys, including Labor Minister José Piñera (a Harvard graduate), imbibed neoliberal ideas during their studies at leading U.S. universities, particularly in Chicago, but also at Columbia, Harvard, and MIT. The program they designed in Chile in 1980–1981 marked a major departure from the country's previous tradition of social insurance. Chile's pension system was experiencing systemic failure in the 1970s. It contained many different systems for different sectors of the economy, with civil servants and well-off individuals receiving higher pension benefits and more generous terms. It was inequitable, bankrupt, and financed by a very high payroll tax of 16–26 percent of wages, depending on the type of job (Edwards 1998, 38). The new system eliminated the old social-security type systems and replaced them with a unified system (though exempting the military) based on individual, private accounts plus a minimum pension guarantee. People who had contributed to the old system received "recognition bonds" from the state that were deposited in their individual accounts and paid a 4 percent interest rate (Edwards 1998, 50). Accounts were managed by pension fund management companies (AFPs) that each established a single pension fund. Contribution rates were set at 10 percent of payroll for pensions, plus an additional 3 percent for disability and life insurance. This substantially reduced payroll tax rates and increased take-home pay, making the program popular among workers.

After implementing pension reform in Chile, reforms faltered as inflation spiraled out of control and a widespread economic crisis in 1982 caused many to question the Chilean model (cf. Edwards 1998). Yet the government held firm to its economic principles, and once the economy revived and began to grow, Chile's pension reform began to bear fruit. Account balances grew rapidly and the reform began to be seen as a legitimate model for other countries, particularly in Latin America (Brooks 2004; Nelson 2004), but also by an international community that had grown more accepting of the neoliberal economic model. The next countries to adopt pension privatization were mostly in Latin America, plus the United Kingdom under Margaret Thatcher. These countries began to consider the implementation of the Chilean model in the early 1990s, in some cases before leading international organizations began to vigorously advocate the Chilean reforms as a possible template (Brooks 2004; Weyland 2005). Still, in many cases transnational policy actors funded the reform teams that considered pension privatization.

Chilean reformers were central to a growing transnational advocacy coalition that supported pension privatization in Latin America. The Chilean government made a major push to publicize its new economic reforms in the 1980s, with special attention to the innovative pension system. This campaign included the sponsorship of academic publications by leading Chilean universities as well as publications, conferences, and activities by leading think tanks, government organizations, and advisers to export the Chilean model. The U.N. Economic Commission for Latin America (ECLAC), based in Chile, contributed by sponsoring a major publication series on pension reforms in Latin America (Demarco 2004, 87). Chilean investment fund companies (AFPs) that managed the private, individual accounts under the system also undertook substantial efforts to spread pension privatization ideas, including an annual conference that brought economists and practitioners together to promote these reforms (interview with Estelle James, June 28, 2005).

Leading Chilean pension reformer José Piñera played a key role in this effort. Piñera (1991) set forth the ideology of the Chilean pension reforms and proved to be a fantastically successful spokesman among Latin American policy makers (Demarco 2004, 87ff.). Piñera established his own think tank and has made a career of promoting pension privatization worldwide. He speaks frequently at events organized by the World Bank and USAID to promote pension privatization, provides *pro bono* advice to governments, organizes study trips to Chile, and often meets with top governmental leaders to convince them of the principles of pension privatization. Piñera has also worked with the Cato Institute to advance pension reforms in the United States and worldwide. Piñera has met with U.S. President George W. Bush, Russian President Vladimir Putin, Peruvian President Alberto Fujimori, and many other world leaders in his advocacy role. He is credited with convincing many Latin American presidents to support reform (Müller 2003, 34, 46).

POLICY DEVELOPMENT: THE WORLD BANK COMES ON BOARD

A turning point in the development of the transnational coalition for pension privatization came in 1994 with the publication of *Averting the Old Age Crisis*, which brought the World Bank and its resources fully on board with the campaign for pension privatization. This publication was the result of a research project initiated by World Bank Chief Economist Larry Summers in the early 1990s. Summers had become concerned with issues of old age finance and the impact of demographic aging on pension systems worldwide. Nancy Birdsall was research director of the World Bank at the time and appointed Estelle James, an academic economist who had just joined the Bank, to lead a team tasked with writing a major report on pension system design worldwide (interview with Estelle James, June 28, 2005).

Averting represented a turning point in the global pension reform effort. It was important for two reasons: first, it represented a major advance in pension reform thinking and, second, the process of writing and disseminating the work helped to establish a large group of pension privatization experts and a broad consensus within the World Bank on pension privatization methods. In the terms suggested by Barnett and Finnemore (2004), *Averting* was important because it created new knowledge about pension reform that allowed the World Bank to reshape preferences and behaviors of actors. It established the World Bank as the foremost authority in pension reform research and thinking. The Bank later backed up this expert authority with substantial resources devoted to pension reform technical assistance and lending (World Bank 2006).

Averting precipitated a measurable shift in World Bank pension policy. Before its publication, the World Bank did not consistently advocate pension privatization and individual pension accounts in its policy advice. World Bank pension advice prior to 1994 was more similar to its style in areas such as health care, where a multiplicity of advice was given by individual consultants and reform teams (Deacon 1997; Nelson 2004). In a systematic search of all publicly available project documents related to pensions on the World Bank documents Web page, it is clear that several World Bank publications as late as 1993 warned against pension privatization, arguing that it would not solve fundamental problems facing systems in Central and Eastern Europe. These publications were written by Nicholas Barr, a frequent consultant to the World Bank who is a well-known scholar and critic of pension privatization. Between 1994 and 2004, no project documents by the World Bank were inconsistent with pension privatization, indicating that a policy shift within the Bank took place in conjunction with the publication of *Averting*.

Averting reshaped pension reform debates primarily by turning attention to the newly defined problem of demographic aging. Such classification and reclassification techniques are a key part of how international organizations and other bureaucracies extend their authority through knowledge creation (Barnett and Finnemore 2004, 31–32). Generating a new problem definition around demographic aging provided a key justification for radical reforms. *Averting* found that a tripling of the global elderly population (over age sixty) between 1990 and 2030 from 500 million to 1.4 billion would put growing pressure on existing pension arrangements in developed and developing countries alike (World Bank 1994, 1). A global pension crisis was in the making. The experience of this crisis differed from country to country and region to region. In mature industrialized countries in Europe, pension expenditures placed an overwhelming burden on the national budget, exceeding 10 percent of GDP in many countries and projected to rise dramatically. In most developing countries, with the exception of Central and Eastern Europe, pension expenditures were far lower, but still increasing. Pension systems in these countries often faced serious difficulties in reaching the poorest of the poor, who were often not working in the formal economy and thus had little or no access to state-operated pension systems. Dramatically rising pension expenditures, though low in relative terms, tended to benefit relatively well-off segments of the formal labor force and prevent governments from responding to a variety of pressing development-related priorities.

Averting synthesized a neoliberal critique of existing welfare state arrangements. It argued that existing social security–type pension systems were unable to cope with emerging demographic pressures. With demographic aging, as the number of people receiving pensions increases and the number of workers declines, budget deficits occur. As a result, social security systems were going to face long-term fiscal crises. Second, *Averting* highlighted administrative and political challenges to the stability of social security systems. It showed that the usual manner of balancing budgets in social security systems by changing parameters of the program tended to create inconsistent benefits over time and undesirable forms of redistribution. Certain cohorts gained far more from social security systems than others, and not always in ways anticipated by program designers. The report further argued that in developing countries in particular, pay-as-you-go systems are vulnerable to moral hazard on the part of politicians. Politicians have a tendency to promise more pensions in the future than pay-as-you-go systems can deliver, compounding fiscal crisis. State social security agencies often experience severe administrative difficulties. For instance, state-managed pension funds provide negative returns in many countries (World Bank 1994, 128). Overall, *Averting* argued that social security systems provide low returns on investment and leave many people uncovered, tending to benefit already privileged sectors of the labor force, particularly in developing countries.

Most important, *Averting* developed a comprehensive and attractive alternative to public social security–type pension systems that promised to rationalize the delivery of income-related benefits while enhancing redistribution. To achieve these multiple goals, *Averting* advocated what it calls a "multi-pillar" or three-pillar approach to pension reform that neatly divides redistributive and income-related benefits into separate "pillars." *Averting* called for

1. A first pillar of state-provided, redistributive benefits, such as a flat, minimum pension, pension guarantee, or reduced social security system
2. A second pillar of mandatory pension savings in privately managed individual accounts
3. A third pillar of voluntary savings in funded individual or occupational pension plans.

The pension privatization model advocated by *Averting* differed significantly from the Chilean model. First, *Averting* did not advocate a complete replacement of the former pay-as-you-go pension system, as had been done in Chile. Instead, *Averting* offered a broad policy template that could be mixed and matched in a variety of formats to suit individual country conditions. Importantly, it opened the way for so-called mixed reforms that reduced the public pay-as-you-go system and replaced it only in part. By making advice more flexible than doctrinaire advocacy of the Chilean approach of complete replacement of the existing social security system, *Averting* made the transnational policy approach more appealing to a broader array of countries while maintaining an emphasis on individual, privately managed, funded accounts.

Averting argued that a primary benefit of pension privatization was not only to better fulfill the insurance and poverty-reduction aspects of pension systems, but also to facilitate capital market development and investment in developing countries. It argued that countries could attain a major benefit for development through the creation of large pools of domestic pension capital that could be used to finance private sector development and growth. Although there has been widespread debate about the extent to which pension fund savings actually increases average savings rates in an economy, this was one of the clear objectives of *Averting*—to use pension savings to increase economic growth and thus absolute pension levels in the long run. The creation of large pools of publicly mandated, privately managed savings has been a primary reason for the interest from international financial institutions and multi-national corporations involved in the management of private pension funds, such as Citibank, ING, and other large banking and investment companies.

Other organizations in the pension privatization coalition followed the lead of the World Bank in mainstreaming the innovative Chilean model. In 1994, for instance, the Inter-American Development Bank (IDB) also published a book that called for three-pillar reforms in Latin America, echoing the approach in *Averting*. It argued for increasing the linkage between contributions and benefits and increasing reliance on funded, privately managed pensions (De Oliveira 1994, 8–13). USAID generally followed the World Bank's lead on broad reform strategy as well after 1994. USAID has tended to emphasize the financial sector development aspects of pension reform in the countries where it has worked (interview with Charles Becker, May 2005), making its pension reform assistance part of its financial sector development projects. OECD has produced an extensive publications series and organized conferences to promote pension privatization ideas in developed and developing countries.

As in other areas of reform, the transnational advocacy coalition for pension privatization was not without opponents. It was opposed by a second coalition composed primarily of the International Social Security Association (ISSA) and the International Labour Organization (ILO), organizations deeply involved in the spread of social security model pension systems. These competing coalitions occasionally debated one another head on (Beattie and McGillivray 1995; James 1996). They also competed in the field. However, the ILO-led coalition has had far less funding than the World Bank and was not successful in blocking its norms creation and diffusion mission (interview with Elaine Fultz, May 2005). As the World Bank–led coalition moved from success to success, the ILO-led coalition increasingly looked like it was fighting a rearguard action. In 2000, the ILO issued a book (Gillion et al. 2000) accepting pension privatization as one possible option for reform, while pointing out its faults. Increasingly, the ILO provided support on pensions to countries where the World Bank did not advocate pension privatization, particularly in poorer developing countries in Africa, Asia, and Europe. In only a few cases did it directly oppose pension privatization in countries where the World Bank was active, as in Hungary (see chapter 5 below). In recent years, the World Bank and ILO have attempted to engage in more dialogue and less confrontation in the field (Holzmann and Hinz 2005, 61). After all, both organizations in theory operate under the larger U.N. umbrella. Nelson (2004, 50) suggests that the pension reform debates in Latin America lacked the "multiple models, with contested strengths and weaknesses" that characterized debates over education and health care reform. No doubt, the transnational advocacy coalition in favor of pension privatization was particularly focused around a clear platform for change after 1994, but it did face, and overcome, opposition. It was helped by the fact that the opposition it faced was not as well organized or resourced.

In sum, pension privatization ideas has been developed by a transnational advocacy coalition of policy actors including Chilean reformers, U.S. economists, U.S. government agencies, and the World Bank and other multi-lateral international organizations. This powerful coalition issued its manifesto in 1994 and gained the full resources of the World Bank at that time. This campaign has been organized and coordinated among the main actors through various international conferences, donor meetings, and individual contacts. Through the efforts of individual proposal actors and their cooperation, this coalition has advocated the transfer of pension privatization policies to countries around the world.

POLICY DEVELOPMENT: INTERNAL DEBATES

The World Bank–led coalition for pension privatization faced substantial internal debates about its policy direction in the years between 1994 and 2007. These debates have led to changes in the advice offered to countries and have contributed to determining the outcomes of reform in various countries. Changes in World Bank policy preferences have arisen from internal debates at the Bank as well as from the interaction with and observation of country experiences over time. Counter to the claims of Haas (1990), who found that the World Bank had no institutional capability to learn as a result of input and experience, this study finds significant evidence of learning (see also Ramesh 2007). This adaptability has played an important role in making pension privatization attractive to a wide variety of countries and domestic interest groups.

While *Averting* was commissioned by World Bank Chief Economist Lawrence Summers, his successor Joseph Stiglitz opposed pension privatization. Stiglitz organized an internal World Bank conference in 1999 to discuss the Bank's work in promoting pension privatization and presented a paper with Peter Orszag entitled, "Rethinking Pension Reform: 10 Myths about Social Security Systems" (Orszag and Stiglitz 2001). Stiglitz and Orszag had previously served on President Clinton's Council of Economic Advisors and had resisted implementing pension privatization in the United States. This should complicate the perspective of those who believe that the U.S. government has been the primary actor pushing pension privatization overseas (interview with Richard Hinz, World Bank Social Protection Unit, 2005). While USAID has played an important role in spreading pension privatization, the U.S. government was not always fully supportive of these reforms during the period under investigation. When Stiglitz left the White House, he brought his skepticism of pension privatization to the World Bank, an organization that had become visibly committed to these reforms. He tried to dampen the organization's enthusiasm.

In pursuing this agenda, Stiglitz and his team faced off against the group of pension reform economists established around the *Averting* project and subsequent policy implementation teams in Latin America and Central and Eastern Europe and Central Asia. The Chief Economist's 1999 conference produced a clash between these two perspectives that was played out openly within the Bank's pension reform community. Orszag and Stiglitz's conference paper argued that the Bank had advocated an ideological, cookie-cutter approach to pension reforms that did not suit all countries and did not take a broad enough view of viable pension reform options. They suggested that systems of private, individual pension savings accounts were not right for all countries and that there should be a return to the more contextual advice given in the pre-1994 period. Pension reform advocates at the Bank argued that the Bank did take country circumstances into account and wished to use the occasion to learn more about what was working and what was not, and how to correct any problems in the future. They debated issues such as fees in private individual accounts, issues of gender equity, and methods of public and private management. Overall, the pension privatization team defended the World Bank's advice, showed an appetite for constructive criticism, and suggested that Orszag and Stiglitz, coming out of the White House, did not fully understand developing country circumstances, where pension privatization could be particularly beneficial by spurring capital market development and solving old age crises before they became acute.

Orszag and Stiglitz's offensive against pension privatization was mostly rebuffed by the pension reform community within the Bank. The head of the Social Protection division within the World Bank, Robert Holzmann, eventually co-edited the book that came out of the 1999 conference (Holzmann and Stiglitz 2001) and sponsored a mid-course correction in the Bank's work that took some of Orszag and Stiglitz's points on board, but not others. Holzmann's 1999 essay, "The World Bank Approach to Pension Reform," emphasized that the Bank did not provide one type of advice to countries and addressed many of the concerns Stiglitz raised without appealing for a fundamental change in Bank practices in technical or policy advice. The 1999 conference did cause some changes in the Bank's practice, rendering it more willing to consider a variety of options proposed by countries, and making a focus on management fees for private pension accounts a high priority for the Bank. It also reinforced concern about implementing pension privatization in countries without strong financial markets. The Bank advised countries to write lower fees into subsequent legislation and initiated a review of Latin American country experiences to put pressure on some of the countries with the worst fee excesses.

By 2005, more substantial revisionist challenges had grown within the World Bank, leading to the publication of three books and one internal report that again questioned aspects of the Bank's work on pension privatization (Ramesh 2007, 114–118). First, Gill, Packard, and Yermo (2005) raised questions about the World Bank's efforts to support pension privatization in Latin America (see also Shah 1997). The book focused on weaknesses in the Latin American privatized pension systems, particularly the high administrative fees charged in individual pension savings accounts and how fees placed an undue burden on the first generation of retirees in the system, which lost a large percentage of their eventual retirement income. Second, a book edited by Barr (2005) emphasized the substantial benefit of reforms to existing social security systems and argued that these often had the potential to do more good than the creation of privatized pension systems. Third, Holzmann and Hinz (2005) responded to internal critics by showing that the World Bank did not advise all countries the same way, but tailored advice to country conditions. It argued that the Bank did not coerce countries to enact pension privatization but, on the contrary, tried to support reforms that were either appropriate or requested in particular countries. It used a variety of internal data sources to suggest that the Bank had been equally active in recommending reforms to social security systems, rather than advocating pension privatization everywhere. Finally, the World Bank's Operations Evaluation Department issued a report in 2006 that substantially criticized the tenor and direction of World Bank policy advice. This report argued that the Bank had by and large emphasized the pension privatization approach even in countries where financial markets were not fully developed and where such systems were unlikely to work (World Bank 2006). On the basis of this, it seems fair to conclude, as O'Brien (2002, 145) does, that "international organizations are both a tool for implementing policy of powerful actors and an arena for contesting the content of that policy."

The World Bank also confronted serious debates with the International Monetary Fund over its new pension reform advice. Starting in the mid-1990s, IMF officials questioned whether pension privatization placed an undue burden on countries' fiscal policy. Financing the transition to pension privatization typically requires governments to borrow substantially, something that may not be healthy for a highly indebted developing country. A 1998 IMF paper by Cangiano, Cottarelli, and Cubeddu (1998), for instance, warned that it would be wrong to ignore the "potential risks implicit in fully funded systems, in particular those related to financial risk and inadequate supervision." Ultimately, however, the IMF agreed to support the World Bank's pension privatization campaign through assistance with fiscal projections and planning, though with greater misgivings about its fiscal impact. Pension privatization advocates suggested that concerns with the fiscal impact of these reforms were somewhat of a chimera. They argued that the reforms simply made explicit an "implicit pension debt" represented by government promises to retirees, rather than creating new debt.

While the IMF took a supportive but somewhat ambivalent stance on pension privatization, the World Bank became a consistent advocate after 1994. This was reflected in the Bank's work, though it did take into account different country circumstances. At the same time, the norms according to which the Bank operated were continuously challenged internally starting in 1999. These debates do appear to have had an impact on the type of advice the Bank gives. In particular, there has been greater attention to the issue of high administrative fees and the question of whether pension privatization is suitable for all countries, regardless of wealth, capital market development, and other circumstances. The World Bank appears to have become somewhat more hesitant over time to advise the adoption of pension privatization in countries where capital market infrastructure is weak, as in poorer former communist countries in Europe and Eurasia, such as Serbia, Armenia, and Uzbekistan (interview with Hermann von Gersdorff, World Bank Social Protection Division, 2005). On the other hand, the Bank is still subject to pressures to provide technical advice to countries that wish to implement World Bank–style reforms, regardless of circumstances.

Transnational actor interventions in domestic policy decisions are driven to a large extent by these transnational actors' own ideas, resources, and decision-making procedures. The World Bank has had a unique impact on pension policy development through *Averting* and later reports. However, different transnational actors have different ideas, opinions, resources, and capacities. USAID, for instance, differs greatly from the World Bank in not having a great deal of policy development expertise in house. USAID does not have the extensive publication series the World Bank has, including books, working papers, and the like. It does very little in the area of norms creation, though it does develop sectoral strategies, periodically assess its own work, and commission papers that may be used to direct its policy activities (interview with Denise La-maute, July 5, 2005). With limited internal expertise, USAID relies heavily on the World Bank and other norms-creating organizations to develop pension reform ideas and expertise (see section on organizational cooperation below). USAID officials attend World Bank training sessions to learn the latest thinking and techniques for the new pension reforms. USAID similarly sponsors country officials to attend World Bank training conferences. Such cooperation suggests that transnational actors specialize in certain competencies and phases of the reform process, such as norms creation, policy development, policy advice, and implementation. By coordinating with other actors who have different organizational capacities and strengths, they magnify their influence.

Pension privatization is more than a set of free-floating ideas: it represents a coherent policy program developed by transnational actors and influenced by the internal norms, behaviors, and resources of these organizations. It has been developed in a transnational policy space by a specific coalition of actors, giving specific shape to these reforms. The following sections explore the role of transnational actors in the transfer and implementation of these reforms in countries around the world.

Policy Transfer

The transnational advocacy coalition for pension privatization began to score high-profile successes in policy transfer starting in the early 1990s. As Brooks (2004) and Weyland (2004) have pointed out, some of these came about as Chilean reformers spread their reform ideas in Latin America without much assistance from major IFIs. However, starting in the early 1990s, as World Bank support for pension privatization coalesced with the publication of *Averting*, the World Bank, USAID, and the Chilean reformers increasingly joined forces in advancing the pension privatization program. Additional international organizations were brought into the fold, including the regional development banks, IDB and ADB, the IMF, and multi-national companies. Even the ILO began to view mandatory, private pensions as one legitimate option for reform (Gillion et al. 2000). As a brief look at the country evidence shows (see Table 4.1 below), it was not uncommon for two or three different organizations to be involved in some capacity in advocating pension privatization in each reforming country.

In most cases, such assistance was carefully coordinated. Coordination took place in a variety of ways. For instance, in planning its pension reform assistance, USAID always would begin by assessing current involve-

ment by other transnational policy actors. This was done to avoid dupli-
cation of efforts and to identify the most critical tasks (interview with
Denise Lamaute, July 5, 2005). Organizations tended to specialize and
rely on one another for specific roles and tasks. For instance, USAID and
the World Bank often asked Chilean promoters of pension privatization
to give pep talks to reformers in other countries. In one example, José
Piñera, the leading Chilean pension reformer and transnational advocate,
gave a talk in 2000 that was beamed via satellite to World Bank offices
in Bulgaria, Latvia, Lithuania, and Uzbekistan, where it was viewed by an
audience comprised of local Bank staff and leading government officials.
Coordination among transnational actors has been a routine practice in
the transnational campaign for pension privatization.

Müller (2003) shows that in the eight countries selected for her study,
all had substantial direct involvement from multiple transnational policy
actors. Müller's study looked at two countries from each of four sub-
regions: Central Europe, Southeastern Europe, the Andes, and the Southern Cone of Latin America. Chief among the transnational policy actors
pushing pension privatization was the World Bank, actively involved in
every global reform process except for Uruguay, where the World Bank
ultimately loaned $100 million for reform implementation. While there
still may be selection bias, her study gives a good sense of the level and
types of involvement of various transnational policy actors. In addition
to the World Bank, transnational policy actors included leading Chilean
economists, notably José Piñera, the former Chilean Minister of Labor,
who "personally convinced more than one Latin American president to
embark on pension privatization" (Müller 2003, 117), the IMF, USAID,
the Inter-American Development Bank, the United Nations Development
Program (UNDP), and the Asian Development Bank (ADB). Many of
these organizations are headquartered in Washington, D.C.

In every case studied by Müller (2003), government reform teams planning pension privatization were financed by external actors and provided
with extensive technical assistance. Table 4.1 details the types of involvement of transnational policy actors in the diffusion of pension reform in
the countries she studied. It suggests that transnational policy actors made
a coordinated effort to spread pension privatization worldwide, with a
regional focus on Latin America and Central and Eastern Europe. In all
countries, several transnational policy actors have played complementary
roles in the reform process. The table underlines the ubiquitous involvement of multiple transnational policy actors in pension privatization processes in Latin America and Central and Eastern Europe. Their involvement extends from pre-reform technical advice to mid-reform public
relations campaigns to assistance with reform implementation.

TABLE 4.1
Involvement of Transnational Actors in Pension Privatization

Country	Transnational actor involvement
Argentina (1994)	• Chilean economists play advisory role • World Bank finances reform team • United Nations Development Program provides technical assistance • IMF includes pension reform in loan conditionality
Uruguay (1996)	• Chilean economists play advisory role • IDB finances planning of reform by Uruguayan and foreign economists under leadership of a Brazilian economist • IDB provides $150 million loan to finance transition to funded system • World Bank provides $100 million to finance transition to funded system
Peru (1993)	• Chilean economists play advisory role • IDB provides technical support and advice • World Bank provides technical support and advice
Bolivia (1997)	• Chilean economists play advisory role • USAID funds pension reform team • World Bank provides technical assistance and finances pension reform experts • World Bank requires pension privatization as part of loan conditionality • Spanish banks dominate pension fund system
Hungary (1998)	• World Bank finances reform team and provides technical assistance • USAID provides technical assistance to pension fund regulator • World Bank provides loan to finance transition

MODES AND MECHANISMS OF TRANSNATIONAL ACTOR INFLUENCE

What are the modes and mechanisms by which the World Bank and other transnational actors have attempted to influence countries to adopt pension privatization? As discussed in chapter 3 above, transnational actors typically use a variety of techniques to exert pervasive influence across phases of the policy process. I argue that they can best be described as "proposal actors," using a combination of ideational suasion and material incentives to encourage domestic actors to support reform and

TABLE 4.1 (*cont'd*)
Involvement of Transnational Actors in Pension Privatization

Country	Transnational actor involvement
Poland (1999)	• World Bank finances reform team • World Bank employee appointed to head Polish Office of the Plenipotentiary for Pension Reform • World Bank and USAID sponsor trips for decision makers and opinion leaders to Argentina and Chile • World Bank provides loan to finance transition
Croatia (2002)	• Chilean economists play advisory role • World Bank finances critical conference on reform organized by East-West Institute bringing Chilean and other international experts to advocate pension privatization • IMF and World Bank provide technical advice • World Bank employee appointed National Coordinator of Pension Reform in Croatia
Bulgaria (2002)	• IMF and World Bank conditionality requires pension reform • World Bank provides $24 million for technical assistance, study tours, and consultants • USAID funds and provides technical assistance for reform preparation and public information campaign

Sources: Orenstein 2000 and particularly Müller 2003.

achieve pension reform outcomes. Because transnational actors do not hold a formal veto over national pension policies, they seek to change or promote the policy preferences of domestic actors through a wide variety of means, hovering over reform processes like nervous parents.

In the first place, World Bank and other transnational actor officials seek to identify promising candidates for reform and country officials who are potential partners. In the language of the Bank, they seek out countries that have the "political will" to reform. This is done through a variety of means. One method is to use conferences and seminars on pension privatization typically held at Harvard University, Oxford University, or the University of Pennsylvania, to get to know a wide variety of pension reform officials from countries around the world. This helps World Bank officials to identify which countries may be serious about pension reform and to recruit new allies to their cause. The World Bank, through its World Bank Institute (formerly the Economic Development Institute) has run a large number of such seminars over the years, training thousands of social policy and finance officials from dozens of countries in pension privatization ideas (Brooks 2004; Holzmann and Hinz 2005, 60; interview with Gustavo Demarco, World Bank Institute, 2005). The World Bank and other organizations also have developed substantial publication series on pension privatization, including a "pension reform primer" intended to train country officials in the workings of pension privatization. It is presented in simple language and provides a wide array of country and topical units. Conferences and publications often provide national pension officials with their first contact with pension privatization ideas. In the case of Kazakhstan, for instance, described in detail in chapter 5 below, senior reformer Grigori Marchenko first learned of pension privatization at a 1996 World Bank conference where he heard a lecture on individual accounts by Chilean reformer José Piñera (Ellerman 2001). Although he had been in the midst of leading a different type of pension reform program for Kazakhstan, he immediately scrapped the old plan after this meeting and began to implement a new pension reform model in Kazakhstan (Orenstein 2000; interview with Marchenko, 1998).

Conferences, seminars, and publications can be seen as part of a strategy of "inspiration" (Jacoby 2004) to recruit and develop new partners in national government—and shape their policy preferences. However, transnational actors focus most of their resources on countries where they have already established willing partners. Here the emphasis shifts to providing these partners with resources to elevate their political fortunes ("partnership"), creating incentives for other domestic veto players to join the reform bandwagon ("subsidy"), and training new pension reform officials in the technical tasks of administration. According to an official World Bank report, "Once the seeds for pension reform are sown, the challenge is to train technicians in the new skills required in administration, regulation, and supervision" (Holzmann and Hinz 2005, 60). Though transnational actors are by their nature not domestic veto players, they can shape the preferences of veto players and provide them with resources and technical competencies that make them more likely to succeed.

One of the key contributions of the World Bank to pension privatization reform efforts worldwide has been the provision of sophisticated modeling software that enables officials to enter parameters and make projections about the future of a country's pension system under different scenarios. This modeling software, which is typically customized for each individual country, provides a unique power resource. Because such complex models are technically demanding to create, they can provide a distinct advantage to reformers who are able to better demonstrate the benefits of their own ideas, undercut the reform proposals of their opponents, and display their greater technical acuity and resources in expert debate (interview with Robert Palacios, World Bank, 1998).

Other ideational resources provided by transnational actors also act to bolster the political power of domestic reformers. Access to high-powered legal experts and consultants can help domestic reformers to out-gun their opponents in public or intra-governmental debate by providing more sophisticated ideas, proposals, and promotional material. In this way, ideas become a political resource (Blyth 2002). Provision of transnational technical support to a particular government ministry can make that ministry the center of pension reform discourse and elevate it over its rivals in technical expertise and political salience. For instance, the World Bank in Hungary and Poland initially provided support for pension reform working groups to the Ministry of Finance, which had not historically had first responsibility for pension reform. Instead, that responsibility lay in the hands of the Ministry of Labor and Social Affairs. However, support from the World Bank helped to place Ministries of Finance in these countries in the driver's seat for pension privatization.

The World Bank, IMF, USAID, and regional development banks have frequently provided loans and assistance to countries on the condition that they implement pension privatization. In the early stages of implementation, tax revenues must be diverted to fund individual accounts, but current pensioners still must be paid. This creates enormous financial burdens in the early stages of reform, so-called transition costs, that must be funded somehow, often through additional borrowing. The World Bank, Inter-American Development Bank, International Monetary Fund, and Asian Development Bank have all provided major support for these transition loans. As with all loans, they are relatively fungible, providing ready cash for governments to spend on priority items. Loans are therefore highly desirable. Countries also may see such a loan as a vote of confidence in their economies, an important selling point for international investors and creditors. Müller (2003, 8) suggests that such international signaling has played a significant role in reform calculations in Argentina, Hungary, and Croatia. A large loan may also change the calculus of reform decision makers, reducing the costs of reform implementation and increasing its attractiveness.[1]

Table 4.2 shows the distribution and amount of World Bank pension reform loans by region between 1984 and 2004. This table shows that World Bank pension reform work has been concentrated in Latin America (where loan sizes have been larger on average) and Central and Eastern

[1] Transition costs of switching from a social security system to a private pension system are immense, because the government often must continue paying current social security recipients while directing a share of current worker premiums to individual accounts. The government must finance the difference through issuance of bonds or other means, including loans from international lenders.

TABLE 4.2
Regional Distribution of World Bank Pension Lending, 1984–2004

Region	Number of countries	Value of pension component of loans (in millions of US$)	Number of loans
Sub-Saharan Africa	14	122.2	26
East Asia and Pacific	4	518.4	7
Europe and Central Asia	25	1,626.2	93
Latin America and Caribbean	15	3,067.5	57
Middle East and North Africa	6	76.0	9
South Asia	4	59.0	12

Source: World Bank 2006.

Europe, the regions of the world that have seen the greatest spread of pension privatization. The IMF has often made implementation of pension privatization a condition of its own loans, but has not provided direct assistance for transition costs.

The significance of loan conditionalities in influencing countries to adopt pension privatization is controversial. While there is no doubt that these loan conditions have been important factors, in every country they have been combined with normative influences in a broader program of transnational actor influence. This makes it difficult if not impossible to rigorously divide the influence of resource leveraging versus normative influence on country decisions. While making a strict distinction would help to settle debates about the power of material versus normative influence on policy, the reality is that transnational actors need to combine both elements in order to have influence on country officials—and one another. Resources certainly help these organizations to achieve their normative goals, but they are clearly insufficient in and of themselves. Transnational proposal actors have always needed to use normative suasion in addition to resources to persuade countries to adopt reform. As Juliet Johnson (2008) shows, this may be because different methods may work with different types of domestic actors. Some may be more open to normative suasion, while others require material incentives to comply.

In addition to "resource leveraging," "norms teaching" strategies are commonly used. Transnational proposal actors advance their advocacy agendas, for instance, by sending state bureaucrats, party leaders, journalists, and other opinion leaders on jaunts to attractive locations in South America for seminars with leading reformers. Chilean reformer José Piñera has often set up such visits as a favor to national governments he is advising (interview with author, 2006). The World Bank and USAID have also sponsored numerous study trips. For instance in Poland, USAID spent $1.4 million on a public education strategy to encourage passage of reform legislation. This money paid for distribution of leaflets to trade unions and employers, the creation of an educated core of journalists knowledgeable about the reforms, and study tours for journalists, parliamentarians, and government officials to Argentina, Chile, Denmark, and other countries. Participants on these excursions were selected by Poland's Office of the Plenipiotentiary for Pension Reform. The trips were the most expensive item in this campaign, but they also had high impact, helping to reshape the perspective of participants (interview with Vicki Peterson, USAID Warsaw Office, 1998).

One often overlooked channel of World Bank support to government pension reformers has been through personnel policies. The World Bank has not only seconded or released its own employees to participate in the reform teams for pension privatization in Hungary and Poland in the late 1990s; it has also hired prominent pension reform officials onto its staff. Hungarian finance minister Lajos Bokros joined the World Bank after implementing a series of unpopular financial reforms, including pension privatization. Another top member of the Hungarian reform team, Csaba Fehér, joined the World Bank to work on pension reform. Argentine reformer Gustavo Demarco has led the World Bank Institute's pension reform training effort. Two prominent Croatian reformers were hired to spread pension reform ideas to the rest of the Balkans and elsewhere. In other cases, domestic officials have had long-standing relations with the international financial institutions that may result in lucrative employment opportunities at the World Bank's main office in Washington, D.C., or as consultants attending conferences or visiting countries to share their experiences and advise on reform methods. Opening a revolving door between leading transnational actors and national governments creates individual incentives for top reformers to participate in the pension privatization campaign and also helps to provide high-level personnel resources to reform teams. It further enables neighboring countries to benefit from local knowledge and social learning provided by natives of their own or nearby peer countries.

While much transnational actor assistance is focused on deliberation within governments over pension privatization, transnational actors are often heavily involved in public advocacy as well. While in the early stages of the policy process, transnational actors seek to identify domestic partners and strengthen their technical resources, in later stages, emphasis shifts to winning broader public debates. It is helpful to break the domestic policy process down into three phases: commitment building, coalition building, and implementation. In commitment building, the main focus of reform advocates is getting a government to commit to reform, usually through a vote of the full cabinet. At that point, the policy process enters a new stage of public deliberation aimed at winning diffuse public support for reform. This stage ends with legislation being adopted—or not adopted—by the parliament. Transnational actors often seek to influence public deliberation through sponsoring sophisticated public relations campaigns, sending legislators and journalists on study trips to Chile and other countries in Latin America, and through direct negotiations with interested and even opposing parties, seeking compromises and subsidies that will win their support for pension privatization.

There are numerous examples of major public relations campaigns for pension privatization being financed by USAID and other transnational policy actors. Bulgaria, Croatia, Poland, and Kazakhstan all had major public relations campaigns funded by USAID (see Table 2.2 above). In Kazakhstan, USAID funded a road show in which public officials answered questions about the new pension reforms in "town hall" style meetings. Interestingly, although the U.S. government has sponsored public relations campaigns in other countries organized by leading U.S.-based public relations firms, the Bush administration did not launch a similar campaign of TV commercials and other media to promote pension privatization in the United States in 2004 and 2005.

In addition, transnational policy actors have been deeply involved in implementation of privatized pension systems in countries worldwide. This commitment to smooth reform implementation is a critical part of the transnational campaign for pension privatization. Setting up a privatized pension system is a major administrative challenge, particularly for developing countries. While pension funds themselves are established by private entities, the state plays a very substantial regulatory and administrative role. In the first place, the state must create a system for collecting payroll tax revenues and depositing these in the correct individual accounts. In some countries, like Kazakhstan, this has required the creation of a new system of social security numbers. In many cases, this requires all employers in a country to adopt new practices for paying and assigning social security contributions. Aside from this monumental data-gathering and administrative role, state institutions also must carefully regulate private pension funds, ensuring that they are operating within the constraints of the law and in the best interests of stakeholders. Regulatory agencies must deal with the closure, failure, or merger of funds and other issues that may arise in the initial years. Often, laws and regulations must be refined to cope with new situations that arise.

As a result, transnational actors have typically remained involved in countries they advise for many years after the initial reform. Indeed, Holzmann and Hinz (2005) point out that most World Bank assistance for pension privatization takes place after the reform decision is made. For this reason, they argue that the World Bank should be seen as playing a supporting role, rather than a dominant one in the reform decision. However, there is a strong case to be made that the promise of extensive implementation assistance influences policy makers' calculations about the prospects for reform. In particular, the expectation of post-reform assistance may help to convince decision makers in a country with low administrative capacity that reform is possible. If they believe that transnational actors will not abandon them, anxieties about the possibility of costly failures may be reduced. Second, post-reform technical assistance reduces the chance of reform failure and therefore increases the probability that these reforms will be viewed as legitimate in neighboring countries. Because transnational policy actors want reform to succeed, even in countries where they would not have recommended reform to begin with, they will invest to avoid explosive reform failures. This appears to be an important logic behind World Bank intervention in Kazakhstan in the 1990s (see chapter 5 below). The World Bank has played a major role in reworking reform in Kazakhstan, Peru, and Russia (Cook 2006, 135), pointing out shortcomings of programs, urging reformers to fix them, and attempting to use resource leveraging and moral suasion to get the desired changes. USAID has often spent as many as eight years working on reform implementation in countries that it has advised. Such activity makes sense in the context of the promotion of a larger transnational policy campaign, where prominent failures could provide a potent negative example and disincentive to further countries.

Some new transnational policy actors typically become involved in reform after implementation, particularly local and multinational fund management companies. Such companies may lobby regulatory agencies for changes and team up with other transnational actors. Transnational actor support for reform implementation is not neutral technical support. Instead, it is a key part of the transnational campaign for pension privatization, creating incentives for policy makers to adopt reform and preventing the emergence of failed cases that could slow the spread of reform by negatively affecting the perception of reforms in neighboring countries.

CONCLUSION

This chapter has sketched the role of transnational policy actors in the development of the multi-pillar pension privatization model, its transfer to countries around the world, and implementation. It has explored the development of a loose transnational advocacy coalition of international organizations, bilateral organizations, think tanks, and Chilean advisers who developed and spread pension privatization ideas in a transnational policy space.

Transnational proposal actors seek to have a pervasive influence on the process of policy transfer, identifying domestic partners, strengthening their resources and technical abilities, providing ready-made solutions, and working with them to win governmental commitment, parliamentary legislation, and administrative implementation for pension privatization. This process often takes years and costs millions of dollars. Transnational policy actors' support for reformers has been vital in country after country, as described in detail in the case studies in chapter 5 below.

The following chapters explore the interaction between transnational and domestic actors in depth in three countries and then analyze a global set of cases to show that direct interventions by transnational policy actors have been decisive in many cases. It is impossible to understand the spread of pension privatization without considering how transnational actors influence the domestic politics of reform.

CHAPTER FIVE

Domestic Enactment of Pension Privatization

TRANSNATIONAL POLICY actors develop reform ideas in a global policy space, but often they must be enacted in a specific national context. This raises questions about the relations between transnational policy actors and domestic reformers. Who takes the lead in the transfer of pension privatization ideas? How do transnational policy actors exert influence over domestic actors? What is the relative importance and nature of transnational versus local contributions to reform? To what extent do transnational actors determine specific features of reform in particular countries?

While previous chapters focused on the transnational campaign for pension privatization, this one shifts to the domestic level of analysis. At the domestic level, I portray transnational policy actors as proposal actors who seek to influence domestic veto and proposal actors at various stages of the domestic policy reform process. While previous sections divided transnational policy processes into stages, this one analyzes domestic policy processes across three stages: coalition building, commitment building, and implementation. I apply these concepts to detailed case studies of reform in three post-communist countries, Hungary, Poland, and Kazakhstan, following the veto and proposal actor model presented in chapter 3. These case studies bolster the case for transnational actor influence by emphasizing the role of transnational actors in placing pension privatization on the policy agenda. They provide evidence that transnational actors have shaped the preferences of domestic veto players and partnered with them to achieve reform outcomes. The case studies reveal five main mechanisms of transnational policy actor influence in domestic reform processes. These become the basis for further inquiry into transnational actor effectiveness in chapter 6 below.

The following case studies show that transnational proposal actors influence domestic policy processes by developing and framing policy proposals, accessing internal governmental debates at an early stage in the policy process when many domestic political actors are excluded, forming alliances with governmental actors, and providing resources that help them to win domestic struggles. Many reform outcomes can be directly traced to transnational proposal actors. Transnational actor influence is often mediated by governmental partners who receive inspiration, subsi-

dies, and technical assistance to help facilitate passage of their policy proposals. It tends to be pervasive, across all stages of the policy process, to
compensate for the lack of a concentrated veto power. Finally, the methods that transnational actors use differ from case to case and by stage in
the policy process, though transnational actors appear to be most influential at earlier, agenda-setting stages.

STAGES IN THE POLICY PROCESS

As with the transnational policy process discussed in the previous chapter,
I adopt a three-stage division of the domestic policy process for pension
privatization, dividing the policy process into phases of commitment
building, coalition building, and implementation (Orenstein 2000).

- *Commitment building* is defined as the stage between the first
  discussion of pension privatization proposals by a government to
  formal government commitment to adopt such reforms, usually in
  the form of a cabinet vote, white paper, or other such formal
  mechanism.
- *Coalition building* is defined as the stage between formal adoption
  of a reform proposal by a government to the eventual
  implementation of reform by legislative act. This process involves
  much political bargaining with reform partners, compromise, legal
  and technical work, and public information campaigns.
- *Implementation* is defined as the early stages of reform
  implementation, lasting between five and ten years, in which the new
  system is planned and implemented. During this stage, numerous
  adjustments, changes, and re-reforms are generally conducted,
  making it a highly complex part of the reform process.

This framework has proved to be a useful heuristic for understanding
the different phases of transnational policy actor involvement in pension
privatization processes (Holzman and Hinz 2005, 134). It highlights the
fact that policy processes unfold over time (Pierson 2004) and that different actors and forums for deliberation can be important at different
stages. Actors that have an effective veto at one stage may lose it at a later
stage. Conversely, actors may become involved at a later stage. Decisions
reached at one stage of the process may structure opportunities for decisions reached at later stages.

What follows are detailed case studies of pension privatization in three
postcommunist countries, Hungary, Poland, and Kazakhstan. The first
two were fairly consolidated democracies at the time of reform, while the
latter was an authoritarian regime with some democratic characteristics,

such as an elected president and parliament. These case studies show how transnational and domestic policy actors interact in shaping pension privatization. The postcommunist countries share some similarities. In each case, transnational proposal actors played a central role in placing pension privatization on the agenda, whereas in Latin America, the Chilean reforms were widely known prior to any major transnational campaign. In all cases, prior pension systems suffered from significant fiscal crisis resulting from post-communist transition. However, the post-communist cases analyzed here are fairly representative of other cases in other regions of the world. They present typical examples of the transnational campaign for pension privatization. Chapter 6 uses a global sample of countries to control for any biases implicit in analyzing these post-communist cases. This chapter first explores in detail reform processes in Hungary, Poland, and Kazakhstan, and then draws general lessons about the modes of transnational policy actor influence.

These case studies emphasize each of the three main factors thought to influence pension privatization: (1) economic factors, (2) domestic politics, and (3) transnational policy actors. They break the domestic policy process into three stages (commitment building, coalition building, and implementation) and show that different actors are influential at each stage. Likewise, forums for debate shift over time from the government to parliament to other public forums, with each stage characterized by different deliberative forums. Transnational actors are shown to be important in assisting their domestic government partners at all stages of the process, but their influence is particularly powerful in setting policy agendas within governments at the early, commitment-building stages. Once a government is committed to reform, particularly in a democracy, it must engage in debate, discussion, and compromise with powerful social groups. In this stage, transnational policy actors often play an important, but largely supportive role, as in policy implementation as well. Taking a close look within the domestic policy process for pension privatization helps to understand the nature of the influence transnational proposal actors wield and the conditions under which they are most effective.

PENSION PRIVATIZATION IN HUNGARY

In the mid-1990s, Hungary was facing a severe and worsening pension system deficit. The country charged very high payroll tax rates by international comparison and spent a high proportion of overall GDP on pensions, 10 percent in 1994 (Simonovits 2000; Augustinovics et al. 2002, 30). The number of pensioners was increasing rapidly and the average pension was falling at similar rates, by about 25 percent in real terms between 1990 and 1995 (Cangiano et al. 1998). The ratio of the number of pensioners to the number of contributors jumped from 51 percent to 84 percent in 1996, due to the rise of open unemployment and early retirement (Augustinovics et al. 2002, 30). Hungary had been coping through ad hoc changes in pension levels, which weakened the link between pension contributions and benefits. Both institutionally and fiscally, the Hungarian pension system faced severe challenges (see Palacios and Rocha 1998 for a complete discussion). Reform of the pension system was very much on the agenda thanks to its contribution to fiscal crisis.

A first step toward reform came in 1993, when Hungary created a system of voluntary pension funds in the form of "mutual benefit societies," funded largely by tax advantages. The idea of creating voluntary pension funds in the form of mutual benefit societies was, for the most part, a domestic policy initiative with limited involvement from transnational actors, though some international advisers were involved in advising the Hungarian government on this reform (interview with Antal Deutsch, pension reform adviser, July 1998). The voluntary pension system intended to build civil society by allowing groups of citizens to found their own pension funds. Organization of these voluntary mutual benefit funds had a significant impact on the course of later pension reform in Hungary. However, the creation of voluntary pension funds did not address the underlying fiscal problems of Hungary's pension system.

Further progress on pension reform in Hungary began when Lajos Bokros was appointed Finance Minister in early 1995. Bokros was appointed after a year of rule by the Socialist Party under Prime Minister Gyula Horn, during which time the government wavered over economic reforms. The Socialist Party had won parliamentary elections in 1994 on a platform that promised negotiations toward a broad socio-economic pact. Although the Socialist Party held a slight majority in parliament, it formed a supermajority coalition with the liberal Alliance of Free Democrats. This social-liberal (Orenstein 2001) government tried to negotiate a social pact with its social partners in the second half of 1994 (Héthy 1995). But as Hungary edged closer to a fiscal and currency crisis, Prime Minister Horn shifted tack and appointed Bokros Finance Minister to implement a neoliberal austerity plan in 1995 that became known as the Bokros package, supported by the IMF and the World Bank. The Bokros package included major cuts in social sector expenditures, especially in Hungary's system of family allowances, which had been a primary source of poverty relief during the transition from communism. Two prominent leftists within the Socialist Party, Minister of Welfare Pal Kovacs and Minister for National Security Affairs Béla Katona, resigned in protest against these cuts (*Financial Times*, March 14, 1995, p. 2). This signaled the ascendancy of liberals within the governing

TABLE 5.1
Veto and Proposal Actors in Hungary: Commitment Building

	Proposal actor	Veto actor
Ministry of Finance (World Bank–funded)	X	X
Ministry of Welfare	X	X
Pension Insurance Fund	X	
Prime Minister/Socialist Party		X
Alliance of Free Democrats		X
Total	3	4

coalition and set the context for a new, more radical approach to social sector reform. Hungary's fiscal crisis and the political response to it set the stage for radical pension reform.

Commitment Building

The process of commitment building in Hungary was complicated by the existence of three major proposal actors: the Ministry of Finance (with a World Bank–funded reform team), the Ministry of Welfare, and the Pension Insurance Fund (see table 5.1). These three actors put forward pension reform proposals in 1995–1996 (see table 5.2). The distance between them can be seen by looking at their opposing positions on implementing a private, funded pillar. Only the Ministry of Finance pushed for a system based on private, individual pension savings accounts, while the Ministry of Welfare and the Pension Insurance Fund advocated rationalization of the state "pay-as-you-go" system (Nelson 2001). Opposition was intransigent, creating a rather polarized debate.

As Hungary faced an imminent financial and currency crisis and the government considered three different strategies for reforming the expensive pension system, the World Bank sought to influence the debate by providing financial and technical support for the ministry proposing the creation of mandatory, individual, private pension savings accounts—the Ministry of Finance—under its Japanese grant facility. This support began at the earliest stages, when the Ministry of Finance developed its reform proposals, and continued throughout the process of reform. At first, the Ministry of Finance working group on pension reform was placed under the leadership of Adam Gere, an investment banker whose firm had a

TABLE 5.2
Pension Reform Proposals in Hungary, 1996

	Ministry of Finance	Pension Insurance Fund	Ministry of Welfare
Goals of reform	• Reduce role of state • Make state guarantee partial • Increase self-reliance • Reduce burden on budget • Decrease employer contributions	• Ensure pensions proportional to number of service years and amount of contributions paid • Wage indexation of benefits • Long-term stable financing	• Income security for aged • System that is uniform, mandatory, and based on insurance principles
Characteristics of model	• Three-pillar system • Basic PAYG pension, financed from employers' contribution • Mandatory private pillar financed from employee contribution • Means-tested state pension • Voluntary private funds	• Two-pillar system • Universal basic pension paid from state budget • Earnings-related PAYG pension replacing 60% of prior income, based on point system • Voluntary private funds	• Two-pillar system • PAYG pension based on insurance principles • Contribution split between employer and employee • 57–58% replacement rate • Complementary state social assistance • Voluntary private funds

large share of the business managing Hungary's voluntary third-pillar funds. With funding from the World Bank, the Finance Ministry working group initially discussed a complete phase-out of Hungary's pay-as-you-go system and its replacement with a system based on private, individual pension savings accounts (interview with Gere, May 5, 1998). However, other members of the working group opposed Gere's efforts on grounds of finance and political feasibility.

After extensive debate, the Finance Ministry proposed a pension system that would be 50 percent social security and 50 percent funded (*Magyar Hírlap*, January 29, 1996). The proposal would have reduced total social contributions from 54 percent to 44 percent, with 25 percent earmarked for pension insurance and 19 percent for health. Within the 25 percent pension contribution, the 15 percent employer contribution

TABLE 5.2 (cont'd)
Pension Reform Proposals in Hungary, 1996

	Ministry of Finance	Pension Insurance Fund	Ministry of Welfare
Financing	• Contribution base same as income tax base • Employers' contribution decreases; employees' increases • Pension system expenditures decrease	• Earmarked income tax to finance basic pension • Employer and employee pay for insurance pension • State budget guarantees full payment • Decreased contribution rates	• Contribution base equivalent to taxable wage income between minimum and maximum limits • Pensions become taxable
Pace of reform	• New system starts immediately, workers under forty have to join	• Principles of new pension system to be worked out by June 1996	• New system starts in one to two years
Transition period	• Widen contribution base • Introduce minimum contribution base • Increase retirement age to sixty-five by 2012 • Price indexation of benefits	• Determine contribution base • Uniform retirement age for men and women • Linear pension scale • Continue indexation	• Point system to determine pensions • Uniform retirement age • Restrict early retirement conditions • Keep individual records

Sources: Magyar Hírlap, "Secure Pensions, A Comparative Table of the Pension Reform Concepts of the MoF, MoW, and Pension Insurance Fund," April 5, 1996; Orenstein 2000, 31; Augusztinovics et al. 2002, 35–37.

would be applied to the social security system and the 10 percent employee contribution to mandatory private funds. People aged forty and under would be obliged to participate in the new system (*Napi Gazdaság*, December 2, 1995). Members of the working group who had initially been skeptical of pension privatization, including the chairman of the supervisory board for the voluntary pension system, supported it after it was decided that the organization of the new pension funds would mirror those of the already existing voluntary pension system in Hungary, and would be placed under the same regulatory authority (interview with László Urbán, May 6, 1998).

World Bank assistance to the Finance Ministry working group was critical to putting pension privatization on the policy agenda in Hungary. Prior to the formation of the Finance Ministry working group, almost no one in Hungary had heard of pension privatization. Working group leader Adam Gere was regarded as an economic radical. Financial support from the World Bank to the working group elevated the quality of its work and helped to mainstream pension privatization proposals in Hungary. Gere was eventually replaced by a more moderate figure. Indeed, World Bank policy makers themselves advocated a more moderate, mixed model than the one Gere proposed. Ultimately, the Finance Ministry proposal came closer to the "mixed" model advocated by the World Bank than the "substitutive" model supported by Gere. By financing proposal development by a group of economic radicals in the Ministry of Finance, the World Bank was able to develop a well-elaborated proposal for pension privatization in Hungary and begin to win allies within the Hungarian government, political parties, and general public.

At the same time (1995 and early 1996), two other proposal actors in Hungary developed pension reform proposals without the benefit of World Bank technical assistance and with a more conservative agenda. The Ministry of Welfare developed a competing proposal with the help of German advisers. The Pension Insurance Fund (PIF) supervisory board, an elected body made up mainly of trade union representatives, developed a third proposal. While the Ministry of Welfare was part of the Socialist/ Liberal government, the PIF was outside direct government control, though connected to the Socialist Party through the trade unions.

Deliberation within the government over these three proposals resulted in a deadlock that lasted through the beginning of 1996, when Finance Minister Bokros resigned from the government. He later took up a position with the World Bank in Washington, D.C., helping, among other things, to advise on pension privatization in other countries around the world. While Bokros's resignation could have changed the finance ministry's position, the new Socialist Finance Minister Péter Medgyessy remained equally committed to pension privatization. Pressure and conditionalities from the IMF and World Bank contributed to this continuity. However, Medgyessy also was more willing to compromise with other veto and proposal actors within the government in order to reach an acceptable compromise on pension privatization.

In early April 1996, the government committed itself to developing a unified pension reform proposal by the end of the month (Népszabadság, April 3, 1996). Pressure from international organizations, in particular the IMF and the World Bank, played an important role in setting this deadline. These organizations saw pension privatization as vital to secure the country's fiscal stability as it stood on the edge of crisis. Prime Minister

Horn wanted credibility in the West for his Socialist Party, and Hungary had agreed with the IMF to develop a pension privatization program by December 31, 1996. Hungary's electoral timetable also influenced this decision. New elections were scheduled for May 1998. The government therefore wanted to implement reform in January 1998, which did not leave much time. It is not clear whether the government anticipated that the reform would be popular and provide a boost in the electoral campaign (Hasselman 2006) or whether it simply felt a need to pass the reform in order to avoid a damaging financial crisis.

Medgyessy invited representatives of the Ministries of Finance and Welfare to his office on April 9, 1996, and told them they had to agree on the outlines of a joint program. During the meeting, Minister of Welfare György Szabó accepted a partly funded system, if a way could be found to finance it *(Magyar Hírlap*, April 10, 1996; *Budapest Business Week*, April 15–21, 1996). A compromise was reached, in which the World Bank–sponsored Ministry of Finance program became the main framework document, but the size of the mandatory private system was reduced from about one-half to one-third of total contributions. The use of a point system (as in Germany) for reforming the social security system was taken from the Ministry of Welfare program, along with a lower labor period to qualify for a social security pension, twenty years, rather than the thirty-two or thirty-five proposed by the Ministry of Finance. The social security pension would be financed by an 18 percent employer contribution and the mandatory private system by a 10 percent employee contribution *(Magyar Hírlap*, April 24, 1996). The reformed system would produce an estimated average replacement rate of 55 to 60 percent.

However, the independent Pension Insurance Fund remained outside this government compromise. Welfare Minister Szabó wanted to find a way to get the PIF to agree, at least in principle, with the outlines of reform. However, this proved impossible. Instead, with the main ministries now agreed on the outlines of reform, the government decided to move ahead in order to implement reform before the end of the parliamentary term.

The Ministry of Finance, backed by World Bank resources, emerged victorious with the main lines of its reform proposal intact and a government commitment to establish mandatory, private pension savings accounts in Hungary. World Bank support had enabled the Ministry of Finance to develop a credible plan for pension privatization and ensured continuity of this plan through changes in leadership at the Ministry of Finance. Ferge notes that "the better opportunities and resources of the Ministry of Finance . . . had a dominant impact on the whole process" of reform (Ferge 1997, 11). In particular, Ferge points to Finance Ministry dominance in technical capacity, personnel, and attracting media atten-

TABLE 5.3
Veto and Proposal Actors in Hungary: Coalition Building

	Proposal actor	Veto actor
Interministerial Working Group (World Bank–funded)	X	X
Prime Minister/Socialist Party		X
Alliance of Free Democrats		X
Trade Unions/Interest Reconciliation Council		X
Pension Insurance Fund	X	
Total	2	4

tion. Alternative proposal actors did not have access to comparable re-sources and the number of proposal actors overall was very few.

COALITION BUILDING

The April 1996 reconciliation of the two government programs started a new phase in the development of reform. Coalition-building in Hungary (see table 5.3) was mainly a process of working out differences within the government coalition itself, which held 72 percent of seats in parliament. At this stage, the two partisan veto actors were the Socialist Party, a for-mer communist party with leftist and liberal elements within it, and the Alliance of Free Democrats, a liberal party that was favorably predisposed to fundamental economic reform. Because of divisions between leftists and liberals within the Socialist Party, the voice of the Socialist-affiliated trade unions (MSZOSZ) became highly influential. Some Socialist parlia-mentarians refused to vote for reform unless it was first approved by the Interest Reconciliation Council (IRC), a tripartite representative body in which the Socialist trade unions had a decisive voice. This shifted delibera-tion on pension privatization from the parliament to the IRC. Discussions in the IRC took longer and produced more compromises than those in parliament. Negotiations in the coalition-building stage in Hungary caused some watering-down of reform proposals, among other things a reduction of the contribution rate to the private pension system from 10 percent to 6 to 8 percent.

During the coalition-building stage, a new inter-ministerial working group for pension reform became the main forum where government re-form proposals were elaborated and legislation drafted. The World Bank was heavily involved in establishing, funding, and assisting this inter-ministerial working group and working toward a political compromise in Hungary. As a measure of the priority the Bank accorded to these activities in Hungary, it provided two of its own employees—Robert Palacios and Roberto Rocha—to work full time with the working group for the duration of the reform process. These World Bank representatives participated in the thirty-member working group as observers, but provided much of its technical modeling capacity as well as coordinating other World Bank assistance. USAID was also involved in providing technical assistance to the reform team, providing training on pension fund administration, sponsoring public opinion research, helping to develop public relations campaigns, and coordinating other technical assistance.

Membership of the inter-ministerial working group on pension privatization in Hungary was cast fairly widely. Experts from the Ministry of Welfare were included, helping to prepare changes in the first pillar. A prominent investment banker, Csaba Lantos, was chosen to head the "investment team" charged with drawing up portfolio management rules and principles related to the introduction of the private funded pension system (Pension Team, May 30, 1996). Addressing opposition from the Pension Insurance Fund was a key concern of the government. In July 1996, Minister of Welfare György Szabó and State Secretary Tibor Draskovics of the Ministry of Finance wrote that the PIF had to be involved in the reform process, in order to help with necessary data collection and eventual implementation (Ministry of Welfare, July 1996). However, the government working group continued its work without participation from PIF experts. The distance between the two proposals was too great to allow for meaningful collaboration. Interestingly, the PIF also had access to a World Bank loan that had been processed earlier and used the technical assistance component of this loan to conduct its own reform agenda.

World Bank assistance to the inter-ministerial working group intensified, allowing the employment of numerous foreign experts as consultants. By December 1996, the working group had created models of the new private pension system, with flexible parameters and a highly detailed legislative proposal. World Bank and USAID assistance enabled the Hungarian working group to draw on the expertise of national and international legal experts. With the support of sophisticated technical and public relations advice, the working group dominated expert debate within the country, with cohesive argumentation in a number of important expert and public forums (interview with Roberto Rocha, May 6, 1998).

In parliament, a special parliamentary group became the main forum for ironing out differences between the two partisan veto actors. The Coalition Parties' Working Group on General Government Reform was founded by reformers from the Hungarian Socialist Party and the Alliance of Free Democrats toward the end of the Bokros period, dedicated to pushing a liberal reform agenda. Powerful centrist members of the Hungarian Socialist Party also joined the group, including Sándor Nagy and Judit Csehak, key figures in social policy making (interview with Klára Ungár, May 1998). The coalition parties' working group had initially been undecided about pension privatization. In early April, it began to lean toward supporting the Ministry of Finance proposal *(Népszabadság,* April 3, 1996).

On April 23, 1996, after the forced reconciliation of the Ministry of Finance and Ministry of Welfare proposals, the Coalition Parties Working Group on General Government Reform formally considered the joint proposal of the government, and after extensive discussions, lent its full support to the program. These deliberations proved crucial, because several parliamentarians with important roles in social policy committees had to be convinced of the wisdom of the government plan. One key player who came over to the government side was Judit Csehak, chair of the parliament's social policy committee and a former welfare minister under communist rule. She would play a critical role in forging compromises she judged acceptable to parliament, and later in selling the program to a wider audience. It should be noted that Csehak, like other major players in the pension reform debate in Hungary, was also involved in setting up third-pillar voluntary mutual benefit societies, and thus had business interests in the sector. Csehak had strong views on the role of fund managers and was conscious of public acceptability of the program (interview with Tibor Parniczky, May 7, 1998). The coalition parties' working group replaced, to a certain extent, deliberation within parliament itself, creating a level of agreement among coalition parliamentarians.

Parliament also held several debates that allowed room for broader public discussion of the government's pension reform plans. The first was on May 8, 1996, the day before the government approved the joint concept of the Ministry of Finance and Ministry of Welfare. Parliament considered a draft of the government's proposal in July and held another debate day on October 13, 1996, called for by the Hungarian Democratic Peoples' Party (MDNP). This enabled parties to repeat their already clear positions on the pension privatization program *(Magyar Hírlap,* October 14, 1996). But by this time, a critical mass of coalition parliamentarians supported the reform (interview with Roberto Rocha, May 6, 1998). Interestingly, the leading right opposition party, the Young Democrats (FIDESZ), was split over the government's pension privatization program. While some deputies spoke out against the reform, others stayed quiet during the pension reform process. These reformers did not want to support unpopular changes contained within the program, such as increases in the pension age. On the other hand, they did not want to object to the fundamental precepts of the program, which some within FIDESZ saw as desirable (interview with László Urbán, May 6, 1998). The position of the main opposition party became important during the implementation phase as FIDESZ, after winning the 1998 elections in Hungary, enacted several important modifications to the privatized pension system.

Once the working group had finished its legislative drafting and modeling, winning the support of the key partisan veto actors, it set out at the start of 1997 to engage in a broad public relations effort intended to rally diffuse support for reform and bring skeptical interest groups on board. The government launched a public relations campaign with USAID and World Bank support and organized a series of meetings between different interest groups and top officials from the working group. Minister of Finance Péter Medgyessy was prominent in many of these meetings, along with working group leaders István Györffy and Mária Major. World Bank advisers chose to not take an active role in public discourse, to avoid the perception that the reform was foisted on Hungary by the World Bank (interview with Roberto Rocha, May 6, 1998). A partial list of meetings between working group members and various social groups, compiled from Ministry of Finance documents, indicates where the government saw potential interest group opposition and significant actors in the debate (see table 5.4).

The most powerful interest group was the Socialist-affiliated trade union federation, MSZOSZ, which was represented both in the Pension Insurance Fund board and within the Socialist party parliamentary group itself. However, the socialist trade unions also had their own independent base of support, and a credible strike threat. MSZOSZ also dominated the Pension Insurance Fund board, and thus had a significant stake in the pre-reform system. The main forum for reaching an agreement with the trade unions was Hungary's Interest Reconciliation Council (IRC), a tripartite body bringing together representatives of government, labor, and business for regular meetings on economic and social policy issues. In the first of a series of IRC meetings on February 4, 1997, the government proposal met with fierce resistance from the MSZOSZ trade union leadership. Some trade union representatives supported the Pension Insurance Fund plan for a reformed PAYG system, and at the start of negotiations, MSZOSZ trade union leader László Sándor expressed opposition to channeling one-third of payroll tax contributions to a mandatory private system. Employer representatives questioned pension privatization as well, on the basis of transition finance. Finance Minister Medgyessy tried to counter these arguments by focusing on the time pressure reformers were under, arguing that pension reform had to happen in 1998, before the upcoming elections (*Népszabadság*, February 5, 1997). A key sticking point was the half-price, half-wage pension indexation (called "Swiss"

Table 5.4
Hungarian Inter-Ministerial Working Group Officials' Public Meetings on Pension Reform, 1997

January 6: Coalition parties

January 7: Pension Insurance Fund

January 8: Parliamentary representatives

January 14: National Alliance of Pensioners

January 15: Council of the Elderly

January 21: Child and Youth Interest Reconciliation Council

January 22: Board of Directors of SZEF state and municipal employees' trade union

January 29: Board of Directors of MSZOSZ trade union

January 30: Hungarian Socialist Party members of parliament

February 4: Interest Reconciliation Council

February 7: Interest Reconciliation Council

February 13: Conference organized by Sándor Nagy (former head of MSZOSZ and PIF)

February 17: Hungarian Democratic Peoples' Party (MDNP)

February 19: Hungarian Socialist Party Left Group

February 21: Board of Directors of SZEF trade union

February 26: MSZOSZ Council of Alliance leaders (including PIF President János Vágó)

February 28: Interest Reconciliation Council

March (various dates): Hungarian Socialist Party MPs

 Hungarian Socialist Party Board of Directors

 Alliance of Free Democrats (SZDSZ) MPs

March 11: Pension Insurance Fund

March 12: Interest Reconciliation Council

indexation) of pensions proposed in the government bill. Other issues included whether to adopt the first-pillar point system proposed by the PIF, whether years spent raising children and studying at universities should count as service years, and the benefit formula used in the first pillar *(Vilaggazdasag,* February 10, 1997).

The two sides were so far apart that MSZOSZ leader Sándor announced that he would lead the workers out on strike if the government submitted its original proposal to parliament *(Napi Gazdaság,* February

8, 1997). However, a number of significant compromises were reached in the Interest Reconciliation Council. The government agreed to a more generous benefit formula for the first pillar, to create a state guarantee for the private funds, and to allow people the option of paying into the private pillar during years spent in child raising or studying at universities, and to count these as service years that qualify for minimum benefits. The transition to Swiss indexation was delayed until 2000, and in the meantime the government agreed to several above-inflation adjustments to pension rates *(Magyar Hírlap*, February 13, 1997).

Further compromises were made at a conference on February 13 organized by Sándor Nagy, a former head of both MSZOSZ and the Pension Insurance Fund. Nagy criticized the government for not paying more attention to the PIF proposal, and yet worked out a deal that would allow pension privatization to go ahead. While the government had been proposing a 10 percent contribution to the mandatory private system, and trade unions wanted 3 percent, a compromise was reached whereby the initial contribution rate would be 6 percent, but phased up to 8 percent in two years (interview with Klára Ungár, August 1998; interview with Roberto Rocha, May 6, 1998, interview with Mihály Kökény, August 1998). Other compromises reached in February 1997 IRC meetings included increased state guarantees for the private system, changes in the rates for crediting years worked under the mixed system, additional maternity years counted toward pension eligibility, and a two-year waiting period before special occupation groups' retirement conditions were reregulated (Ministry of Finance documents, February–March 1997). Thus trade unions had a moderate but significant impact on reform. Their effectiveness was determined by their strong links with Socialist Party leaders such as Nagy, and their presence within both the Socialist Party parliamentary group and the PIF. Despite these agreements in February, resistance from the Pension Insurance Fund and the trade unions continued until the end of April 1997, when pressure for an agreement intensified as the government prepared to submit its proposal to parliament at the beginning of May. The Interest Reconciliation Council reached a final agreement in its last scheduled session *(Magyar Hírlap*, April 30, 1997).

On May 12, almost exactly a year after the first parliamentary debate day, the government submitted its pension privatization plan *(Népszabadság*, May 13, 1997). It consisted of five laws and two parliamentary decree proposals. The government pushed for the package to be voted on immediately by parliament, after two weeks of study, but the opposition refused. Deputies complained that the laws were drafted in a very opaque fashion, and working group head István Györffy agreed, but blamed it on the PIF *(Népszabadság*, May 23, 1997). Parliamentary debate began on June 3 and continued until July 15, with the opposition voicing doubts over financing the transitional pension deficit, and whether private pension funds would really bring much benefit to the economy *(Népszabadság*, June 11 and July 16, 1997). The five laws were passed on July 15, 1997, with support from 55 to 58 percent of deputies (Ferge 1997, 13).

A number of observers have criticized the closed and elite nature of the policy process in Hungary that led up to the acceptance of pension privatization legislation in July 1997 (cf. Ferge 1997, 13). There is no question that the process was mainly one that took place within the government coalition and its transnational policy advisers, with some consultation with interest groups connected with the Socialist Party. World Bank and other experts played a leading role in formulating programs, drafting laws, and consulting to the interministerial working group, while discussions in the Interest Reconciliation Council produced only a moderate level of compromise on the parameters of reform. Public discussion was taken into account only toward the end of the process, during a time when the government's priority was to sell the reform through a concurrent public relations campaign. Yet the main partisan veto actors themselves contained a fairly wide range of interest groups. Coalition debate was fairly open, and allowed for a wide range of expert views to be expressed. Opponents of the original Ministry of Finance proposal within the government coalition had to be won over, and eventually a wide cross-section of experts were included in the inter-ministerial working group. Opinions of the Pension Insurance Fund were not accepted in whole, but some compromises with it were reached. The PIF could have rallied support in parliament, but did not. In sum, while pension reform in Hungary was indeed an expert or elite process, it was also a relatively open and democratic one of deliberation within a super-majority government coalition. Ultimately, the World Bank–led coalition for pension privatization managed to push through reforms in Hungary, though with some significant compromises on the size of the new private system.

Implementation

Hungary's new pension system was implemented in January 1998. New elections later that year brought a change in government. While "[t]here is no reason to assume that the pension reform had any effect on this outcome" (Augustinovics et al. 2002, 49), there is also no reason to think that pension privatization enhanced the popularity of the outgoing Socialist/Liberal government. While some FIDESZ leaders supported the broad outlines of pension privatization (interview with László Urbán, May 6, 1998), they also seized the opportunity to enact substantial changes to the pension system on taking office. First, they brought the semi-independent Pension Insurance Fund under the control of the Ministry of Finance. Second, they transferred collection of social security contributions from the PIF to the State Tax Collection Agency. Third, they extended the option for older workers to switch back to the public social security system. Fourth, they eliminated the "Swiss" indexation of benefits in 1999 and reverted to a yearly ad hoc indexation, as before. Fifth and most important, the FIDESZ government froze contribution rates to the private system at 6 percent of employee wages and reduced total contributions to the pension system from 24 percent to 18 percent. In November 2001, the government made it voluntary to join the new system, even for new entrants to the labor market (Augustinovics et al. 2002, 49–50). Such changes show the importance of decisions taken in post-reform implementation.

During the early years of reform implementation, several problems emerged with the new private system. First, administrative issues proved to be more difficult than expected. The main problem concerned the crediting of contributions to individual accounts (Augustinovics et al. 2002, 60–61). A further problem concerned the negative rate of return in the Hungarian private pension funds since 1998. Augustinovics et al. (2002, 77) found that the gross return on pension assets in the private funds in 2000 was 7.5 percent, well below the inflation rate of more than 10 percent. Below-inflation returns have persisted in Hungary through 2004 (interview with Elaine Fultz, May 2005).

USAID and the World Bank continued to provide Hungary with substantial implementation assistance from 1998 to 2001. USAID worked closely with the supervisory body for pension funds, and the World Bank provided post-implementation technical assistance. Meanwhile, several prominent Hungarian reformers were hired to the World Bank staff to promote pension privatization in other countries. In addition to finance minister Lajos Bokros, reformer Csaba Fehér joined the World Bank's social protection team after reform implementation.

Transnational policy actors played a critical role in Hungary's choice of pension privatization. The World Bank helped to put pension privatization on the domestic political agenda in Hungary by inspiring and supporting the Ministry of Finance reform team at a time when few in Hungary had ever heard of pension privatization. World Bank and USAID financing enabled the Hungarian government to hire transnational consultants to help write its reform legislation and to participate in expert debate within the inter-ministerial working group on pension reform. The World Bank even took the extraordinary step of sending two of the authors of its 1994 report to Hungary for many months to work with the government on crafting pension privatization. Their support enhanced the work of the inter-ministerial working group and helped to push through pension privatization in various deliberative forums. USAID and other transnational policy actors also provided funding for a public relations campaign to sell the reforms to the Hungarian public and later provided crucial technical support to pension fund supervisory bodies. Transnational policy actors exerted a pervasive influence on the reform process in Hungary, from inspiration to the recruitment of partners to providing them with the technical and financial support they needed to succeed with reforms to implementation. Domestic economic and political factors also had a powerful role in shaping reform in Hungary, as well as past policy legacies and economic conditions. However, the design of pension privatization in Hungary owed more to the World Bank and its allied organizations than to any other single actor. These reforms probably would not have been implemented in Hungary and certainly not in the same way without the support of transnational policy actors.

Pension Privatization in Poland

In the mid-1990s, Poland's pension system suffered from prior policy decisions that drastically expanded eligibility for early retirement and disability pensions, causing a rapid rise in the dependency ratio. As opposed to most post-communist countries, the proportion of a worker's income that the pension system typically replaced increased from about 60 percent to about 75 percent between 1990 and 1993 (Andrews and Rashid 1996, 9). Both of these trends caused pension spending to skyrocket. Pension spending in Poland ranked among the highest of any European country in 1993, despite Poland's relatively favorable demographic profile (Andrews and Rashid 1996; Cain and Surdej 1999). Poland also inherited a widespread system of special pension privileges, a history of ad hoc changes in cost of living indexation rates, and an emerging demographic problem. Payroll tax contribution rates for all forms of social insurance reached 45 percent, placing a large burden on formal employment. The pay-as-you-go state pension system was managed by a special pension insurance institution, ZUS. A special farmers' pension system, KRUS, was heavily indebted and kept afloat almost entirely by government subsidies.

As early as 1991, ZUS president Wojciech Topiński and Marian Wiśniewski (1991) proposed a partially funded pension system for Poland. However, this proposal was rejected by the World Bank's top pension adviser to Poland at the time. Nick Barr, a highly regarded U.K. social security expert, was a leading skeptic of pension privatization. Barr joined the Bank when it required pensions experts to help advise in Central and Eastern Europe and left once the Bank unequivocally began to support pension privatization a few years later (interview with Nick Barr, February 5, 2007). Barr's ability to quash consideration of pension privatization in Poland in 1991, though, shows the strong influence of the Bank in Poland. Government officials could not adequately pursue pension privatization domestically without the resources and legitimacy conferred by World Bank support.

Poland was the only post-communist country where there is any evidence of expert consideration of pension privatization proposals prior to 1994. Despite this early consideration of the pension privatization, politicians in Poland perceived pension reform as an issue that was too controversial to tackle. Instead, as pension spending increased from 8.6 percent to 15.5 percent of GDP between 1990 and 1994, the Polish government used ad hoc measures to control spending by changing benefit formulae, indexation levels, and rules on additional allowances. Poland's Constitutional Tribunal put an end to these practices by issuing decisions that declared ad hoc changes illegal and forced the government to repay any lost benefits. Only then did government officials take the pension crisis seriously, and begin to work toward comprehensive reform. (Chłoń et al. 1999, 12; Hausner 2001). An emerging fiscal crisis and legal constraints on the government's handling of pension finance contributed to Polish policy makers' willingness to consider pension privatization in 1994.

Commitment Building

When Poland began to consider fundamental reform in 1994, four distinct proposals were elaborated, including a Ministry of Finance proposal whose development was sponsored by the World Bank. The proposals of the Ministry of Finance and Ministry of Labor and Social Affairs were by far the most important. However, it is notable in Poland that two civil society actors formulated their own proposals. A proposal by the Solidarity trade union was seriously debated, while a proposal by the Institute of Labor and Social Policy had a minimal impact. Still, the presence of alternative civil society proposal actors sets Poland apart from other countries in the region, indicating a higher level of public involvement in the pension privatization process. Ultimately, it was the World Bank–supported Ministry of Finance proposal that prevailed in Poland (see table 5.5).

During the commitment-building stage of reform, the government remained the main forum of the pension reform debate. Governmental struggles over the shape of reform were intense, characterized by a year-and-a-half long standoff (late 1994 to mid-1996) between the Ministry of Finance and the Ministry of Labor and Social Affairs over opposing proposals for reform (Chłoń et al. 1999, 12). This suggests that both min-

TABLE 5.5
Veto and Proposal Actors in Poland: Commitment Building

	Proposal actor	Veto actor
Ministry of Finance (World Bank–funded)	X	X
Ministry of Labor and Social Affairs	X	X
Prime Minister/Democratic Left Alliance		X
Polish Peasant Party		X
Solidarity Trade Union	X	
Institute of Labor and Social Affairs	X	
Total	4	4

istries were true veto players. While Finance Minister Grzegorz W. Kołodko proposed a fundamental reform of the pension system in his June 1994 "Strategy for Poland," and later developed a precise proposal in collaboration with World Bank policy advisers, Minister of Labor and Social Affairs Leszek Miller wanted to preserve, yet rationalize, the existing social security–type system. Because Miller was an important figure within the governing Alliance of the Democratic Left (SLD), while Kołodko was an independent economic expert with ties to the party, Miller initially had the upper hand within the government. The government approved the Ministry of Labor's proposals for rationalization in May 1995, which provided for

- establishing a basic pension of 30 percent of average wage for everyone
- an additional insurance-based pension for all those who had contributed to the system for more than fifteen years, proportional to an individual's earnings and work period
- supplementary pensions based on voluntary contributions
- equalizing indexation rules for the uniformed services
- limiting and partially eliminating branch privileges
- gradually increasing the contribution rate to the farmers' pension system
- capping contribution rates at 250 percent of average wage
- splitting contributions equally between employees and employers
- introducing more restrictive rules for disability qualification, and
- gradually increasing the retirement age to sixty-five for both men and women.

The Ministry of Finance strongly opposed the Ministry of Labor's program as being too conservative and quickly formulated an alternative proposal for pension privatization, with World Bank support. The new pension reform proposal was conceived by Marek Mazur, an advisor to Minister Kołodko who had a reputation as a neoliberal economist. Mazur had no previous experience with pension privatization, but had begun doing research on it in 1994. Mazur made a study trip to Peru, Colombia, Argentina, and Chile sponsored by pension privatization advocates and came back supporting a dominant funded pillar. World Bank Social Protection Division chief Robert Holzmann further reviewed the Ministry of Finance proposal as it was drafted in 1995 (interview with Marek Mazur, July 1998). Thus the World Bank–led coalition provided its expert technical and logistical support to the Polish Ministry of Finance and helped to convince key officials to push for pension privatization.

The Ministry of Finance was helped by the fact that extensive public opinion research, sponsored by USAID, showed that Poles found the Ministry of Labor's proposal too timid and wanted more radical reform. In the autumn of 1995, the government changed course and recommended the preparation of a pension privatization program that would include mandatory, funded, individual pension savings accounts (Hausner 2001). Now on the defensive, the Ministry of Labor exercised its veto power, and the reform process remained at a standstill.

In January 1996, the Institute of Labor and Social Affairs convened an expert conference to discuss and reconcile the competing governmental and non-governmental proposals. The main principles of each concept are presented in table 5.6, with the Ministry of Finance and Ministry of Labor proposals on the two extremes, and the ones formulated by non-governmental organizations situated between these two. The conference ended with recognition that each of the programs had its flaws and that a new approach was needed.

An end to the stalemate finally came in February 1996. As a result of a cabinet reshuffle and the appointment of a new Prime Minister, Włodzimierz Cimoszewicz, Labor Minister Miller was transferred to the Interior Ministry, while Deputy Minister Andrzej Bączkowski was appointed Labor Minister in his place. Both the new Prime Minister and Labor Minister supported pension privatization. Bączkowski also had been a Solidarity activist, and thus provided a link between the left government and the main opposition proposal actor, the Solidarity trade union. Bączkowski had demonstrated unusual negotiating skills and been appointed chairman of the new tripartite commission for socio-economic affairs in 1994. Bączkowski proposed creating a special office for pension reform, called the Office of the Plenipotentiary for Social Security Reform, that would improve coordination within the government, render pension re-

TABLE 5.6
Pension Reform Proposals in Poland, 1995–1996

	Ministry of Finance	Solidarity Trade Union	Institute of Labor	Ministry of Labor
Basic pension	Flat pension of 20% of average wage	Basic pension with two elements: flat pension financed from taxes and earnings-related pension from contributions	Based on contributions from employer and employee with maximum limit; benefit depends on length of contribution and amount	Based on contributions from employer and employee with maximum limit of 250% of average wage and state subsidy
Additional pension	Mandatory saving in private pension funds	Mandatory saving in pension funds supplemented by privatization bonds given to all employees	Voluntary savings in pension funds by people earning more than average salary; tax preferences	Voluntary savings in private funds for people with highest income
Transition	Mandatory participation for new entrants, choice between systems for employed, high transiton costs	Expected transition period for forming pension funds, social security contribution divided between systems, budget subsidies	Immediate changes; lower replacement rate in pension system when contributions start to voluntary private system	Gradual implementation; no reduction in costs of basic system

Sources: *Gospodarka i Przyszlosc,* special edition on Social Security; Orenstein 2000, 4.

form independent of any ministry, allow non-governmental experts to be involved in the drafting, and indicate government commitment to fundamental reform (Chłoń et al. 1999, 13). Bączkowski was appointed Plenipotentiary as well as Labor Minister, taking overall political responsibility for the reform.

The World Bank was asked to assist in the creation and funding of the Office of the Plenipotentiary, which it did. A Polish World Bank official, Michał Rutkowski, was appointed head of the Office of the Plenipotentiary, taking responsibility for the day-to-day running of its activities and the drafting of reform proposals. He took a leave of absence from the World Bank. However, he retained close ties to the World Bank and eventually returned to play a leading role in the Bank's policy advisory activities in other countries. Rutkowski's close ties to the World Bank clearly facilitated the flow of financial and technical resources to the plenipotentiary's office in Warsaw. The fact that the World Bank is sometimes able to place its own people in high-ranking national government offices provides evidence of the extent to which it has been able to influence reform processes in countries worldwide. It also reflects the unusual credentials of the individual involved and the priority accorded to reform in Poland by the World Bank as well as the personnel policies of the World Bank, which are often employed to facilitate reforms. World Bank resources ensured that the Office of the Plenipotentiary had everything it needed to convince potential allies and defeat potential opponents in public and technical debate.

The establishment of the Plenipotentiary and the World Bank–funded (and –led) Office of the Plenipotentiary marked a major breakthrough in the pension reform effort in Poland. The appointment of a pro-reform prime minister, the reassignment of Minister Miller, and the creation of a single governmental office for pension reform reduced the number of veto actors within the government, indicated strong commitment to reform, and allowed the process of technical drafting to move swiftly ahead. The World Bank and its allies contributed enormously to winning government support for pension privatization in Poland. However, the numerous actors involved and the long delay in reaching government commitment to fundamental reform meant that Polish reformers had to race against the electoral clock, with parliamentary elections scheduled for September 1997. Unanticipated events and further government shake-ups meant that Poland could not pass the whole legislative package for pension reform in one parliamentary cycle. Poland's coalition-building process therefore was divided into two distinct phases.

Coalition Building: Phase One

Poland is somewhat unique in that pension privatization legislation was passed by two successive governments and parliaments, representing most major parties at one time or another. The first phase of coalition building (table 5.7) lasted from April 1996 to August 1997 and resulted in the passage of three pieces of legislation that regulated the organization of the new second and third pillars, and the use of privatization revenues to finance the transition. The second phase lasted from September 1997 to December 1998, under a new center-right government, which approved

TABLE 5.7
Veto and Proposal Actors in Poland: Coalition Building Phase One

	Proposal actor	Veto actor
Office of the Plenipotentiary (World Bank-funded)	X	X
Prime Minister/Democratic Left Alliance		X
Parliament		X
Solidarity Trade Union	X	
Total	2	3

laws overhauling the first pillar and withdrawing special pension privi-leges. Support of partisan actors across the political spectrum is particular to Poland, and demonstrates a particularly democratic reform dynamic.

The World Bank–funded Office of the Plenipotentiary's work on the new pension program, "Security through Diversity," began in September 1996 and was completed in February 1997, three months after the sudden death of Andrzej Bączkowski in November 1996. The loss of Bączkowski endangered the progress of reform. Bączkowski 's successor at the Labor Ministry, Tadeusz Zieliński, was skeptical of the reforms. However, the Office of the Plenipotentiary persevered with continued prime ministerial support. The government appointed Jerzy Hausner, a former adviser to Finance Minister Kołodko, Plenipotentiary for Social Security Reform and moved the whole Office of the Plenipotentiary to the Council of Min-isters, where Hausner was Secretary of State.

During legislative drafting, the Office of the Plenipotentiary engaged in deliberation within the government on a wide spectrum of issues (see Hausner 2001). The Ministry of Finance was involved in discussing meth-ods of financing the transition to a funded system and the use of privatiza-tion revenues. The State Treasury was consulted on privatization-related issues. In contrast to Hungary, Poland's Social Insurance Institution (ZUS), the institution that manages the pension system, did not oppose a multi-pillar reform. This was partly for institutional reasons and partly due to its leadership. Reform plans in Poland gave the ZUS a substantial new role as clearinghouse for all pension payments, administrator of the pay-as-you-go pillar, and manager of a new system of individual social insurance records (Hausner 2001). Therefore, the ZUS was not as threat-ened institutionally by reform plans in Poland as the Pension Insurance Fund was in Hungary. The ZUS President was also a political appointee, whereas the Pension Insurance Fund in Hungary was an independently elected body with substantial trade union representation and intransigeant leadership. Because it more or less went along with reform, the ZUS was consulted on administrative matters, although it did not prepare sufficiently for a reform that would transform its own work significantly.

The Office of the Plenipotentiary's Security through Diversity program was tacitly approved by the government in March–April 1997 as an amendment to its previously introduced plans. According to the program, drafted under the guidance of a former World Bank employee and supported by extensive financial and technical assistance from the Bank and USAID, the new pension system would be multi-pillar, with a large, but reformed, social security–type pillar, a new private pillar funded by approximately one-third of the old-age payroll contribution, and a reformed, voluntary, third pillar. It is not surprising that the proposal clearly reflected the program first published in *Averting*. The transformed first pillar would be based on a notional defined contribution (NDC) system. Security through Diversity proposed a mandatory, private, funded second pillar, based on defined contributions. It also called for a comprehensive reform of Poland's voluntary pension savings. For political reasons, as in other reforms, people above the age of fifty would not participate in the new system. Younger workers, below thirty years of age, would be required to join the second pillar, while those between thirty and fifty would have the choice of switching to the multi-pillar system or being covered only by the NDC first pillar.

Security through Diversity won general support from Poland's Tripartite Commission in April 1997, including representatives of business associations and trade unions, some of whom were persuaded to give up their opposition to reform. Why did trade unions support pension privatization in Poland? Part of the answer has to do with the division of Polish trade unions between the center-right Solidarity and the former communist OPZZ. The Solidarity trade unions had actually supported pension privatization from the beginning, with their political wing drafting reform proposals that called for the establishment of a private, funded pillar. While the former communist OPZZ was initially opposed and supported the Ministry of Labor position, leading officials of the OPZZ were ultimately convinced to support pension privatization, while defending the primacy of the social security–type system. Essentially, pension privatization advocates in Poland convinced trade union officials that trade unions would be able to form their own pension funds, a move that gave the trade unions a clear business interest in the reforms. Although neither of these trade unions was a formal veto actor, each was closely allied with leading political parties and their voices were critical to attaining the high degree of parliamentary and public support garnered both on the government and opposition sides.

TABLE 5.8
Veto and Proposal Actors in Poland: Coalition Building Phase Two

	Proposal actor	Veto actor
Office of the Plenipotentiary (World Bank–funded)	X	X
Solidarity Electoral Action	X	X
Freedom Union		X
Total	2	3

To move ahead with reform before elections in September 1997, the government decided to focus on passing the least controversial elements of reform legislation, while tying Poland to a timeline that would force the next government to pass reform by the middle of 1998 and to start implementation in 1999. Between June and August 1997, the first set of implementing legislation was passed, on regulating and organizing the second and third pillars, and on the use of enterprise privatization revenues to finance the transition. The second-pillar law provided for the establishment of a pension fund regulatory agency (UNFE) in May 1998, a licensing process for private pension funds to start in August 1998, and pension funds to begin operations in January 1999. This created powerful constituencies that would force the next government to complete reform legislation. ZUS also awarded an expensive contract to a Polish company, Prokom, to develop a computer system to manage the privatized pension system. This reform legislation passed in parliament with support from 90 percent of deputies, and across the political spectrum (Hausner 2001). Only a few right-wing deputies connected with the Christian national wing of the Solidarity movement voted against fundamental reform. Otherwise, all the major current and potential partisan veto actors supported reform. This proved important when the center-left coalition was overturned after elections in September 1997 by a new center-right coalition of the Solidarity Electoral Action (AWS) and Freedom Union (UW), initiating a second phase of the coalition-building process.

Coalition Building: Phase Two

While both center-right parties broadly supported pension privatization, the change of government changed the veto and proposal actors involved in reform (see table 5.8) and disrupted the coalition-building process in Poland, delaying further legislation until the new government recommitted to the specific reform ideas contained in Security through Diversity. Solidarity Electoral Action still supported the original Solidarity trade union proposal for reform, and in particular wanted the government to reconsider how to use enterprise privatization revenues to finance the pension system, a key aspect of the Solidarity proposal. Freedom Union support for Security through Diversity was less problematic, because a number of Freedom Union–affiliated experts served on the World Bank–funded Office of the Plenipotentiary team. Still, it took a while to appoint a new government plenipotentiary, which slowed the process of legislative drafting. Civil society interest groups began increasingly to mobilize against reform, particularly the influential Federation of Trade Unions of Polish State Railway Employees, which opposed folding the railway workers' pension system into the general one. Meanwhile, the broad political consensus that led to the overwhelming passage of the first set of legislation began to break down (cf. Hausner 2001). The new government refused to work directly with the outgoing Alliance of the Democratic Left (SLD). Former Labor Minister Miller was elected to lead the SLD parliamentary caucus in opposition and, having never supported the new pension reforms, tried to mobilize the party against them. Work on the new information technology system for ZUS also slowed down, eventually causing a delay in the launch of the second pillar until April 1999.

Despite these problems, the coalition agreement signed by Solidarity Electoral Action and Freedom Union in November 1997 recommitted the government to pension reform as part of an aggressive package of four major reforms, including pensions, health care, education, and local administration. The World Bank lobbied behind the scenes for follow-through with promised reforms. A new minister was appointed to coordinate the social sector reforms, Teresa Kamińska of Solidarity Electoral Action (AWS). Ewa Lewicka of AWS was appointed Plenipotentiary for Social Security Reform as well as a Secretary of State in the Ministry of Labor. With her appointment, the Office of the Plenipotentiary returned to the Ministry of Labor. Lewicka fully and enthusiastically accepted the Security through Diversity program and intensified the work started by her predecessors (Chłoń et al. 1999, 14). The prime minister also appointed a new president of ZUS, Stanisław Alot (AWS). This meant that all the important for social security system posts were taken by AWS, disturbing the Freedom Union, which wanted its candidate appointed president of ZUS.

The new government, dominated by Solidarity appointees, made few significant changes in the design of reform. For the most part, it retained the outlines of the Security through Diversity program and jettisoned key elements of previous Solidarity proposals, such as the use of privatization revenues to fund the pension system. ZUS president Alot did re-negotiate the infornation technology contract and launched personnel changes in ZUS—an enormous bureaucracy with 40,000 employees—ostensibly to prepare it for becoming a clearinghouse for pension payments, but also to replace many midlevel managers with political appointees. AWS also adopted a new policy on the retirement age. In line with the party's conservative social values, AWS recommended keeping the retirement age at sixty for women and sixty-five for men, rather than sixty-two for both men and women as proposed in Security through Diversity. While a notional defined contribution first pillar had always been part of the Security through Diversity program, the government made the strategic decision that the first pillar law should not just be amended, but completely rewritten, to cover all the regulations concerning the old-age and disability pensions for the entire population covered. This slowed down the deliberative process in parliament and changed one of the basic political strategies of the pension reform up to that point: to leave the present first pillar rules intact in order to avoid lengthy debates. Rewriting the first pillar law allowed the government to combine a slew of previously enacted legislation and rules into one single text, and also allowed the incorporation of two new groups into the first pillar: employees of the uniformed forces born after December 31, 1968, and judges and prosecutors. Judges and prosecutors, a key state interest group, later managed to avoid inclusion in the new system.

Public deliberation with civil society interest groups produced additional changes. The second set of draft laws was presented to the Tripartite Commission at the beginning of March 1998. Some of the main issues discussed concerned the legal status of ZUS, which the trade unions wanted to be kept strictly separate from the state budget. However, many other aspects were discussed, and government legislative drafts were deeply refined and revised during tripartite negotiations. Some differences proved impossible to reconcile. Within the tripartite working group on pension reform, union representatives also expressed concerns about the pension rights of people with occupational privileges, which were to be abolished for younger workers. The unions also differed from the office of the plenipotentiary on benefit indexation and on equal retirement ages for men and women. The Office of the Plenipotentiary was unsuccessful in trying to convince the unions of an equal retirement age. The OPZZ trade union complained that it could not keep up with rapid changes in the draft laws and that it did not have time to consult on the proposal with all its constituents. Therefore, the Tripartite Commission did not work out a final common position on the first pillar and pension system laws. Both major trade unions sent qualified negative opinions to parliament, especially on the first pillar law, expressing their concern about the issue of the occupational privileges. However, the unions did not mobilize to oppose pension privatization. Instead, a pact was reached between the government and the trade unions to allow the legislative process to go ahead, with the thorny issue of how to adapt special privileges to be negotiated with union representatives starting in the middle of 1998.

Poland launched a major public relations campaign in April 1997 with $1.4 million in financing from USAID (interviews with Vicki Peterson and Rafał Szymczak, July 1998). In its first stage, until September 1998, the campaign focused on creating a general image of the reform and informing the main groups involved—unions, employers, public opinion leaders (politicians and media)—about the main principles of pension privatization. Journalist education seminars and materials were supplemented by study tours to Argentina and Chile for journalists, parliamentarians, and government leaders selected by the Office of the Plenipotentiary. PR activities in the first stage included conducting opinion polls about the old pension system, creating a reform logo and graphic informational materials, training Office of the Plenipotentiary and ZUS employees in communication techniques, and preparing a pension reform Web page for the Office of the Plenipotentiary.

During this campaign, the government continued its internal consultations on the new pension legislation. Most of the comments came from the Ministry of Finance and related to financial aspects of the proposed system. Other discussions on system coverage concerned the Ministry of National Defense and the Ministry of Labor. A series of informal meetings took place with the representatives of the Catholic Church, concerning covering the clergy by the mandatory social security system. Before the draft laws were sent to parliament, judges were excluded from the mandatory system, as a result of their constitutional right to the proper remuneration after the end of an active career, which was pointed out by the legislative department of the Prime Minister's office. This illustrates the power of well-placed state interest groups in pension reform.

The government approved the two second-phase laws on April 28, 1998, and sent them to parliament, asking it to form an Extraordinary Commission to discuss the government proposals, as with the first set of laws. This time, however, the government did not ask for a quick process of discussions. The issues covered by the laws were, in the opinion of most decision makers, too complex to allow for such a procedure. The extraordinary commission of parliament for pension reform began its meetings in May 1998. However, a dispute broke out among the partisan veto actors over who to appoint as President of the Commission. Freedom Union argued that it should chair the committee, because the AWS held all the main social sector posts in the government. However, one AWS deputy thought that she should have recognition for her involvement in the reform process (she was a member of Solidarity team that prepared the union's proposal for reform and participated at the meetings of tripartite commission). Discussions on this issue lasted for a couple of weeks. Finally, a Freedom Union MP, Jan Lityński, was appointed president of the commission with votes from the Freedom Union and the opposition Alliance of the Democratic Left. This indicated that pension reform would not rely solely on votes from coalition deputies, but would include some representatives of opposition parties as well. In addition to the two coalition parties having slightly different views on several issues, some AWS deputies did not support the reform in full. Meanwhile, the Democratic Left was split between a managerial faction that supported radical change and trade unionists who opposed key aspects of the reform.

As a result of these differences among the key partisan veto actors, when the commission started work on the first pillar law, it had to focus on each paragraph, discussing it in detail. This was mainly a result of Democratic Left Alliance (SLD) strategy. Because its government had initiated reform, the party could not turn against the law directly. But in opposition, left-wing deputies tried to delay the process and avoid approving difficult changes in first pillar rules, which were against the interests of affiliated trade unions. The party opposed lowering replacement rates, eliminating income redistribution, and eliminating occupational privileges in the mandatory system. As a result, discussions in the extraordinary commission took much longer than expected.

While the key partisan veto actors were finalizing reform legislation in parliament, new actors were being created as a result of implementation of the second pillar law. In mid-1998, the regulatory agency for the second pillar, UNFE, was established with several million dollars in support from USAID (interview with Vicki Peterson, USAID, July 1998). Cezary Mech, a member of the Christian National Union, a constituent party of Solidarity Electoral Action, was appointed president. Cooperation between UNFE and the Office of the Plenipotentiary was very difficult, because Mech proved to be a great fan of Chilean-type reform and did not want to accept the mixed approach expressed in the Polish pension laws. Some degree of cooperation was finally established by the end of 1998. UNFE was the first of the new policy actors to be created in the early implementation stage of reform. As a result of the stalemate in parliament, the government decided to delay launch of the second pillar until April 1999. However, the licensing process for pension societies and pension funds started as planned in August 1998. This enhanced the irreversibility of the reform process, because most of the Polish and international companies operating in the Polish market (banks, investment funds, and insurance companies) became stakeholders in the new pension funds.

Because of upcoming local elections and the shrinking time until implementation, the parliamentary commission decided to stop discussing the first pillar law and switch to the Social Security System law in August, the so-called mother law. The final version of this law was accepted in October. Major changes introduced in parliament included covering only new entrants to the uniformed forces and excluding prosecutors from the mandatory system. Parliament returned to the first pillar law in October. The main issue remained how to deal with special occupational pensions granted under the old regime. Trade unions began to exert pressure at the beginning of December, when the Solidarity miners' trade union protested against the proposals being discussed. After several meetings with the Minister of Labor and the Plenipotentiary, miners' concerns grew, and they decided to take protest measures.

Representatives of the miners' union occupied the Ministry of Labor for two days, demanding that the government extend early retirement options for miners by adopting so-called bridging pensions before the first pillar law was implemented. Miners' concern about the pension system was enhanced by the process of coal industry restructuring that was closing down some mines. Negotiations also included the mining employers' organization. Employers promised to finance a part of a future bridging arrangement. The unions were partially satisfied with the solution; however, they demanded a legislative solution before the first pillar law was adopted. Finally, the Polish Senate adopted a slight change in Article 41 of the first pillar law, which promised to include bridging pensions in another legal act. The miners left the Ministry building.

Deliberation in parliament produced additional changes. An amendment to the first pillar law allowed a lower retirement age for those who fulfilled the work experience criteria for retirement but had not reached the normal retirement age. This provision reflected increased dissatisfaction from both the OPZZ and Solidarity trade unions. A final dispute concerned indexation rates. Parliament decided that "notional capital" in the individual first pillar accounts would be indexed quarterly to 75 percent of total wage fund growth, as opposed to the less generous half-price, half-wage indexation proposed by the government. Coalition deputies provided the votes to adopt the first pillar law on December 17. President Aleksander Kwaśniewski, a former leader of the opposition Democratic Left Alliance, signed the law on December 29, and on January 1, 1999, Poland's privatized pension system entered the implementation phase.

While domestic actors also shaped pension privatization legislation in Poland, the World Bank, USAID, and its transnational allies played an instrumental role in putting pension privatization on the agenda. The experience of 1991, when World Bank official Nick Barr prevented the government from moving ahead with funded pensions, shows that World Bank support was a necessary condition for reform in Poland. Starting in

1994, the World Bank inspired, educated, and supported the first reform advocates in Poland, employing and equipping them to initiate a radical shift in the domestic debate. The World Bank helped to establish Poland's Office of the Plenipotentiary for Pension Reform and provided all manner of resources to ensure the completion of reform, including the office's Polish leader, Michał Rutkowski. World Bank and USAID support in Poland continued for more than four years, showing that transnational actors have deep reserves of resources and patience in navigating domestic policy processes. Transnational actors provided continuity for the reform effort through multiple changes of government and cabinet reshuffles. The influence of these actors was truly pervasive and deeply influential. While independent domestic policy actors also influenced the reform process, this often amounted to either delaying the reform (in the case of Minister of Labor Miller) or altering a small number of provisions (in the case of the Solidarity government). The main lines of the reform were inspired by and conceived with World Bank participation and advice. They were drafted into legislation and supported by extensive technical and financial assistance. This could not have been achieved without powerful domestic allies, nor without the long-term assistance of transnational actors.

Implementation

Transnational policy actors continued to intervene deeply in pension reform implementation in Poland in an effort to set up administrative and regulatory systems and ultimately to prevent this leading reform country from turning into a high-profile disaster story.

Key features of the Polish reform are the change to a "notional defined contribution" first pillar, the establishment of mandatory, private second pillar funds for pension savings, and the creation of a legal framework for new types of third pillar voluntary funds (see Chłoń et al. 1999 for a complete description). For employees participating in the new system, a payroll tax of 12.22 percent of gross wages began to be contributed to an individual notional capital account and 7.3 percent to a private pension fund of the employees' choice. An additional payroll tax of 17.48 percent continued to fund the disability pension system and a few other benefits paid by ZUS. Employees aged thirty and under were required to participate in both the new first and second pillars. Workers between the ages of thirty and fifty could choose whether to participate in the second pillar or only in the reformed first pillar. People over fifty remain outside the new system. Several possibilities were created for the third pillar, including individual pension insurance and employer group funds that may be set up and managed by consortia of employers and workers' representatives, including trade unions. The Solidarity trade union was involved in setting up the first such consortium, in cooperation with several leading financial institutions.

Some major design decisions continued to be made in the early implementation phase. In early 1999, the government renewed negotiations with trade unions over a "bridging law" that would resolve the thorny issue of occupational privileges. A special medical committee prepared new criteria for early retirement, forming the basis for bridging arrangements to be negotiated among the government, unions, and employers. These criteria allow early retirement for those who work in special conditions (such as underground or underwater work) that might influence the health status of the employee and those who perform work of a special character (such as airplane pilots and train engineers), that requires good psychological and physical conditions for public safety.

In October 1998, the implementation stage of the USAID-funded public relations campaign started. The main goal of this campaign was to inform people about pension privatization rules and the choices for different age groups. It created a call center, starting in March 1999, through which anyone would be able to order a brochure about the new pension system and have basic questions answered. In February, a media campaign was launched to inform people about the call center, to explain how the reform affects different age groups, and to promote the new ZUS. In addition to TV ads, the Polish telephone company sent a reform booklet out with its April telephone bills. A World Bank grant paid for government officials, parliamentary deputies, and journalists to go on study tours to Chile, Argentina, Hungary, and Sweden to learn about pension reform ideas underlying the Polish model and thus to become more effective communicators about pension privatization. In many cases, these tours caused skeptics to become advocates or supporters of pension privatization. On February 16, pension funds were allowed to start their own advertising campaigns, and the scramble for members began. Their activities are monitored by UNFE, a regulatory body heavily supported by outside advice, which intervenes in cases of improper advertisement.

Although Poland did not experience the substantial post-reform changes in program design that occurred in Hungary, it faced severe administrative problems. Poland threatened to become a high-profile scare story to other countries attempting to implement pension privatization. The early implementation stages showed ZUS and its information technology system to be unprepared, resulting in widespread public outcry about failed allocation or misallocation of pension contributions, although this did not stop millions of Poles from joining the new, private pillar (Chłoń-Domińczak 2002). Initially, all ZUS branches and offices were flooded by customers eager to get forms, software, and information. ZUS prepared new rules on sending information to ZUS and special software for employers to send information via computer data transfers. The pension fund regulatory agency UNFE also began its work in February 1999, monitoring the activities of the pension funds, their advertising campaigns, and registering fund agents. ZUS proved unable to manage the demands of individual record keeping and system redesign. It failed to credit contributions to the right accounts for several years and introduced administrative changes that made it impossible to verify contributions in 1999, leading to a sharp decline in contribution rates. With World Bank assistance, administrative improvements were made over time and new computer systems became operational, but the administrative chaos at ZUS turned public opinion decisively against the reforms (Chłoń-Domińczak 2002). While the World Bank provided extensive assistance to ZUS, USAID focused its efforts on the private pension fund regulatory body, UNFE (interview with Vicki Peterson, USAID, July 1998). These efforts lasted for several years and cost millions of dollars in transnational donor money.

Another problem with privatized pension system implementation in Poland was that the private pension funds experienced negative returns in the first years of system implementation (Fultz 2004, 13). Chłoń-Domińczak (2002, 189) shows that internal rates of returns in the private funds (minus fees) ranged from −3.54 percent to −13.76 percent in the period from January 2000 to June 2001. Such results have convinced a number of advocates of pension privatization to be more cautious in promoting them and to pay greater attention to the design of administrative systems (Barr 2005; Holzmann and Hinz 2005). Transnational proposal actors remained deeply involved in Poland during reform implementation, helping to solve the worst administrative problems in a way that ensured the continued viability of the new pension reforms. While they faced serious challenges and growing skepticism, the future of the reforms does not appear endangered despite poor performance in its early years.

PENSION PRIVATIZATION IN DEMOCRATIC COUNTRIES

The experience of reform in Hungary and Poland shows that these democratic countries have been heavily influenced by the World Bank and USAID through the financing of reform teams and the provision of pre-reform and post-reform technical assistance. Such assistance has strengthened the hand of domestic pension privatization advocates, altered the preferences of actors, and tipped the political balance within both countries in favor of reform. Reformers and their transnational allies have been deeply involved in negotiation with domestic opponents and potential opponents of reform and have made numerous compromises in order to get reforms passed through the legislature. They have also made use of externally funded public relations campaigns to convince people to support reform. As a result, in both Hungary and Poland, reform passed with substantial public support (Hasselman 2006), but subsequently became deeply unpopular as administrative problems and negative returns in the private funded system came to light (Fultz 2004, 13).

Reform processes in both countries clearly reflect the priorities of transnational policy actors in conjunction with the current government and, to a lesser extent, other powerful political parties and social actors. While both countries faced severe economic and fiscal crises that spurred a search for reform solutions, it is also evident that these problems could have been solved in a number of ways, with or without pension privatization (Augustinovics et al. 2002). Thus, to explain the implementation of pension privatization requires attention to the agendas and actions of transnational policy actors, particularly the World Bank and USAID, and domestic political actors. We will see that much the same can be concluded for the non-democratic reforming country in our sample, though the role of alternative proposal actors has been less significant.

Pension Privatization in Kazakhstan

In the mid-1990s, Kazakhstan experienced a dramatic pension arrears crisis—meaning pension obligations simply were not paid on time. Kazakhstan, like Russia (Cook 2006, 128) and Romania, had initially controlled pension spending by accumulating substantial payment arrears to current pensioners (Cangiano et al. 1998, 10) and by not indexing pensions to keep up with inflation. In 1996 and 1997, Kazakh pension arrears were so severe that mass protests of pensioners broke out in cities across the country. A collapse in state ability to tax was a large part of the problem, reflecting the extent of the so-called gray economy, as well as a steep decline in production. Few small private businesses paid any pension payroll tax at all. System failure seemed to call for radical measures, and the Kazakh government responded with a radical pension reform, introduced in tandem with an effort to pay off all existing pension arrears.

Commitment Building

The process of commitment building in Kazakhstan shows the powerful role that transnational actors can play in inspiring domestic policy makers

TABLE 5.9
Veto and Proposal Actors in Kazakhstan: Commitment Building

	Proposal actor	Veto actor
Governmental Working Group	X	X
President		X
Total	1	2

to undertake radical reforms. Kazakhstan began its reform process with full governmental commitment to finding a way out of its pension crisis. The solution Kazakhstan adopted was heavily influenced by transnational actors but was facilitated by the small number of veto players in its strong presidential political system (see table 5.9). With authoritarian political institutions and a centralized policy style, Kazakhstan was able to circumvent open disputes between different ministries and government agencies that characterize the reform process in consolidated democracies. Reformers in Kazakhstan won presidential approval for the reform at the outset of the reform process and set up a special interministerial commission for pension reform that monopolized authority within the government, under the political sponsorship of the prime minister, thus simplifying commitment and coalition building.

The reform process started in November 1996 when President Nursultan Nazarbaev and Prime Minister Akezhan Kazhegeldin appointed Grigori Marchenko chairman of the National Securities Commission and Natalya Korzhova head of a newly consolidated Ministry of Labor and Social Protection. Marchenko was put in charge of the special governmental working group on pension reform that included the prime minister, deputy prime minister, Minister of Finance, Chairman of the Central Bank, Minister of Labor and Social Protection, head of the National Securities Commission, two persons from the private sector, and two members of parliament (Majilis). Chief reformer Marchenko had previously worked at the National Bank of Kazakhstan and was a protégé of reformist Prime Minister Kazhegeldin. Marchenko reports that it was important to get people from different agencies to head off potential misunderstandings and lack of coordination down the road (interview, July 1, 1998).

Transnational actors, particularly USAID, the World Bank, and the Asian Development Bank, provided policy ideas and direct technical assistance to the pension reform working group. Chief reformer Grigori Marchenko reported being heavily influenced in his thinking about pension reform by reading *Averting the Old Age Crisis* and attending World Bank–sponsored conferences (interview, July 1, 1998). In particular, Marchenko attended a World Bank sponsored conference where he was inspired by an address by the Chilean reformer José Piñera (Ellerman 2001). Piñera convinced Marchenko of the benefits of the Chilean system, and Marchenko returned to Kazakhstan committed to establishing similar reforms in Kazakhstan. This commitment was reinforced by World Bank and USAID support for Kazakh reformers, including technical analyses and study trips to Chile and other reforming countries.

The basic framework for pension reform in Kazakhstan was thus transmitted largely through reformers' own interpretations of World Bank and USAID policy ideas. Direct technical assistance to the pension reform working group was provided by USAID. USAID technical assistance gave the working group important advantages. Given the lack of technical expertise in Kazakhstan and the lack of resources on the part of civil society groups, "no one else was technically in a position to develop a model" for analyzing or developing pension reform proposals (Marchenko interview, July 1, 1998), and thus the working group easily dominated expert debate. Secrecy also enhanced the working group's monopoly on reform proposals in Kazakhstan, sharply restricting the ability of civil society or other interest groups to influence reform. Even high-ranking government officials in affected ministries were not informed of the progress of working group deliberations. This helped to allow the government to develop a more radical reform program than in other post-communist transition countries.

After four months of deliberation, the working group on pension reform had prepared the outlines of a radical reform program in the form of an eight-page "draft concept" that was published in the Kazakh press on March 20, 1997. In essence, the draft concept proposed changing the Kazakh pension system from a pay-as-you-go system paid for by a 25.5 percent payroll tax to a private, funded system based on a 10 percent employee contribution with a minimum pension guarantee. The pay-as-you-go system would be phased out over a ten-year period. Later amendments, however, extended the transition period. Disability and survivor benefits would be transferred to the central budget, all special privileges eliminated, and new recording and financial mechanisms put in place. Private pension funds would collect and invest employee contributions, aiding the development of Kazakh capital markets.

Kazakhstan's reform development process was swift, marked by the quick formation of a working group on pension reform that brought together all the key governmental actors. Full presidential support and the lack of alternative veto or proposal actors within the government enabled the working group to produce the most fundamental reform of the three

TABLE 5.10
Veto and Proposal Actors in Kazakhstan: Coalition Building

	Proposal actor	Veto actor
Governmental Working Group	X	X
President		X
Total	1	2

cases. Later stages of public and parliamentary deliberation did not substantially change the basic outlines of reform, agreed in the working group's secretive four-month session.

Coalition Building

The rest of the reform process in Kazakhstan was characterized by cursory public and parliamentary deliberation. Although the government was obliged to submit the reform program to some debate, Kazakhstan's strong presidential system meant that there were no real partisan or civil society actors who could exercise a veto (see table 5.10). Parliament was the main deliberative forum, but had no actual veto power, either. Interest groups still managed to influence the process to some extent, but only within bounds set by the administration.

The Kazakh government allocated less than two months for public discussion of the new, private pension system. Public deliberation began on March 20, when the government published its draft concept paper in the press, and lasted until May 12, when the government approved a revised concept for pension reform. During this time, a deputy minister of labor and social affairs solicited and considered public commentary, collecting approximately two hundred letters and interest group comments. However, the same deputy minister, a former opposition trade union leader, notes that the government had not previously intended to consult with interest groups and that this was undertaken on her own personal initiative (interview with Sivriukova, July 6, 1998). In addition, two teams of government representatives toured the country in April and May with funding from USAID to promote the pension privatization concept and gather public reactions in town hall–style meetings that were widely reported in the press. Public deliberations also took place in tripartite council meetings with trade unions and employers in April. The main trade union federation expressed dissatisfaction with the government proposal

(*Kovcheg*, May 1, 1997). The leader of the second leading trade union accepted reform, believing it to be a fait accompli. Still, trade unions criticized the rushed deliberative process, saying it deprived interest groups of voicing their concerns (*Kovcheg*, May 1, 1997).

The government ignored widespread public opposition expressed in the press and public opinion polls. Groups such as the Federation of Kazakh Trade Unions, the association of labor and war veterans, and several pensioners' associations came out against the reform. Some government social security officials also expressed opposition (*Kazakhstanskaya Pravda*, April 25, 1997), reflecting limited support and deliberation within the government itself. There is no evidence that the government concerned itself with rallying popular support, as only limited resources, mostly provided by USAID, were allocated to public relations and public awareness campaigns. Public support would have been difficult to obtain, because the government was dealing at the same time with a massive pension arrears crisis, causing mass protests around the country. In one instance, on August 18, 1997, a crowd of several hundred angry pensioners demonstrated against pension arrears in the central square of Taraz, a city in Southern Kazakhstan. They gathered in front of the mayor's office, blocking traffic on one of the city's main thoroughfares for three hours, chanting slogans including, "Give us pensions!," "We want to eat!," and "We don't believe you! You lured away our kopeks!" (*Express K*, August 19, 1997).

The government chose to trade off extensive deliberation for quicker implementation of reform. Its main imperative was to submit pension reform legislation to parliament in time to begin implementation in January 1998. Legislative drafting had started already in April, while public deliberation was under way. Nonetheless, public deliberation did produce a handful of changes. Most of these were technical, including ten to twenty instances of rewording for consistency and other technical reasons, and about ten alterations made after consultation with various international organizations. However, four new provisions clearly reflected the impact of special interest groups, while seven appeared to respond to broadly expressed public interest concerns.

Initially, the Kazakh reform intended to eliminate all special pension privileges, which were numerous under the Soviet regime, something that was recommended by the World Bank as part of the pension privatization process. However, between March and May 1997, military and internal affairs officers managed to make their voices heard. Four new provisions granted special exemptions and benefits to the military, employees of the Agencies of Internal Affairs, and the State Investigation Committee (former KGB). The so-called power ministries were the only lobby able to gain a guarantee of special treatment under the proposed new system.

The May 1997 draft exempted anyone with ten years of service or more from being affected by the change to the new pension system. The power ministries also won a lower retirement age and higher benefits for their employees under the new system. New entrants into the military, security, and intelligence services and those with less than ten years of service would participate in the new system, but were awarded a 20 percent contribution to their pension funds, paid for by the state, double the 10 percent for all other categories, paid for by employees themselves from pre-tax earnings.

Several changes also addressed broad public concerns expressed through multiple deliberative channels. Kazakhstan's privatization experience, in which many voucher coupons became worthless, left the public with a low regard for private investment funds. This translated into a mistrust of private pension funds, expressed time and again in public meetings held around the country (interview with Marchenko, July 1, 1998). In response, the government introduced in its revised program a State Accumulation Fund that citizens could choose over private, non-state accumulation funds. The State Accumulation Fund would provide greater security through tighter investment controls and a state guarantee, with the trade-off of potentially lower returns. This provision proved to be very important, as 85 percent of citizens initially trusted their contributions to this state fund, severely limiting the extent of private management in the funded pillar and showing widespread public suspicion of pension privatization. The State Accumulation Fund's dominant share of the "private" market had declined to approximately 70 percent by late 1999. The May 1997 draft concept also promised price indexation of benefits to beneficiaries of the old state system, an improvement over the ad hoc indexation of previous years.

The May 1997 draft increased from 10 percent to 15 percent the amount of payroll contribution allocated to the old state system, and increased from ten to fifteen years the length of time to phase out this tax. The May 1997 draft also included a vital promise to repay pension arrears, a condition demanded by the World Bank for its continued assistance to Kazakhstan and by USAID to reestablish confidence in the pension system (USAID 1997). The new concept reduced the requisite work periods for minimum pension eligibility and promised no decline in take-home pay as a result of the transition to the new system.

Public deliberation had only limited impact on the outcome of debates on pension reform in the Majilis, Kazakhstan's lower house of parliament. Parliament was not a veto player in the reform process, but it provided an important deliberative forum nonetheless. Kazakhstan's president submitted the draft pension reform law to parliament marked "urgent," a legislative procedure that meant that the parliament had only one month to debate, amend, and pass the law or risk being dissolved by the president. In this case, the law would be passed by presidential decree. Threat of dissolution militated against making major changes to the law. As one Kazakh newspaper explained, the dissolution threat presented the deputies with a difficult dilemma: if they voiced public concerns and voted against pension reform, they would lose their positions and pension reform would be accepted by decree. If the deputies voted for reform, they would face public outrage in upcoming parliamentary elections in September. Constituents in several districts had threatened to recall deputies who voted for reform (*Express K*, May 29, 1997).

Deputies tried to resolve this dilemma by expressing public concerns and even outright opposition, but at the same time accepting the constraints the government reform team placed around acceptable compromises. Parliamentary deliberation thus took two forms: purely rhetorical deliberation and a parallel, somewhat more secretive, process of actual reform amendments that were few in number. Very few parliamentary deputies spoke in favor of the reform program, and the pro-reform side was represented directly by the government reform team itself. One newspaper described the debate as "fervent" but also said that the attempt of the deputies to paint the reform as "anti-social" tended to break down when facing the "threatening" faces of the government team (*Kustanaiskiye Novosti*, May 27, 1997). Parliament voted overwhelmingly for the reform in June, despite the hostility of many parliamentarians to the reform in full or in part, in order to guard against dissolution.

In the course of deliberation, the government was forced to concede a few points to parliament. The main changes were to the system of state guarantees, the phasing-out of the old state program, the retirement age, and special benefits. The Majilis voted not to increase the pension age to sixty-five as proposed in the government draft, but to end a phased increase already in progress in 2001, when the retirement age would reach sixty-three for men and fifty-eight for women. Majilis deputies had protested increasing the retirement age further on the grounds of low and decreasing life expectancy in Kazakhstan.

Second, the Majilis managed to get two special interest provisions included in the law. Lower retirement ages were granted to (1) citizens who lived in zones of extreme and maximum radiation risk (the top two radiation risk zones) for not less than ten years between 1949 and 1963 (victims of the Soviet Union's nuclear test program), and (2) women in rural areas with five or more children. Interestingly, the Majilis voted against extending special pension benefits to employees of the interior ministry and state investigation office (former KGB) (*Selskaya Novi*, June 12, 1997). However, special benefits for these two groups were reinstated in the Senate, a body more closely controlled by the president. The government lobbied insistently for the reinstatement of these special benefits, despite the declared goal of the reform to eliminate special pension privileges (*Panorama*, June 13, 1997). Efforts by senators to grant special benefits to other groups, including steel workers, miners, prosecutors, and judges, failed.

Despite enormous limitations on the legislative process, parliament also succeeded in making a few important general interest alterations to the pension reform law. Most important was the decision to extend the phase-out of the old state system indefinitely and to grant state guarantees for moneys deposited in the State Accumulation Fund.

Still, the government managed to preserve the fundamentals of its pension privatization program throughout the rapid, two-month deliberative process. Reformers in Kazakhstan and their transnational advisers set out to implement a Chilean-style pension reform and were successful in pushing through pension privatization. The Kazakh reforms replaced the social security–type system with a minimum pension guarantee and a mandatory, funded system based on private accounts (Rutkowski 1998). The law called for price indexation of the minimum pension twice a year, but no automatic indexation. From the start of reform on January 1, 1998, all Kazakh employees were required to invest 10 percent of their earnings in pension funds. An additional 15 percent of payroll continued to be paid by employers to the existing state pension system. Previously, the 25.5 percent contribution rate was paid entirely by employers. Under the reform, the contribution rate was reduced slightly and 10 percent was paid by employees from pre-tax income. All workers who contributed for six months into the old pay-as-you-go system would also receive benefits from it, making the phase-out period last for decades until the last contributor dies. Workers entering the labor force less than six months before the January 1, 1998, starting date would derive their entire benefit from the new system.

Implementation

Kazakhstan passed one of the quickest and most radical pension privatization programs in the former communist countries. However, the accelerated legislative process in Kazakhstan had some downsides in terms of legislative quality and implementation (Rutkowski 1998). Major problems included

- low contribution compliance in the first months of implementation
- failure to set up private pension funds in time for the start of reform
- failure to issue all workers needed identification numbers

- more general failure of administrative computer systems
- lack of public information on how the new system works, and
- lack of confidence in private pension funds or reform more generally.

Lack of preparedness for reform implementation was related directly to the speed of reform. The government was determined to complete pension reform before parliamentary elections in September 1998 and presidential elections in 1999. However, this left little time to draft legal regulations, inform the public about the program, or allow prospective pension funds to establish themselves and work out business plans. All of these things began to happen as reform was already under way.

As a result, Kazakhstan experienced serious administrative lapses in the early months of implementation. In January 1998, few contributions were collected, leaving the state center for benefit payments with a substantial deficit. The first private pension funds were not founded until March 1998. Issuance of individual contributions with social identification numbers continued several months into the implementation process. Many regulations needed to supplement the pension reform law were drafted while the reform was in progress during 1998, with USAID providing vital technical assistance (interview with William Baldridge, USAID, July 2, 1998). For instance, the regulation "on qualification requirements applied to the licensee, founders and managerial staff of the accumulative pension funds" was registered on February 11, 1998. Similarly, the regulation of the National Pension Agency that provided for issuing licenses to owners of greater than 25 percent of shares of open pension funds was registered on March 18, 1998. Public information about the reform would have been distributed sooner and more extensively had a longer public debate occurred.

More inclusive deliberation may also have stymied anti-reform civil society mobilization in the early implementation stage and increased public confidence in the new private pillar. Already in July 1997, air traffic controllers and pilots began efforts to reinstate special privileges they had enjoyed under the old system (*Panorama*, July 11, 1997). In September, miners' representatives traveled to Almaty to press their demands for reinstatement of special retirement provisions (*Panorama*, September 5, 1997). In November, steelworkers, miners, and pilots threatened a nationwide strike on behalf of those professions that lost special retirement benefits (*Kazakhstanskaya Pravda*, November 11, 1997). These claims attracted substantial support in parliament and in mid-1998 a group of deputies began to consider legislation to reinstate a number of categories of special privileges that it had taken away a year earlier. USAID simulations showed that workers in hazardous professions had in fact lost about half their benefits under the reform, but argued that special benefits were not affordable. Instead, USAID recommended that the government should pay for actually disabled workers through the disability system (USAID, April 23, 1998).

Interestingly, Kazakhstan chose pension privatization without having its reform team funded by the World Bank. However, World Bank ideas were still influential, particularly through lead reformer Grigori Marchenko's participation at a World Bank conference supporting pension privatization, where he picked up *Averting the Old Age Crisis* (World Bank 1994) and heard a pitch from Chilean pension guru José Piñera. World Bank resources came to Kazakhstan only after major design decisions were made. USAID, however, was deeply involved in Kazakhstan's pension reform from the outset, pushing pension privatization ideas through internal consulting reports and working with the government on implementation issues for a period of approximately seven years, from 1998 to 2005.

After a rocky start, Kazakhstan's pension systems began to benefit from dramatic real economic growth from 2001 to 2004, accompanied by high levels of foreign direct investment (Becker et al. 2005, 25). While Kazakhstan had planned to phase out its pay-as-you-go pension system, replacing it with a minimum pension, wage growth caused a dramatic increase in social tax collections. Thus, greater funds were available and the government decided to dramatically increase payments to current retirees under the pay-as-you-go system. In 2003, the Kazakh government increased statutory minimum pensions by 27 percent. A second sharp increase in minimum pensions by 59 percent was planned for mid-2005. In addition, pension benefit levels were recalculated based on 2002 wage data for the industry in which a pensioner worked prior to retirement, causing the wage basis for calculating pensions to double (Becker et al. 2005, 27).

However, while social security payments have recovered, economic growth in Kazakhstan has not so far helped returns in the new private accounts. Because most investment in the oil sector came from foreign direct investments, investment opportunities for private pension accounts have not kept pace with their growing balances. Since 1998, a majority of pension fund investments have been in short-term government bonds and bank deposits, which began to earn negative real interest rates (Becker et al. 2005, 29). Essentially, with Kazakhstan's weak financial markets, there have not been sufficient investment opportunities to put the new pension funds to work, and foreign investments have become less attractive with the appreciation of the tenge against the dollar. Thus, Kazakh pension accounts have been, like their Hungarian and Polish counterparts, experiencing negative returns.

One notable success of the Kazakh reform has been in the area of financial market development. Thanks to the pension reform, Kazakhstan has a far greater supply of investment capital, and this has been good for the banks and other financial sector organizations. Because the pension funds have required strong regulatory oversight, pension reform has also enabled improved government supervision of the financial sector more generally. The Kazakh experience thus accords with the arguments of Madrid (2003) and Brooks (2004; 2005) that pension privatization is often undertaken more to spur financial sector development than to benefit pensioners. Becker et al. (2005, 23), for instance, shows that most Kazakh pensioners would have been much better off keeping the old pay-as-you-go system, because most of the benefits of pension privatization accrues to high-income earners.

Transnational and Domestic Actors in Pension Privatization

This chapter has put forward a conceptual model for analyzing transnational policy actor involvement and examined in detail the collaboration of international and domestic actors in pension privatization. It has shown that transnational actors rely on domestic partners to push forward with reform processes in specific domestic contexts. However, it has also shown that domestic reformers rely on international organizations to get reform through. International influence comes in several forms:

1. changing the way leading reformers think about pension systems by introducing new ideas and information about pension privatization and its alternatives
2. funding reform teams through grants and loans that dramatically increase their technical and intellectual capacity in ways that allow reformers to defeat their domestic opponents
3. providing technical advice during the process of commitment building and coalition building for reform on numerous topics, ranging from pension system design and modeling to public relations and political advice
4. providing loans and technical assistance post-reform to enable countries to cope with difficult implementation problems and to finance costs of transition to a system based on individual pension savings accounts, and
5. affecting the career paths of domestic reform officials by creating new opportunities to consult and work for transnational policy actors in spreading the new pension reforms to other countries.

As described in the model presented in chapter 3, transnational policy actors have an impact in countries by exerting a pervasive influence on governments to adopt a pension privatization model. Because transnational policy actors are not domestic veto actors, however, they often cede control over specific design issues to domestic actors. In each case investigated here, many policy design issues have been developed in-country by reform leaders or through compromises with alternative veto and proposal actors or interest groups in domestic political debate. Some authors have found these limitations to be evidence of the rather limited power of transnational actors (Weyland 2005). To a certain extent, that is true: transnational policy actors are not domestic veto actors and have no direct authority to make domestic policy decisions. Nonetheless, this chapter has shown that transnational actors exert power over reform decisions through pervasive influence on the process of reform, working with multiple actors over multiple stages. Transnational actors have pursued agendas by finding domestic partners, inspiring them with reform ideas, strengthening the hand of domestic partners in domestic political debate, and following through with loans and technical assistance that tend to prevent or correct reform errors and problems in implementation. The result is reforms that conform closely to transnational actor advice.

The following chapter seeks to test the generalizability of these conclusions by studying a broader sample of countries, including not only countries that implemented pension privatization, but also cases of non-reform. This is important because some countries may have reformed without transnational actor involvement, while others that experienced major transnational actor campaigns may not have adopted pension privatization. Only by exploring such cases will it be possible to make general conclusions about how necessary transnational actors are to the pension privatization trend. The following chapter seeks to provide a global evaluation of the impact of transnational actors and the conditions for their effectiveness.

CHAPTER SIX

Transnational Influence and Its Limits

CHAPTER FIVE EXPLORED THE ROLES of transnational policy actors in the domestic policy process in three postcommunist countries. These case studies showed that the World Bank and USAID played a major role in each country in all three domestic phases of reform: commitment building, coalition building, and implementation. Perhaps the greatest influence of transnational proposal actors came during policy development and commitment building within governments. These case studies showed that transnational policy actors used at least five distinct mechanisms of influence: disseminating reform ideas through conferences and seminars, funding reform teams during the planning of reforms, providing technical assistance to reform teams, providing loans and technical assistance for reform implementation, and affecting the career paths of reformers. The use of these mechanisms varied from case to case; however, a variety of methods was used in each case.

The present chapter extends this analysis by exploring the use of these mechanisms in a global sample of cases. While a number of works on the political economy of pension reform have presented case study analyses, few have sought to locate these cases in global context. This work sets out to do this by analyzing cases of transnational policy actor involvement and non-involvement in all countries where pension privatization has been implemented. It further seeks to analyze the level and type of involvement of transnational actors in all countries where they have been engaged in promoting pension privatization. This helps to test whether the findings for transnational actor influence in chapter 5 can be generalized.

This chapter presents findings from a global database of pension reform experiences compiled from World Bank and USAID sources. On the basis of this research, I develop a simple typology of countries where transnational policy actors were involved in putting reform on the policy agenda, cases where transnational policy actors supported reform once under way, and cases of non-involvement. Shorter case studies then analyze a selected sample of pension reform experiences from each category. The findings of this chapter are clear: transnational policy actors have exerted influence in the vast majority of reforming countries in multiple ways. Cases that disconfirm transnational actors' influence do exist: I find three clear cases where countries rejected transnational policy campaigns to implement pension privatization (though these countries may reform in the future); and in several OECD countries pension privatization has been implemented without substantial transnational policy actor involvement. However, there is strong evidence that the transnational policy campaign for pension privatization has had a substantial impact on most countries in which it has operated. There would not be thirty countries in the world with privatized pension systems at the time of this writing without transnational actor interventions.

A GLOBAL SAMPLE

To test the applicability of findings from the detailed case studies in chapter 5, I have compiled a new global pension reform database from primary sources at the World Bank and USAID and supplemented by secondary sources from the case study literature. Data on World Bank conferences and seminars come from the World Bank Institute, compiled by its lead pension trainer and former Argentine reformer Gustavo Demarco and Debbie Kim Wang.

Data on World Bank involvement in pre-reform and post-reform technical assistance and loans were obtained from Richard Hinz of the World Bank, co-author of Holzmann and Hinz (2005), which analyzed data collected by the World Bank's Operations Evaluation Department on the Bank's pension reform work. This database contains a complete record of all Bank loans with a pension component between 1984 and 2004, including year of loan, country, type of loan, and the nature of the policy advice or assistance. Coding in the database has been controversial within the World Bank (interview with Richard Hinz, June 2005); it has proven difficult to differentiate pension lending, for instance, from other lending in a financial sector loan instrument. However, there is a high degree of confidence in the coding of pre- and post-reform assistance and whether it involved a loan or technical assistance. Similar data were collected from USAID on completed pension reform projects. These data indicate the year and type of assistance as well as contacts and consultants. Finally, data on the career paths of reformers have been collected from interview sources at the World Bank. This data source substantially underestimates the impact on reformers' career paths, because it includes only reformers who are currently staff members of the World Bank, rather than staff and consultants for the full range of transnational policy actors.

Table 6.1 displays all countries where the World Bank provided pension reform advice between 1994 and 2004 and the extent of transnational policy actor involvement by the World Bank and other leading organizations. Based on this table, a simple typology can be constructed of cases where transnational policy actors were involved in putting pension privatization on the domestic policy agenda (either by providing pre-reform training at seminars and conferences or by funding and providing technical assistance to the reform team during the preparation of reform) and countries where transnational policy actors were involved only in post-reform implementation. In addition, drawing on a broader global sample of cases, we can include cases where transnational policy actors are not involved at any stage of the reform process. Table 6.2 displays a global sample of countries placed into these categories. Again, table 6.2 shows that in most cases, transnational actors have assisted with agenda setting and the provision of technical assistance prior to reform. Only a small number of countries have reformed without transnational actor assistance, mostly in the developed world. Similarly, countries that transnational actors have advised not to reform have mostly not reformed. Only a handful of countries appear to consider these reforms without transnational actor support.

The rest of this chapter discusses a select sample of cases drawn from each category in table 6.2. These case studies explore the role that transnational policy actors play in domestic policy processes. Special attention is given to any cases that show low or limited transnational policy actor influence on domestic reform processes. In particular, these include any cases where transnational policy actors advocated pension privatization, but where such reforms did not take place (Slovenia, Korea), and cases of reform without transnational policy actor involvement (Chile, United Kingdom, Sweden). These case studies, then, provide a clearer view of the impact and limits of transnational policy actor influence.

TRANSNATIONAL POLICY ACTORS AS AGENDA SETTERS

Cases where transnational policy actors helped to shape the pension privatization agenda best support a strong view of their influence. And indeed, transnational policy actors played such an agenda-setting role in most cases. These cases are concentrated in Central and Eastern Europe and Latin America, where transnational policy actors played a major role in putting pension privatization on the agenda. They played this role through (1) sponsorship of conferences and workshops on pension privatization that disseminated the ideas advanced in *Averting* and often brought Chilean reformers to speak; (2) dissemination of publications,

TABLE 6.1
Transnational Actor Involvement in Pension Reform

Country	Prior conference attendance	Reform team funded	Pre-reform technical assistance	Implementation assistance	Reformers hired by World Bank (WB)	Date of reform	Reform type	Type of first pillar [a]
Argentina		WB/UNDP	WB/UNDP	WB	Rofman, Demarco	1994	Parallel	PAYG
Bolivia		USAID/WB	USAID/WB	WB/USAID	Gottret, Revollo	1997	Substitutive	
Bulgaria	WB	USAID/WB	USAID/WB			2002	Mixed	PAYG
China	WB	WB	WB	WB/ADB		N/A	Mixed	
Colombia				WB		1994	Parallel	
Costa Rica		WB	WB			2001	Mixed	PAYG
Croatia	WB	WB	WB	USAID/WB	Plevko, Anusic	2002	Mixed	PAYG
Dom. Rep.	WB		WB			2001	Substitutive	
El Salvador			WB			1998	Substitutive	
Estonia	WB/USAID	WB	WB			2001	Parallel	PAYG
Hungary		WB	WB	WB/USAID/US Treasury	Bokros, Fehér	1998	Mixed	PAYG
Kazakhstan	WB/USAID	N/A	USAID	WB/USAID		1998	Substitutive	Minimum
Kosovo		WB/USAID	WB/USAID	WB/USAID		2001	Substitutive	Minimum
Latvia	WB/USAID	WB	USAID	USAID		2001	Mixed	NDC
Macedonia	WB	USAID/WB	USAID/WB	USAID		2002	Mixed	PAYG
Mexico	WB	WB	WB	WB/IMF		1997	Substitutive	Minimum
Nicaragua				WB		2001	Substitutive	Minimum

TABLE 6.1 (cont'd)
Transnational Actor Involvement in Pension Reform

Country	Prior conference attendance	Reform team funded	Pre-reform technical assistance	Implementation assistance	Reformers hired by World Bank (WB)	Date of reform	Reform type	Type of first pillar [a]
Russia	WB/USAID	WB	WB			2002	Mixed	NDC
Slovakia	USAID	WB	USAID/WB			2003	Mixed	PAYG
Uruguay		IDB/WB	IDB/WB	IDB/WB		1996	Parallel	PAYG
Ecuador	WB					Ongoing	Parallel	
Romania	WB	USAID/WB	USAID/WB			Ongoing	Mixed	PAYG
Ukraine	WB	USAID	USAID			Ongoing	Mixed	PAYG
Lithuania	WB/USAID		WB/USAID	USAID		2002	Parallel	PAYG
Armenia	WB					N/A		PAYG
Brazil		WB	WB/UN/IDB/ILO	WB		1999	NDC	NDC
Cameroon	WB					N/A		
Djibouti	WB					N/A		
Honduras						N/A		
Korea	WB		WB			N/A	N/A	PAYG
Kyrgyzstan		WB	WB			1997	NDC	NDC
Panama	WB					N/A		
Sri Lanka	WB					N/A		
Turkey	WB	WB	WB			N/A		PAYG
W.Bank/Gaza	WB					N/A		
Zambia	WB							
Uzbekistan	WB					2004	Mixed	PAYG
Chile				WB		1981		

[a] PAYG = pay-as-you-go; NDC = notional defined contribution.

TABLE 6.2
Reform Outcomes and Transnational Policy Actor Involvement

	Individual accounts	*No individual accounts*
Transnational policy actors help shape new pension reform agenda by providing pre-reform technical assistance and/ or funding reform team	*Private Savings Accounts* Argentina (UNDP/WB) Bolivia (USAID/WB) Mexico (WB) El Salvador (WB) Kazakhstan (USAID/WB) China (WB) Hungary (WB/USAID) Poland (WB/USAID) Bulgaria (WB/USAID) Croatia (WB/USAID) Kosovo (WB/USAID) Costa Rica (WB) Estonia (WB) Latvia (WB) Lithuania (WB/USAID) Macedonia (USAID/WB) Russia (WB) Slovakia (WB) Dom. Rep. (WB) Nicaragua (IDB) Uruguay (IDB) *Mid-Reform* Romania (USAID/WB) Ukraine (USAID) Serbia (USAID) Montenegro (USAID) *NDC Reform* Brazil (WB)	Korea (WB) Slovenia (WB) Djibouti (WB) Zambia (WB) West Bank and Gaza (WB) Venezuela (IDB/WB)
Transnational policy actors provide only loans and technical assistance for reform once underway	*Private Savings Accounts* Peru (WB) Colombia (WB)	N/A
Transnational policy actors not involved in reform	Chile Sweden United Kingdom	United States
Transnational policy actors oppose reform	Russia	Serbia Armenia Georgia

including *Averting*; and (3) provision of pre-reform technical assistance, often to fund the activities of pension reform design teams.

Conferences

As Queisser (2000, 39) puts it, "the World Bank's involvement in policy advice often begins with sectoral studies, informal contacts or seminars by its training arm, the Economic Development Institute (EDI)," recently renamed the World Bank Institute (WBI). "World Bank staff or experts help governments to analyse the problem of old-age provision and identify and evaluate alternative possibilities for reform and the costs of the various options. The models used are generally designed and developed in conjunction with the competent country institutions, so that they can later be used by the countries themselves for their own simulations" (Queisser 2000, 39). Conferences have often been co-sponsored with other organizations, including universities, institutes, think tanks, and transnational policy advocates.

Conference data supplied by the World Bank Institute show fifty-two pension-related events organized by the World Bank Institute between late 1996 and 2004, though the data are incomplete, particularly for earlier years, and exclude events organized by other units of the World Bank, such as the Social Protection Division. Many of the World Bank Institute events attracted participants from ten to twenty countries, sometimes from a single region of the world, other times from multiple regions. Some of these events were tailored to the needs of a particular country. Topics ranged from general ones, such as "Social Security and Pension Reform: Design and Administration of Pension Systems," to more specific regional and national seminars, such as "Pension Reform Options for Francophone Africa" or "Design and Implementation of Pension Reform in Iran." Many seminars took place in recipient countries, while others were held in Washington, D.C., Boston, or multiple national locations via video conferencing.

While these data are incomplete, they give some insight into the conferences and seminars organized by the World Bank Institute, which have been cited in the academic literature (cf. Brooks 2004; Pinheiro 2004) as a major source of policy advice and a recruiting ground for domestic reform partners. They also allow us to observe whether officials from a particular country took part in a World Bank seminar prior to reform. The seminar data provided by WBI are also interesting because they display a major emphasis on Central and Eastern Europe in the late 1990s. Rising participation from officials from Asia, Africa, and the Middle East in the 2000s may presage an increase in adoptions in these regions of the world. Nigerian officials, for instance, attended a "Pension Reform Executive Workshop" at Harvard University in 2001 and another seminar entitled "Pension Reform Action Plan—Africa 1," in Auckland Park, South Africa, in 2003 prior to the launch of reform in 2004. Officials from eleven African countries attended the latter seminar.

Publications

Transnational policy actors also exert enormous influence through policy research publications. The World Bank's publications budget dwarfs that of most transnational think tanks and organizations. According to Stone and Wright (2007, 9), it "is probably the largest single organizational producer of research on development." They note that a Bank "survey of development courses in leading universities found that fully one-sixth of the references on reading lists came from the Bank" (Dethier 2005, 4, quoted in Stone and Wright 2007, 8). Although it is difficult to quantify the impact of publications, the World Bank has clearly done several things to enhance the transfer of pension privatization ideas through publications. First, it has published major studies, such as *Averting*, that seek to frame the World Bank's pension reform agenda. Second, it has established a Pension Reform Primer series that provides a relatively simple introduction to numerous aspects of pension reform and country experiences. This series is available on the World Bank's pension reform Web site. Third, it has sponsored numerous specialist and technical papers that address all aspects of pension reform finance, administration, and political economy. Taken together, the World Bank has established itself as one of the key knowledge providers globally on pension privatization issues. In addition to providing pre-reform technical assistance, the World Bank has become the leading force in pension reform agenda setting worldwide (Charlton and McKinnon 2002). Observation of pre-reform "inspiration" shows that transnational actors are exerting influence, rather than merely assisting domestic reformers.

Case Studies: Transnational Policy Actors as Agenda Setters

The following case studies provide detailed information about the influence of transnational policy actors in pension reform in a representative set of cases worldwide. These case studies are designed to explore the generalizability of the findings presented in chapter 5 above. As a first step, it is useful to review the three post-communist cases presented in chapter 5 that showed substantial transnational influence over domestic agendas for reform.

Hungary

Hungary is a case where transnational policy actors played a major role in putting reform on the agenda through knowledge-dissemination activities and by funding a reform team in the Ministry of Finance to promote pension privatization. The World Bank played a leading role in these efforts, with additional assistance from USAID. The World Bank later funded the inter-ministerial working group on pension reform that designed the reform legislation. It also appointed two of its own pension reform experts to work full time with the inter-ministerial working group in Hungary, assisting with all aspects of reform design, political strategy, and public relations, as well as coordinating the work of outside contractors. USAID conducted technical assistance projects during the first three years of reform implementation in Hungary from 1998 to 2001, strengthening the regulatory agency for the new private funds and providing a range of other technical support (interview with Denise Lamaute, USAID, July 5, 2005).

Poland

Poland is a country where transnational policy actors played a large role in putting pension privatization on the agenda. The World Bank–sponsored the activities of the Office of the Plenipotentiary for Pension Reform and even released one of its leading pension reform officials, a Polish citizen, Michał Rutkowski, to head this office. The World Bank was deeply involved in all aspects of reform planning. The Bank provided modeling expertise and help with legislative drafting. World Bank and USAID were also critical in reform implementation, as Poland experienced severe administrative difficulties in its social security administration, ZUS.

Kazakhstan

Kazakhstan's reform was spurred by leading reformer Grigori Marchenko's attendance at a World Bank–sponsored conference on pension reform, where he heard the pitch of Chilean reformer José Piñera (Ellerman 2001). Marchenko returned to Kazakhstan convinced of the benefits of a private funded system. USAID provided immediate technical assistance to help in this project, including paying for travel of officials to

Chile and other countries to study global pension system models. USAID also provided reform design services and technical assistance of various types. The World Bank ultimately agreed to support the Kazakh reforms as well, although the Bank was unhappy with several design features and attempted to use loan conditionalities to change them. The World Bank loaned Kazakhstan $300 million to finance transition costs. USAID provided post-reform technical assistance for the first six years of implementation, working on writing and improving regulations and laws, administrative and regulatory systems, and creating better investment opportunities for pension funds.

OTHER CASES OF INTERVENTION AND REFORM

In addition to the three post-communist cases analyzed in chapter 5, I have selected a few additional cases of transnational actor intervention that ended with reform legislation being passed: Romania and Argentina. Romania is a later-stage post-communist case, while Argentina is one of the earliest Latin American cases and one where transnational actor influence has often been disputed. These cases illustrate the wide range of cases of effective intervention.

Romania

Romania exemplifies the persistence of transnational actors in advocating pension privatization in a country and struggling to promote reform with various governments that are not committed to reform. Romania has legislated but not yet implemented its privatized pension system based on individual accounts. Cashu (2005) shows that despite a deep crisis in Romania's pension system in the 1990s and World Bank technical advice to address it, the World Bank initially did not promote pension privatization in Romania. Nor did pension privatization figure on the agenda of the governing Party of Social Democracy from 1990 to 1996. The Ministry of Labor and Social Protection's first proposal designed to address the fiscal imbalances of the pension system did not contain provisions for mandatory pension savings, but rather targeted retirement age, eligibility criteria, and benefit formula. It further supported the development of private, voluntary pension schemes. While the proposal reached the parliamentary stage of the process in the summer of 1996, it received no priority because of the imminent general elections in the fall. The Party of Social Democracy was defeated at the polls by a four-party center-right coalition led by Emil Constantinescu. The new government withdrew the draft pension law from the parliament, but later reintroduced it without significant changes.

The new government began to discuss the creation of a mandatory savings scheme in 1997. Alexandru Athanasiu, the leader of the social democrats in the coalition and minister of labor, became the champion of a mandatory, funded system. At that point, the World Bank granted a loan to the Romanian government to finance reform-related projects. A group representing the drafting team, political parties, and social partners traveled to Chile to study first hand the Chilean model. Also with the World Bank support, the Ministry of Labor held an international conference in Bucharest in 1999 that featured the architect of Chilean reform, José Piñera.

A pension privatization proposal reached parliament, but failed to make any headway beyond the specialized committees. As general elections in November 2000 drew closer, chances of its passage dimmed as the center-right coalition began to disintegrate. Prime Minister Mugur Isarescu then introduced the new pension system through an emergency ordinance, a constitutional provision allowing the executive to approve draft laws pending their formal adoption by the legislature within one year. Parliament then approved pension privatization in early 2000. USAID launched a project to provide technical assistance. However, after new elections, the new government abrogated the Isarescu decree and invoked the need for a conventional parliamentary procedure proportionate to the social importance of this law. The Party of Social Democracy dragged its feet on reform between 2000 and 2004. It finally passed laws on voluntary and mandatory private pension funds in June and October 2004, respectively, only a month before general elections, leaving implementation to the next government. The law did not differ much from the one passed in 2000. At the time of this writing, the World Bank and USAID were involved in setting up administrative and regulatory aspects of the new private pension system.

Argentina

Argentina is sometimes considered a case where transnational policy actors had limited influence on reform. However, closer examination reveals that while Argentina planned its reform in the early 1990s, prior to the publication of the World Bank's *Averting*, its reform team drew on substantial transnational policy actor support in reform planning.

Argentina, like most other countries that have enacted pension privatization, faced a major fiscal crisis in its pension system in the late 1980s and early 1990s. Like other Latin American countries, the financial crisis was caused by demographic aging, contribution evasion in the informal sector, inflation, and macroeconomic instability. When the government responded by reducing the rate of pension indexation, court decisions ruled such practices unconstitutional, furthering the crisis. The government, under the strong influence of neoliberal Economy Minister Domingo Cavallo, decided on a fundamental reform of the social security system (Demarco 2004, 82–84).

Argentina received extensive advice and support from various transnational policy actors in its pension reform process (Müller 2003, 26–32; Demarco 2004, 84). The World Bank and the IMF supported pension privatization, while the ILO and the International Social Security Association supported reforms to the existing social security system. The Inter-American Development Bank and the U.N. Economic Commission for Latin America and the Caribbean (ECLAC) also supported pension privatization in Argentina. The UNDP and the World Bank provided funding for the social policy reform team (PRONATASS) that analyzed and evaluated the Chilean reforms as a potential model (Demarco 2004, 88). The IMF included a requirement to complete pension privatization as a condition of its $40 billion extended fund facility agreement with Argentina in 1992 (Brooks 2004, 70). The World Bank also provided more than $320 million in loans to Argentina to support implementation of its pension reforms in 1996 and 1997 (Tuozzo 2004, 107).

Argentine reform officials carefully evaluated the Chilean model and for policy and political reasons decided on a reform model that departed in significant ways from the Chilean substitutive reform and presaged the multi-pillar model advocated in *Averting*, which was published in 1994, the same year as the Argentine reform. The Argentine reform was based in part on polling (Demarco 2004, 90) and discussions with social interest groups, to gauge and improve its political feasibility. In particular, Argentine reformers believed that complete pension privatization would not be possible in a democratic country and that they needed to design a system that would be accepted by various social actors (Demarco 2004, 89). After political discussions, Argentine reformers realized that a parallel model would garner the greatest political consensus (Demarco 2004, 95). Argentina's reform thus reflected domestic political considerations, particularly in specific features of reform design. However, World Bank and UNDP financing had a major impact on the ability of the government to enact this reform. The advice of transnational policy actors, both for and against pension privatization, also appears to have had a substantial impact on the ultimate reform design.

It should be noted that Argentina's reform is sometimes labeled a "mixed" system, while in fact it is a "parallel" system. New entrants to the labor force continue to have a choice of whether to participate in individual pension savings accounts or to be covered under the state social security system (Demarco 2004, 103; Gill et al. 2005). It is also interesting to note that Argentine reformers have often been hired as consultants and employees of transnational policy actors to spread reform ideas to other countries. Demarco (2004, 100–101) notes at least seventeen countries where Argentine experts have consulted on pension reform in Latin America, Central and Eastern Europe, and Africa for organizations including the World Bank, IDB, ILO, and USAID.

Summary

While some analysts have argued that transnational policy actors have not been very important in influencing reform outcomes in countries despite their extensive involvement in the planning or support of reform, close examination of the case record provides limited support for such arguments. One can surely look at these cases in many different ways and decide that the glass is half-empty (transnational policy actors were not important) or the glass is half-full (transnational policy actors were very important). However, the case studies presented above show strong evidence for transnational actor influence through agenda-setting activities and pre-reform technical assistance.

A stronger refutation of transnational actor influence would be found in cases where transnational actors pushed reform but were rejected by domestic governments. The following studies search for evidence of such phenomena and find only three cases where this clearly occurred. I focus on two of these here: Slovenia and Korea. Venezuela under President Hugo Chavez also rejected pension privatization in 1998 as part of a broader rejection of external neoliberal policies and influences. These cases show that national veto players have the power to reject transnational actor advice. However, the small number of such cases also suggests that countries that begin to consider pension privatization often succeed when they have access to transnational actor resources. Conversely, it may be costly to change direction abruptly.

CASES OF INTERVENTION AND NO REFORM

Cases where transnational policy actors strongly advocate pension privatization and such reforms fail to occur provide the best potential for refuting the thesis advanced in this work that transnational policy actors have been an important determining force for pension privatization worldwide. A careful examination of the global case study evidence, however, finds only three clear cases where this occurred: Korea, Slovenia, and Venezuela. Other cases of transnational policy actor involvement and non-reform have taken place in poor countries with substantial administrative problems that resulted in the World Bank and other donors not pushing strongly for pension privatization. Only Korea, Slovenia, and Venezuela faced a major push for pension privatization that ended in a failure for the World Bank. Brazil is often mentioned as a fourth case; however, Brazil adopted an NDC pension system in 1999 that is consistent with World Bank advice in numerous other countries (Melo 2004, 337). This reform was supported by the World Bank and is broadly consistent with the logic of pension privatization (see discussion in the appendix). The World Bank helped to put the NDC concept on the agenda in Brazil (Pinheiro 2004) and the 1999 and subsequent reform programs have taken place with World Bank support; therefore, it would be hard to categorize Brazil as a country where the World Bank and other transnational policy actors have not been influential. The Brazilian case is also considered below, as are two of the cases that best display the limits of transnational policy actor influence: Slovenia and Korea.

Slovenia

Slovenia is a case where the World Bank was deeply involved in reform discussions with the government, but failed to enact reforms including individual, private pension savings accounts (Novak and Bajuk 2007). While Minister of Labor Tone Rop was initially highly committed to pension privatization (interview with Dušan Kidrič, Slovenian Ministry of Economic Relations, May 11, 1998), the government ultimately stepped back from its plans to switch to a private pension system (Stanovnik 2002, 49). To some extent, this reflected opposing advice given by transnational policy actors and to some extent the threat of domestic labor mobilization and criticisms voiced by the Slovenian Ministry of Finance (Stanovnik 2002, 57).

In the mid-1990s, the World Bank was deeply involved in supporting Minister of Labor Tone Rop in the development of a government white paper that would outline a private pension system for Slovenia. Transnational policy actors, in particular the World Bank and an E.U.-sponsored team of French consultants, were involved in discussions toward a government white paper on pension reform that included individual private accounts. The World Bank supported pension privatization in Slovenia in a number of ways. First, it provided funding for reform preparation through a grant from its Japanese grant facility. This grant funded technical advice on reform preparation and legal drafting, technical support for pension system modeling, including training of staff at the Institute for Macroeconomic Analysis, support for a public relations campaign, and developing a strategy for financing transition costs. To develop elite support for reform, the World Bank sponsored a major conference in Ljubljana in October 1997 to discuss the government's white paper for reform, published in November 1997. The World Bank also sent Slovenian members of parliament to Switzerland and the Netherlands to study private pension funds.

Other transnational policy actors opposed the implementation of pension privatization in Slovenia. In particular, the French consultants supported by EU PHARE generally opposed pension privatization (Stanovnik 2002, 42–45). Italian officials also warned against pension privatization for political reasons; Italy had experienced major protests that brought reforms to a halt a few years before. These transnational policy actors were joined in their opposition by leading Slovene pension experts, the Minister of Finance, who worried about financing transition costs for a new system, and the Free Trade Unions of Slovenia, which organized several demonstrations against the pension reform plans in early 1998 (Stanovnik 2002, 48–49; interview with Dušan Semolic, Free Trade Unions of Slovenia, May 13, 1998). Ultimately, lead reformer Tone Rop dropped the idea of individual, private accounts in response to this opposition.

The Slovene case shows that the World Bank does not always succeed in strengthening its domestic allies in political competition. Sometimes, such a strategy fails. It also suggests that World Bank support tends to go to reforms that include a private, funded system, despite the findings of Holzmann and Hinz (2005), which suggest that the World Bank supports a range of system designs. Müller (1999, 54) has argued that the World Bank had lower leverage over less indebted countries, such as Slovenia. Still, successive Slovenian governments have continued to consider pension privatization.

Korea

Yang (2004, 197–198) shows that pension privatization ideas were proposed by Korean government officials in 1995–1996 under the government of Kim Young Sam and laid out in a Public Pension Development Plan published in 1996. Korea was one of the last countries to implement a national pension system globally, and as a result, a switch to a private pension system would be significantly less costly than for countries with mature pension systems (Myles and Pierson 2001). The Public Pension Development Plan called for a low basic pension for the poor and a large funded system on the model of the United Kingdom (see below). This plan was opposed by social policy bureaucrats from the Ministry of Health and Welfare (MOHW) and National Pension Corporation (NPC). The government attempted to mediate this dispute through the National Council for Social Security, chaired by the prime minister. The council created a body "filled with dozens of representatives of different facets of society including business, labour, farmers, women, the academy, and the press," but ultimately backed the original Public Pension Development Plan. The MOHW continued to oppose it.

However, in 1997 Korea was in the throes of a major financial crisis, and elections in December 1997 brought veteran democratic dissident Kim Dae Jung to the presidency. Kim Dae Jung broadly backed the MOHW (Yang 2004, 199). The World Bank intervened in Korea with a $2.0 billion structural adjustment loan and tried to influence the pension reform debate in Korea. It demanded that a government-wide task force draft a white paper on pension reform that would include a basic and earnings-related component with a funded, privately managed component (Yang 2004, 201). The government created a Pension Reform Task Force in December 1998, but dragged its feet on pension privatization. The task force, which included a majority of representatives sympathetic to the MOHW position, ultimately developed four alternatives for structural reform, including three based on individual, private accounts and a fourth that basically maintains the current system, with the fourth option being the most likely to be adopted as of 2004 (Yang 2004, 201).

The Korean case is interesting because it shows that domestic leaders, at least determined ones in a large and wealthy country, have the power to resist the most extreme leverage of transnational policy actors (Yang 2004, 202). However, Korea is also unique in that government leaders wished to resist such reforms. A main reason appears to be the transformational nature of the Kim Dae Jung government. Kim Dae Jung sought to overturn the authoritarian, technocratic style of government policy in Korea and was hostile to reform plans developed under Kim Young Sam. Pension reform debates continued in Korea in 2003–2005, with different parties and the government offering different proposals for reform. The World Bank and the OECD supported a funded system, while the ILO supported reform of the existing system. Mandatory, individual accounts still do not figure highly in the programs of domestic political actors (Chong-Bum 2005).

Brazil

Brazil is a controversial case in the literature on pension privatization. Some have claimed that transnational policy actors have not had much influence on pension reforms in Brazil (Weyland 2004; Brooks 2005). Others have argued that their influence was substantial (Melo 2004; Pinheiro 2004). What is clear is that Brazil did receive advice from the World Bank, IMF, ILO, ISSA, IDB, UN ECLAC, and other transnational policy actors on pension reform and opted not to adopt individual, private accounts. However, Brazil did enact an NDC pension system (Pinheiro 2004), which (as described in the Appendix below) is part of the new pension reform model advocated by the World Bank. Melo (2004, 337) shows that this reflected World Bank advice to the country in the mid-1990s. Pinheiro (2004) further shows that the World Bank was highly influential in the adoption of the NDC system in Brazil, which is based on individual accounts with "notional" balances, but is in fact based on pay-as-you-go financing. Therefore, it would be incorrect to suggest that the World Bank had no influence on the Brazilian reforms or that they are inconsistent with pension privatization models. In fact, the Bank has supported adoption of NDC systems in several other countries (Latvia, Poland, Russia, Moldova, Kyrgyzstan) and often sees NDC as a step toward a future funded system (Melo 2004, 337), because it creates the infrastructure of individual accounts, recordkeeping, and strict income linkage.

In Brazil, pension privatization ideas were first spread by independent liberal and financial industry think tanks that supported the Chilean model, possibly with the support of Chilean and other Latin American pension fund companies. However, the government of President Collor de Melo (1990–1992), which supported pension privatization, did not have the political backing to move forward with reform. Pension privatization proposals re-emerged with the government of President Cardoso (1995–2002). However, the international financial crisis of 1997–1998 made it impossible for Brazil to contemplate funding the transition costs to a new system. Note that the Brazilian pension system is much larger as a share of GDP than any other system in the Latin American continent except for Uruguay (and Cuba). Thus transition costs were judged to be prohibitive (Pinheiro 2004).

The World Bank started to work on pension reform in Brazil in 1997. By that time, the government was already immersed in a controversial debate over whether to change the pension system benefit formula contained in the Brazilian constitution (Pinheiro 2004, 124–128). In 1997, the Brazilian government set up a working group to discuss pension privatization and considered multi-pillar models similar to those advocated by the World Bank. It concluded that private accounts would over-burden the country's finances and decided instead on an NDC reform in 1999, based on ideas "disseminated in courses and seminars organized by the World Bank with the participation of Brazilian technical staff."

This reform received the support of the IMF, the World Bank, and the IDB (Pinheiro 2004, 134–135). Melo (2004) concurs that the NDC system was first heard of by Brazilian policy makers in World Bank–sponsored seminars.

CASE OF TRANSNATIONAL POLICY ACTOR INTERVENTION POST-REFORM

Holzmann and Hinz (2005) claim that the World Bank is less influential than commonly reported because pension reform assistance is often provided only post-reform. This study disputes those findings. The Holzmann and Hinz (2005) study includes only loan data and not the full range of World Bank influence mechanisms. When one includes conferences and seminars as well as pre-reform technical assistance and similar or overlapping assistance provided by other members of the transnational advocacy coalition for pension privatization, one finds very few cases where transnational policy actors were not involved pre-reform. One of the few cases was Peru, the first Latin American country after Chile to adopt pension privatization in 1993. There is little evidence of transnational policy actor involvement, except for the intervention of Chilean specialists, in the Peruvian reform. However, the World Bank provided substantial post-reform assistance and loans to Peru to make pension privatization a success.

Peru

Peru became the first Latin American country to follow the Chilean model in adopting pension privatization. The policy process was led by Finance Minister Carlos Boloña, a neoliberal who was a strong advocate of pension privatization. He worked to persuade President Alberto Fujimori of the wisdom of pension privatization for Peru and had the help of Chilean reformer José Piñera, who is reputed to have convinced President Fujimori of the benefits of these reforms in a critical meeting. The Peruvian reform differed somewhat from the Chilean model, insofar as participation in the private pension system remained voluntary. A large proportion of the population also remains outside the pension system, due to the large share of informal economic activity in Peru. After the reform, the World Bank provided $500 million in loans to support transition costs and technical assistance, but was not involved prior to reform. Peru's pension system has performed well according to advocates, who point to the contrast with the collapsed state system that it replaced. However, critics have suggested that administrative fees in Peru are exorbitant and participation rates remain low. The World Bank subsequently has worked with Peru to fix various problems of pension fund administration (Shah 1997; Gill et al. 2005).

CASES OF NON-INVOLVEMENT BY TRANSNATIONAL POLICY ACTORS

One of the striking findings of this study is the limited number of cases of reform without involvement by transnational policy actors. Only Chile, the first reformer, and several wealthy, early-reforming OECD countries appear to have reformed without substantial influence from transnational policy actors. This suggests that transnational policy actors are more important in later-reforming countries and in countries with less domestic policy capacity. Wealthy OECD countries can rely on elaborate networks of private and government-sponsored think tanks, academic institutions, and domestic policy entrepreneurs. They are also less vulnerable to transnational policy actors; in the case of pension privatization, the leading organizations spreading these reforms do not work in developed countries. This does not mean that wealthy countries are immune to influence from transnational policy actors. In the United States, officials of the World Bank and USAID have played a substantial role in the domestic policy debate and have translated lessons learned from other countries' experiences. However, this study suggests that wealthier countries are less open to transnational policy actors' advice and influence. Pension privatization would spread without transnational policy actor influence, but far more slowly than has been observed.

Chile

Chile, being the first country to implement pension privatization, was not subject to the same transnational influences as other states. Chapter 3 above demonstrates that the ideas that lay behind the Chilean pension reform were derived from conservative economists at U.S. universities and reflected contemporary neoliberal thinking about welfare state reform. However, there is no evidence of substantial pre-reform technical assistance or funding from transnational policy actors for the Chilean reform.

Sweden

Similarly, Sweden had little involvement from transnational policy actors in its reform process (Anderson and Immergut 2007, 372–380). In Sweden, reform had its roots in a parliamentary committee that studied the pension system and presented its final report in 1990 (Wadensjö 2000, 70). A government committee with representatives from all parliamentary parties was then appointed to formulate a response. This report was published in March 1994 with support from the four liberal and conservative parties that made up the then governing coalition as well as the leading opposition party, the Social Democratic Party. The general principles for reform were adopted by parliament in June 1994 (Wadensjö 2000, 70). The Swedish reform created a funded component of the earnings-related pension scheme with a 2.5 percent payroll tax contribution. These funds could be invested by individuals in as many as five different pension funds. Sweden retains a basic, flat pension and an earnings-related pay-as-you-go system based on NDC principles after the 1994 reform.

The United Kingdom

The UK pension reform of 1986 that introduced private, funded options in place of the State Earnings Related Pension Scheme (SERPS) also appears to have been developed without substantial outside influence (Schulze and Moran 2007, 67–74), though Prime Minister Margaret Thatcher did invite former Chilean Secretary of Labor José Piñera to visit the United Kingdom in October 1981 to discuss pension privatization in Chile (interview with José Piñera, January 19, 2006). The U.K. reforms essentially allowed individuals to choose whether to receive an earnings-related pension from the state, to join a funded employer-sponsored pension scheme, or to open an individual, private account (Emmerson 2003, 174).

Summary of Cases

This chapter has shown that transnational policy actors have been directly involved in supporting pension privatization in countries around the world, including in several countries that sometimes have been used as cases of non-involvement or non-success, such as Brazil. Transnational actor involvement has taken many forms, but primarily the dissemination of reform ideas through conferences and seminars, funding of reform teams planning pension reforms, technical assistance to reform teams, post-reform loans, and technical assistance in implementation. Transnational policy actors also have hired domestic reformers in critical "success" cases to work for them as staff or consultants in spreading the reforms to additional countries, thus providing an additional incentive to government officials to implement pension privatization.

While transnational policy actors have been directly involved and highly influential in the vast majority of countries that established individual, private accounts as part of their pension reforms, this chapter also explored other categories of cases. Importantly, it analyzed cases of countries that received similar advice from the same transnational policy actors, but did not implement private accounts. Slovenia and Korea are key examples of middle-income countries that considered but rejected World Bank advice. Other countries in this category appear to be poorer countries with less developed pension systems, where transnational policy actors did not push so hard for pension privatization. Notably, the number of transnational policy actor failures is far smaller than the number of successes. However, the existence of these cases does show the importance of domestic partners and domestic conditions in explaining the adoption of pension privatization.

This chapter also explored a number of countries that adopted private, individual accounts, but received little or no advice or support from transnational policy actors, where the reform process was truly home-grown. These countries are mainly rich OECD countries, including Sweden and the United Kingdom, as well as Chile, the first reforming country. However, it would be wrong to suggest that transnational policy actors had no impact in these countries. Chilean reformers were linked with transnational policy networks that advocated neoliberal reforms, as were their British counterparts. Debates in these networks clearly had an impact on their reform designs (Demarco 2004). However, these impacts are more indirect. It also bears mentioning that the number of cases in this category is smaller.

Reviewing the data from this global sample suggests that not all cases of reform can be explained by transnational actor interventions. Some countries adopt these reforms without transnational actor support. In others, transnational actor interventions prove insufficient to overcome domestic opposition. However, the vast majority of reforming countries have been heavily influenced by transnational proposal actors at all stages of the reform process. This holds particularly true for middle-income developing countries. Transnational actors have exerted influence in numerous ways and at numerous stages, but particularly in pre-reform inspiration and technical support. This shows that transnational actors have not merely responded to calls by domestic reformers to assist in reform processes already under way, but have seeded the demand for reform by influencing the ideas of domestic reformers.

It seems fair to conclude that many cases of reform would not have taken place without the interventions of transnational policy actors. The pension privatization trend would still exist, but would be traveling much more slowly and not have had such an impact on middle-income developing countries. Cross-regional diffusion would be much slower. While there are clearly limits to their influence, transnational actors have shaped most reform programs. Few countries have adopted pension privatization without them.

The United States provides an interesting case for the analysis of transnational policy actor influence. While the major organizations supporting pension privatization worldwide, the World Bank and USAID, did not pressure the U.S. government directly, they did have some impact. Estelle James, the lead author of the World Bank's *Averting the Old Age Crisis*, served on President Bush's commission for social security reform. Other important pension privatization advocates, activists, and organizations (such as the Cato Institute) also exerted influence on various governmental reform committees. The United States is unique in being the headquarters for organizations advancing pension privatization, yet in not having succeeded in implementing such reforms itself. One can point to a number of policy legacies that may explain this, such as the relatively low level of social security benefits in the United States, the large voluntary private pension system, and the power of interest groups such as AARP. The U.S. experience, though, like the other developed country case studies presented above, suggests that transnational actors are likely to be more influential in developing countries than in developed ones. This may be in part because of stronger policy legacies in developed countries. It could also be because transnational development agencies that spread pension privatization and other economic reform ideas do not operate as advocates so forcefully in developed countries.

Conclusions

This study has used a wealth of primary data from the World Bank and USAID to show that transnational policy actors are ubiquitous participants in pension reform processes worldwide. While most previous studies of pension privatization have taken a regional approach, the research design adopted here provides a global perspective on this trend that encompasses diverse country circumstances. Transnational policy advocates, including Chilean and other policy entrepreneurs and major international organizations such as the World Bank, played an important role in developing pension privatization ideas that were spread to countries around the world. Often acting in concert, these organizations have played a powerful role in policy transfer, together with domestic partners. Transnational policy actors have multiple tools that they use to influence domestic policy processes. These include conferences and seminars to introduce new pension reform ideas, technical assistance and loans to countries to develop and implement reform proposals, and personnel policies that encourage country officials to cooperate with the transnational campaign for pension privatization. The data set analyzed here includes cases of transnational intervention and non-reform (Slovenia and Korea) as well as cases of no intervention and reform (Chile, the United Kingdom, Sweden). While not all cases can be explained by transnational actor interventions, most reforming countries have been deeply influenced by transnational actors at multiple stages of the policy process. Analysis of negative cases shows that developed countries are less likely to be swayed by transnational policy actors. However, the relatively small number of developed country cases suggests that transnational actors have accelerated the pension privatization trend through their advocacy of reform in middle-income developing countries.

While most analysts agree that transnational actors have been involved in pension privatization processes in all corners of the earth, there remains wide disagreement in the literature about the importance of this involvement. Part of this arises from radical differences in the ways scholars identify transnational policy actors. Some authors see no transnational policy actor involvement where others find extensive involvement. This has been documented most dramatically in the cases of Estonia (see chapter 2) and Brazil. Often, observational differences arise from a failure to look at the full scope of the policy process, including policy interventions at earlier stages in the agenda-setting process, or from different understandings about the outcomes of reform. This book has addressed this issue by emphasizing that transnational policy actors are active at multiple stages in both the transnational and domestic policy process. Evidence of transnational actor involvement needs to be sought at all stages with the time dimension of reform fully in mind. Standard measures of transnational actor involvement, such as World Bank loans/GDP, are at best crude measures of the impact of transnational influence.

This work has aimed to develop a more sophisticated understanding of what transnational actors do and how to analyze their behavior. It has emphasized that transnational actors often work in loose coalitions, so that measures that focus on the influence of a single organization may underestimate overall influence. Also, internal decision-making processes by transnational actors may cause them to change their approach over time or vary it according to country circumstances, meaning that variables that assume stable support for one type of reform may tend to underestimate their influence. For instance, if the World Bank advises a country to keep its social security system intact, it still has influence, though this would complicate most statistical models used to date.

Using a process-tracing and comparative case-study method, this book has shown that transnational actors have been highly influential in spreading pension privatization. First, there are few cases of reform in the developing world where transnational policy actors have not been involved in agenda-setting and other phases. Second, there are many more cases of reform in developing countries, though it is developed countries that have more severe problems of population aging. Third, while learning from neighboring countries certainly facilitates diffusion, the inter-regional diffusion of pension privatization ideas from Latin America to Central and Eastern Europe was very quick and clearly facilitated by transnational policy actors. Fourth, transnational actors have been effective in seeding domestic demand for reform by introducing country officials to pension privatization ideas through conferences, seminars, and publications. Finally, transnational actors have been very effective in translating policy advice into reform. Korea, Slovenia, and Venezuela were the only clear examples found of countries where a transnational advocacy coalition campaigned for pension privatization and reform ultimately failed. Even so, pension reform debates continue in these countries with Slovenia again considering pension privatization. Finally, case studies show that transnational policy actors have been responsible for putting pension privatization on the agenda in many countries, particularly in post-communist Europe, where such reforms had not been widely known before the publication of the World Bank's *Averting the Old Age Crisis.*

While transnational policy actors have been influential at all stages of the policy process, they have had their greatest impact in policy development and commitment building, because large multinational organizations such as the World Bank have tremendous power to set global policy agendas through their ability to mobilize expertise and promote ideas through conferences, seminars, and publications. These are unique organizations with the expert and moral legitimacy to establish best practice in social policy worldwide (Barnett and Finnemore 2004). While some transnational actors specialize in policy development, others specialize in policy transfer and implementation. USAID, for instance, has contributed little to development of pension privatization ideas but has been critical in reform implementation in numerous countries. Such activities are important because they allow transnational actors to leverage their resources to advance the chances of reform in multiple countries and to fix problems that could result in negative policy lessons for neighboring countries. Transnational actor interest in pension privatization clearly extends well into the implementation phase, and this concern with achieving good results should be seen not only in the light of a commitment to a particular country, but rather in light of a broader commitment to the spread of a reform trend that can be disrupted by prominent failed cases.

Pension privatization constitutes a revolution in post-war social policy, and it has been spread, in large part, by a loose coalition of transnational actors operating in multiple national contexts to exert influence at all phases of the policy process. This book has provided a wealth of data about the involvement of transnational policy actors in pension privatization processes from policy development to transfer to implementation. Using a policy process-tracing and comparative case study approach, I have explored the extent and limits of transnational actor influence. This work contributes to a debate in the comparative welfare states literature about the national versus transnational influences on reform and to the literature on transnational politics by tracing a single transnational policy process through all stages of its development and diffusion worldwide. It puts forward a model of transnational actor influence on domestic politics and policy that should be generally applicable beyond the pension reform arena.

CHAPTER SEVEN

Analyzing Transnational Public Policy

THE WIDESPREAD IMPACT of transnational policy actors raises questions about power in the international system, the extent of U.S. hegemony, forces of global governance, and the nature of democratic sovereignty. Some have argued that U.S. power is behind the influence of the World Bank and other international organizations (Wade 2002). While the United States obviously has had a substantial influence on the World Bank and other Washington consensus organizations, it would be difficult to argue that pension privatization represents an outgrowth of U.S. state power. While President George W. Bush advocated the adoption of pension privatization in the United States in 2004 and 2005, such reforms ultimately were rejected by U.S. legislators and by the general public. At the time that USAID became actively involved in the promotion of pension privatization abroad, between 1994 and 2000, Joseph Stiglitz and other leading White House economic advisers actively opposed pension privatization. It seems that successive U.S. governments have had no clear or unequivocal policy on pension privatization. Different departments of the U.S. government have pursued different approaches at different points in time. Therefore, the campaign for pension privatization cannot be traced back entirely to U.S. government policy. It is more closely associated with Chilean government policy. While certain U.S. universities, epistemic communities, and government agencies have supported pension privatization, it is not simply a U.S. model.

Pension privatization is the work of an epistemic or expert community (Haas 1992; Bockman and Eyal 2002), not a state. It represents one outgrowth of the neoliberal economic theory developed primarily in U.S. academic departments of economics and adopted by proponents worldwide. After the formative experience of the Chilean reforms in 1980–1981, a coalition of like-minded economists and policy makers began to advocate pension privatization internationally, taking up positions of power in various governments and international organizations or becoming independent policy entrepreneurs to promote pension privatization across national boundaries. This coalition won the full support of World Bank in 1994 and also recruited a slew of other transnational policy actors, including USAID, the Asian Development Bank, the Inter-American Development Bank, OECD, and others. It was the resources and legitimacy of these organizations, more than any other factor, that facilitated the rapid dissemination of pension privatization worldwide after 1994.

It certainly did not hurt the campaign for pension privatization that it could rely on the support, tacit or active, of major international banks and fund management companies. These companies played a role in the promotion of the Chilean model in Latin America and elsewhere, funding conferences and promotional activities. However, the research presented here suggests that international financial companies played a secondary and often not very visible role, at least prior to the enactment of reform legislation. It has been transnational policy actors rather than multinational companies that have been the bearers of pension privatization in country after country, though multinational corporations may play a larger role post-reform, once they have concrete interests at stake.

The rapid spread of pension privatization would not have happened without the active involvement of transnational policy actors. Transnational policy actors helped to develop and publicize pension privatization through joint publications such as the World Bank's *Averting the Old Age Crisis* (1994). They put these reforms on the agenda in many countries through sponsorship of workshops and conferences and by funding reform teams. Transnational policy actors have assisted in designing reforms with domestic partners to suit specific country conditions. They have provided a range of technical assistance, from tailoring pension system modeling software to sponsoring domestic reform allies to designing public relations campaigns, in an effort to sell the reforms. Transnational policy actors have helped to implement reform in many countries, spending as many as eight years in Kazakhstan, for example, to support aspects of regulatory and administrative implementation, changing laws and practices in the process and loaning hundreds of millions of dollars for smoother reform implementation. Transnational actors have been critical players in the creation and dissemination of reform ideas.

SOURCES OF AUTHORITY

This study shows that a leading source of impact of transnational policy actors lies in their ability to set policy agendas through knowledge creation and expert and moral authority (Barnett and Finnemore 2004). While scholars have attempted to distinguish the impact of "norms-teaching" versus "resource-leveraging" activities (Chwieroth 2003; Brooks 2005), modes and mechanisms of transnational policy actor influence often combine ideational and material forms of influence (Epstein 2008; Jacoby 2008). For instance, the training courses and seminars that provide many world leaders with their first understanding of pension privatization constitute one mechanism for the transfer of knowledge and information. Such seminars are primarily a mechanism of knowledge transfer. However, they are also very costly to run. Dissemination of technical know-how globally cannot be done without substantial resources. Costly too are the enormous publication series of the World Bank, whose publications budget exceeds the total budget of many smaller transnational policy actors. It is so large that the Bank has become the largest single source of development-related research in the world (Stone and Wright 2007, 9). Publication activities on this scale require ideas; they also require resources. In many cases, resource-leveraging and norms-teaching methods of influence are analytically inseparable.

Transnational actors not only teach norms, they also help to create them. In the pension reform area, the World Bank publication *Averting the Old Age Crisis* catalyzed thinking within expert communities on the importance of private, funded pension systems. It created new problem definitions (old-age crisis) and new metrics and indicators (implicit pension debt) and provided a comprehensive set of policy solutions to address these problems. It was the World Bank's role in creating new, authoritative knowledge about pension reform that was perhaps most crucial in the spread of pension privatization. This suggests that much greater attention needs to be paid in empirical studies to the ways that international organizations generate authority around the development of new knowledge and how they make decisions about which ideas to promote. This study suggests that these choices may depend on organizational circumstances and the outcomes of internal debates rather than on systematic structural factors alone.

TRANSNATIONAL ACTORS AND THE ROLE OF IDEAS

Many traditional studies of political economy give short shrift to the explanatory role of ideas, treating them, as Marx did, as "epiphenomena" dictated by the interests of powerful groups. Materialist explanations are particularly prominent in rational choice theory in political science and economics. This study gives norms and ideas a more prominent role in causal explanation. It shows that norms and policy proposals pushed by leading transnational actors have had an enormous influence on economic policy in countries around the world. New policy ideas and norms have caused domestic political actors to reshape their policy preferences, imagine new political coalitions, and create new institutions. New ideas have helped to discredit competing policy proposals and win support for new actors in the pension reform policy area (Blyth 2002). The rise of pension privatization cannot be reduced to material interests alone. As case studies have shown, a wide variety of actors have supported the new pension reforms, including those whose material interests would seem to make them likely opponents. Political economy needs to come to terms with the role of ideas and proposal actors in shaping policy discourse, influencing perceptions of interest, and determining policy (Blyth et al. forthcoming). Rational and ideational explanations can and should be combined to make sense of reform outcomes.

Veto and Proposal Actors

Transnational actors are influential bearers of policy ideas worldwide. This study has suggested viewing transnational policy actors as "proposal actors" in domestic policy contexts. A number of policy scholars have analyzed domestic policy processes as arenas for contestation between "veto players" (Immergut 1990; 1992; Tsebelis 2002; Immergut and Anderson 2007). Veto players analysis provides a parsimonious and comparable way to study and compare complex domestic policy processes. However, it tends to focus attention exclusively on veto players while excluding consideration of principled advocates and other non-veto players in policy choice.

In a comprehensive cross-national study that investigates the role of veto players and veto points in pension reform decisions in Western Europe, Immergut and Anderson (2007) back away from the veto players model developed in Immergut's (1990; 1992) earlier work on health care reform. Immergut had hypothesized that differences in pension reform trajectories can be explained by the number of veto points in a country's policy process and the number of veto players involved. After extensive consideration of the evidence from throughout Western Europe, however, Immergut and Anderson conclude that while the veto players perspective provides an important starting place for analysis, "veto points and veto players do not provide an adequate explanation for the dynamics of pension politics" (Immergut and Anderson 2007, 37). They conclude instead—on the basis of domestic political analysis—that some aspects of "political competition" need to be added to make sense of pension reform outcomes, such as the nature of party competition, though "further conceptual analysis is needed to specify this variable more precisely" (ibid.).

What is missing from the veto players analysis is attention to the ways that "proposal actors" operate and shape the preferences of domestic veto players. Proposal actors are defined here as domestic or transnational actors who develop well-elaborated policy proposals and encourage veto players to adopt them as their own. Proposal actors include domestic think tanks, individual policy entrepreneurs, NGOs, specialized government agencies, and transnational actors. Transnational proposal actors develop well-elaborated policy proposals and advocate them in a transnational political space.

Proposal actors have power because veto players often do not have well formed preferences in certain areas of policy or because these preferences can be reordered when proposal actors present new information or proposals that promise to achieve or maximize material interests in ways not previously considered. Blyth (2002, 9) argues that preferences can be highly malleable under conditions of "Knightian uncertainty," "situations regarded by contemporary agents as unique events where the agents are unsure as to what their interests actually are, let alone how to realize them," for instance, in periods of crisis. Under such conditions, proposal actors can be remarkably influential by presenting ideas that help to organize new political coalitions and underpin the development of new institutions. Proposal actors do not supplant the material interests of veto players, but rather exert informational, ideational, or programmatic influence that causes preferences to shift. This perspective is consistent with that of McCarty (2000), who argues that veto players theory suffers from a lack of attention to proposal rights. It is also consistent with constructivist scholarship, which has long emphasized the role of ideas and perceptions in the constitution of material interests (Checkel 2001).

The veto players and proposal actors framework presented here is useful because it enables comparisons between countries, sheds light on the nature of coalitions across the transnational/domestic divide, and emphasizes their joint operations and resources. It provides a clear framework for combining ideational and material analysis and captures the most significant dynamics between transnational policy entrepreneurs and their domestic partners.

COOPERATION AND CONTESTATION IN TRANSNATIONAL AGENDA SETTING

Because transnational policy actors have become highly influential in setting policy agendas worldwide, they have also become critical sites for contestation between competing advocacy networks and epistemic communities. Control over transnational actors provides an important potential resource for policy advocates and entrepreneurs. Gaining key positions in a transnational actor or organization can provide control of transnational actor agendas, positions, resources, and legitimacy. It is not surprising, then, that multiple different expert communities fight to gain ascendancy within transnational actors, resulting in conflict over policy agendas within and between transnational actors.

In the case of pension privatization, a particular epistemic community was able to take positions of power within the World Bank and other influential organizations in order to organize a global campaign. This process has been discussed in chapter 4 above. Nelson (2004) draws attention to the fact that the relatively united transnational coalition for pension privatization set it apart from other social sector spheres such as health policy, where transnational actor advice has been more variable. Prior to 1994, World Bank pension advice also encompassed a range of competing perspectives. This may be the norm in many large transnational policy actors. The creation of unified policy agendas that monopolize the orientation of action within and between organizations may be relatively unusual.

Why did pension privatization advocates take power within the World Bank while other advocacy groups did not achieve such dominance? One might hypothesize that it had something to do with the structure of the policy area, the ideas, or the interests involved. Nelson (2004), for instance, suggests that pension reforms may be less contentious than health sector reforms, where many interest groups are involved in day-to-day administration. However, this study suggests an alternative explanation. It raises the possibility that the rise in power of this particular epistemic community could have depended on more internal organizational factors, such as leadership. The rise of pension privatization may have owed less to structural factors affecting pension systems and more to the idiosyncratic occurrence of a particularly successful World Bank research and advocacy project. Had Lawrence Summers not commissioned a major report on pensions, had Nancy Birdsall not taken charge of it, and had Estelle James not led the pension reform team, it is likely that the spread of pension privatization would have proceeded far more slowly.

Policy outcomes worldwide may depend on the outcomes of internal struggles within transnational policy actors. If this is true, scholars should pay greater attention to conflicts and agenda setting within transnational policy actors and the ways that these actors make decisions, allocate resources, and distribute power. The domestic politics of transnational policy actors is an important yet understudied area (Orenstein and Schmitz 2006).

A Transnational Policy Model

How can one integrate a new understanding of the role of transnational policy actors into standard domestically based models of the policy process? Such a synthesis requires adopting a multi-level model of the policy process that differs from the traditional ones taught in most contemporary policy schools. This work has suggested one such model in chapter 3 above. This model pays greater attention to policy actors whose scope is global, transnational, or regional. It suggests that the involvement of transnational policy actors extends over three distinct periods or phases of reform: policy development, policy transfer, and policy implementation. It shows that transnational policy actors rely on multiple modes and mechanisms of influence, beause they lack the veto power that would give them more concentrated authority.

This transnational policy perspective differs in important ways from the structural political economy model employed in much of the pension reform literature. Instead of focusing on a single decision point, in which domestic reformers are faced with economic crisis and a set of economic and political conditions, the transnational policy model presented here encompasses a longer period of time, in stages, with multiple modes of influence. Domestic actors often do not act alone. Instead, they are connected in transnational or transgovernmental networks or communities of policy makers (Slaughter 2004) that have the capacity to develop well-elaborated policy proposals, tailor them to local circumstances, promote them vigorously, and provide help with policy implementation. Transnational actors do not replace domestic ones in most cases, but are continuously involved in policy decisions in multiple states.

This study contributes to ongoing efforts to cut across the divide between international and domestic politics in political science. While the international and national political spheres often have been regarded as distinct, with different rules and procedures, the boundaries between domestic and international actors and influences increasingly are blurred. New advances in transnational politics and policy scholarship will tend to erode the coding of actors as either international or domestic. For instance, Chwieroth (2003) regards domestic policy actors trained at certain U.S. universities as "neoliberals" and suggests that they have an independent effect on policy. Such actors may be understood as part of transnational epistemic communities, having more in common with their counterparts in international organizations than with many citizens of their own countries. Another useful way of looking at this may be through the lens of career tracks. Some individuals clearly see international organizations and work in foreign countries as part of their career path; this may be becoming more common in an era of globalization. It may be more sensible to divide policy actors into "cosmopolitans" and "locals" (Haas 2006) in ways that cut across the domestic-international divide.

In sum, the transnational policy model presented here suggests a mode of studying policy development that focuses on new actors, new data sources, and new ways of coding variables that leads to a richer and more accurate understanding of the transnationalization of domestic policy.

CONDITIONS FOR TRANSNATIONAL ACTOR EFFECTIVENESS

This model also suggests conditions for transnational actor effectiveness. Given the levels of conflict within and between transnational actors over the right policies to adopt in any given area, one key condition for transnational actor effectiveness is an ability to unify around a certain set of policy ideas. This may occur because a certain epistemic community has taken power within an organization or because a policy development team was particularly skilled in its work. Second, transnational actors need resources to pursue their policy agendas worldwide. This study has suggested that a key to World Bank influence has been its greater policy resources compared with the ILO. Resources are vital to the pursuit of normative agendas and can be used to provide incentives for norm compliance. Because transnational actors are not usually formal veto players in domestic politics, they use a variety of indirect methods to achieve their objectives across multiple phases of the policy process. Such pervasive involvement requires the use of various resources across a wide span of time and can be very costly. Third, adaptability is important. Transnational actors can be more effective if they continually adjust their policy proposals and methods of work over time. In the pension reform area, this study has shown that the World Bank not only advocated a flexible policy template, but also sought to re-evaluate its work periodically in dialogue with reform skeptics. Fourth, transnational actors can enhance their effectiveness by mobilizing other organizations and individuals around their policy ideas, creating a broad campaign coalition with a coordinated division of labor. Fifth, transnational actors are likely to be more effective when their opponents are not as well mobilized or effective. The transnational campaign for pension privatization was particularly successful because of its coherent and adaptable agenda, the way it mobilized a large number of different transnational actors, and the weakness of opposing coalitions (Nelson 2004).

IMPLICATIONS FOR DEMOCRATIC SOVEREIGNTY

One of the key questions raised by studies of global governance is: What are its implications for democratic sovereignty? Transnational actors are not democratically accountable in the way national governments are. Therefore, their policy interventions may be perceived as less legitimate. Yet one of the peculiar ironies of the campaign for pension privatization is that these reforms have been far more prevalent in democratic than non-democratic states. While the first reformer, Chile, was an authoritarian regime at the time of reform, almost all subsequent reforms have been undertaken by democracies. Only six of the more than thirty countries that have adopted pension privatization including systems of individual pension savings accounts have been authoritarian (Chile, China, Kazakhstan, Uzbekistan) or hybrid (Russia, Peru) regimes. This raises an important dilemma: Why are policies that are purveyed by seemingly unaccountable transnational actors more frequently implemented in democracies?

This paradox may be rooted in a commonly overlooked aspect of democracy as a system of governance. If we view democracy, as Karl Popper did, as an "open system" of government, which allows multiple actors and interest groups access to the political process, then we can more easily understand why transnational actors may enjoy greater success in democratic states. Democracies provide more openings not only for domestic interest groups but for transnational policy advocates as well. As governments change, transnational actors enjoy multiple opportunities to influence policy. As the long literature on the democratic peace concludes, democracies are less likely to react aggressively against external threats and influences, particularly from other democracies. They are more likely to adjust through peaceful means, with greater openness of communication. This finding holds implications not only for the democratic peace, but also for the influence of transnational actors. In democracies, they find more fertile ground.

To restate the paradox, democracy, a system of government that is commonly conceptualized as being more responsive to domestic voters, is also more responsive to unaccountable transnational actors.

This suggests that democracy has an international dimension that has frequently been overlooked. Being a modern democracy means participating in a liberal international system that empowers a range of transnational actors that are not strictly accountable to domestic constituencies. Being a democracy is like belonging to a club. In the European Union particularly, but also elsewhere, being a democracy is increasingly less about domestic sovereignty and more about shared membership in the international community. Other authors have spelled out the implications of these trends at some length, discussing issues of democratic accountability, democratic deficits, and the like. This study of pension privatization suggests that policy making in democracies is indeed less domestic than previously considered.

Transnational Politics of the Welfare State

These findings about the power and influence of transnational actors challenge much of the conventional wisdom about the politics of welfare state development and change. While welfare state policies and institutions have often been thought to respond primarily to domestic political and economic influences, this study shows that transnational policy actors are prominent drivers of change. They have deeply influenced the structural transformation of pension systems worldwide—the largest and most controversial welfare state policy area. Models of welfare state development and change need to be revised to take this influence into account.

Fundamentally, this means incorporating a second transnational level of analysis into models of welfare state development and change. Studies need to systematically consider the continuous involvement of transnational actors in welfare state policy and no longer regard them as either superfluous or only implicated in occasional "external shocks." While transnational and other actors may be more influential in times of crisis, they are often stable fixtures of the policy process. Transnational actors are not the sole determinants of welfare state policy—far from it. Rather, this book has shown that they are important agenda-setting proposal actors. Using a variety of means, they have sought to co-determine policy with selected domestic partners. This implies that standard models of the welfare state policy process need to be updated to include consideration of transnational proposal actors' role.

While transnational actors have had a considerable role in policy reform in a wide range of mostly middle-income developing countries, do they have as much influence in developed countries? It is possible that the answer is no. In the two developed country cases considered in this study, Sweden and the United Kingdom, transnational policy actors appear to have had far less significant involvement. The well-known Chilean policy advocate José Piñera did visit the United Kingdom to advise the government of Margaret Thatcher, but it would be hard to argue that transnational advocates were driving reform decisions. Developed countries may be more difficult to influence for several reasons. First, they may have more entrenched interest groups that battle change, as in traditional path dependency explanations. Second, they may have well-developed policy think tanks and institutions that are less vulnerable to the influence of resource-rich transnational actors. Third, certain transnational actors may not be as active in promoting reform in developed countries, as in the case of pension privatization, which have been pursued largely through development organizations.

Nonetheless, findings for transnational actor influence cannot be happily ignored in research on developed country welfare states. Developed countries may face different forms of transnational influence. First, they may be more likely to use their own policy institutions to learn from neighboring countries by employing a process of non-hierarchical social learning. Second, developed countries may be more influenced by organizations, such as the EU and the OECD, that use more subtle means of influence, such as policy benchmarking and the development of common metrics. Third, transnational actor influence may be more important at certain moments in time. In particular, while transnational actor influence on welfare states may have been less important in the fifty years after the Second World War, its influence may be growing at present. Transnational influence may exist, but by different means and at different times. Over time, the transnationalizaton of welfare state policy may become more relevant to developed countries as well.

The Future of Pension Privatization

With the rise of serious debates within the World Bank over the benefits of pension privatization, some analysts have begun to question whether the pension privatization trend may have peaked. Several Latin American countries have begun to make it easier for beneficiaries to move from the private to public systems (Argentina, Peru), while others have established commissions to improve the private system (Chile, El Salvador, Uruguay) or even to consider reverting to pay-as-you-go state systems (Bolivia) (*Hewitt Global Report* 2007). While it is impossible to know the future, my findings suggest that despite low returns and high fees in some countries, the pension privatization trend is in the process of accelerating worldwide. Several observations point in this direction. First, the adoption of pension privatization in Nigeria in 2004 and its serious consideration in South Africa will most likely presage a wave of reforms in Africa. Similarly, the adoption of pension privatization in Taiwan in 2004 will lend renewed vigor to the Asian reform trend. As these reforms take root in previously unfamiliar territory, a greater number of neighboring countries will be influenced by regional reform examples. Second, World Bank Institute policy conferences have initiated officials from many countries in Asia, the Middle East, and Africa into pension privatization ideas in recent years. Thus, the ideas and norms behind pension privatization continue to spread. Third, though there have been strong criticisms of pension privatization, the World Bank and other organizations have not ceased to pursue it. Instead, they have modified and adjusted their advice, while maintaining their advocacy of pension privatization. Fourth, neither the traditional opponent of the World Bank in this area, the ILO, nor any other transnational actor has posed a serious, new intellectual alternative to pension privatization. In the realm of ideas, the World Bank's multi-pillar pension privatization model remains unchallenged. Finally, while serious reform discussions have taken place in Latin America, these are more likely to result in incremental reforms than a dismantling of the private pension fund system. Despite its shortfalls, countries around the world will continue to see pension privatization as an innovation that promises a way out of current pension system issues. Transnational actors will continue to help diffuse this trend as it reaches its ascendancy worldwide in the 2000s and 2010s.

TRANSNATIONAL POLICY AND ITS SKEPTICS

While this study has sought to illuminate the role played by transnational proposal actors in welfare state policy worldwide, many scholars and observers will remain skeptical about the influence of transnational actors. I have tried to speak to skeptics throughout this book, using a careful research design that has looked at all phases of policy development, transfer, and implementation in all countries where pension privatization has been introduced. I have looked at negative cases where these reforms pushed by transnational actors were rejected, in order to avoid a biased research design. I have provided a detailed analysis of the methods of transnational actor influence on policy making in multiple states and new insight into how to measure transnational actor influence in qualitative and quantitative studies.

Despite the evidence presented here, I suspect that the transnational policy model suggested in this book will meet with skepticism among those committed to a more state-centric view of the world, including some (but not all) realist scholars of international relations, neo-Marxist theorists of hegemony, and historical institutionalists in political science. How convinced should readers be of the importance of transnational policy, and how can these findings be integrated with these existing scholarly perspectives?

The transnational policy approach challenges some of the core tenets of state-centric realist thinking. In making the argument that transnational policy actors are relatively autonomous from nation-states and co-determining of policy in nation-states, the perspective departs from strictly realist approaches. However, some realists accept that transnational policy actors have a place in analyses of world affairs, particularly in areas of policy that do not challenge core security or economic interests of states. This transnational policy approach also may appeal to neo-Marxist realists, who see transnational policy as an offshoot of U.S. hegemony. While characterizing the international financial institutions and other transnational policy actors as fundamentally representing U.S. interests and U.S.-based global governance, some analysts in this tradition (Wade 2002) may agree that transnational policy actors are nonetheless relatively autonomous and need to be analyzed in their own right. The transnational policy model also suggests amendments to historical institution-alist scholarship. Historical institutionalism (Hall 1989; Mahoney and Rueschemeyer 2003) has typically studied how national policy elites react differently to similar transnational trends. The transnational politics model presented here suggests that institutions at the global level have a substantial impact on policy, despite these domestic differences. It is there-fore important to analyze the historical development of their policy ideas and policy interventions in order to provide a better understanding of how they transmit their models differently to different states. Historical institutionalist work on transnational actors would enrich scholarship on transnational politics and historical institutionalist analyses of national politics by introducing new sources of domestic variation.

It may be difficult to imagine a world in which an imperfect form of global governance has come into existence, but that is the world in which we now live. Transnational policy does not affect all countries equally, nor all policy areas. It is often not based entirely on formal/legal authority or explicit delegation of tasks by nation-states. It lacks veto power in territorial states and other sorts of formal authority. Yet this study of pension privatization shows that transnational policy actors can be pow-erful and co-determining of policy within nation-states. The realm of transnational policy exists and is more important in areas of "domestic" policy, such as pension reform, than has previously been recognized. It is time to integrate a deeper understanding of transnational policy processes into our analyses of policy reform in countries around the world.

Appendix

Understanding Pension Privatization

PENSION PRIVATIZATION represents the most controversial development in welfare state politics in recent decades. This appendix further analyzes how privatized pension systems differ from traditional social security systems. It highlights controversial distributive issues and those concerning the transition between systems. The central argument is that with pension systems, the devil is in the details. Specific design features, as well as the choice of system models, can make the difference between what one might define as a "good" or "bad" reform. Therefore, to analyze the impacts of reform fully, it is critical to understand the effects of different parameters of pension system design.

During the writing of this book, a controversy broke out in the United States with President George W. Bush's announcement at the end of 2004 that reforming the U.S. social security system would be a key initiative of his second term in office. The controversy turned on whether pension privatization would make social security more sustainable and who would gain from such reforms. After much internal debate, the Bush administration proposed to allow contributors to opt out of the social security system partially and contribute to a system of private individual accounts. This amounted to a "parallel" type reform. Shortly thereafter, a major public relations campaign was launched by reform opponents, including a solid block of the Democratic Party. Some conservative columnists also criticized Bush's reform as doing little to resolve the real issues facing social security in the future. Bush's proposal for a small, optional private system on top of a reduced social security system failed to ignite popular support. Though the president himself spent weeks campaigning for pension privatization, public opinion polls showed that most Americans were not convinced and hardened their support for social security. Ultimately, the president decided not to pursue these reforms in the face of negative public opinion.

Thus, the United States represents a failed case of pension privatization and therefore differs from the more than thirty countries that have adopted fundamental reforms to their social security–type systems. However, it would be wrong to assume that pension privatization was more controversial in the United States than elsewhere. In fact, pension privatization has proven highly controversial in most countries in which it has been proposed, for the following reasons. (1) It radically alters a key part of the post-1945 social contract; (2) pension systems account for a large part of the overall economy in many countries; and (3) pension privatization imports a neoliberal policy approach into an area previously dominated by New Deal social thinking (Minns 2001).

Pension privatization represents a radical path departure from the global pension policy regime established after the Second World War (often with advice from the ILO). Until recently, most pension systems worldwide were based on the social security (or "pay-as-you-go") model familiar in the United States. The essential innovation of pension privatization is to fund pensions through individual, private, pension savings accounts. Pension privatization creates these accounts and increases reliance on them as a means of funding retirement benefits over time. Private pension savings accounts are meant to achieve several goals that are consistent with neoliberal economic policy:

- to increase overall savings and economic growth
- to provide a more sustainable means of financing pensions in the face of demographic aging
- to reduce the role of the state in pension provision, and
- to give individuals greater choice and control over retirement decisions

Critics emphasize that pension privatization

- often reduces government and corporate commitments to pension provision (and benefits overall)
- benefits wealthy individuals and pension fund companies rather than the average pensioner, and
- creates inequality and makes individuals more vulnerable to social risk (Barr and Diamond 2006, 36–37)

However, the nature and implications of pension privatization are complex. Social security and privatized pension systems are financed differently, administered differently, calculate benefits and pay them differently, allocate risk differently, and have different implications for labor markets, coverage rates, and the economy as a whole. What follows is a brief side-by-side description of both types of systems.

Traditional social security pension systems in most countries of the world today are based on six principles:

- The state and/or employers administer collections and benefits.
- Financing is "pay-as-you-go," where current payroll tax revenues are used to pay current beneficiaries.
- Benefits are defined in advance with predictable retirement benefit levels.

- Benefits are often redistributive within and between generations and in many cases are oriented toward preventing poverty.
- Benefits are also linked at least in part to lifetime income to support a retirement consistent with a retiree's previous lifestyle.
- Risk is pooled to provide "social security" against a variety of risks, including lacking old-age income, disability, and survivorship.

By contrast, privatized pension systems depend in part on mandatory savings in privately managed individual accounts. Private pension savings systems have the following features:

- The private sector administers individual pension savings accounts in a manner similar to mutual funds.
- Financing is "pre-funded," with pension benefits paid from funds collected ahead of time and invested in private accounts.
- Benefits are not defined in advance, but depend on investment returns and fees in private accounts.
- Benefits are linked strictly to past contributions and investment returns.
- There is little or no redistribution within or between generations, though other redistributive mechanisms may be preserved or created.
- Risk and reward is individualized, with individuals taking greater risk for their own retirement, but potentially realizing greater returns as well.

Social security and privatized pension systems both require mandatory payroll tax contributions and both provide state-mandated savings for old-age security. However, they do so in very different ways with very different economic consequences, reflecting different philosophies of welfare state provision. Social security systems are an outgrowth of European traditions of state social provision. They emphasize solidarity of citizens within the nation-state. Privatized pension reform systems emphasize individual saving and individual responsibility and incentives, choice, and returns. They reflect skepticism about the role of the state in social provision and a concern about the impact of state social provision on economic efficiency and redistribution. The following sections present a brief description of the major differences between social security and privatized pension systems in financing, administration, redistribution, and risks and returns.

FINANCING

Differences in the financing of state social security and privatized pension systems are portrayed in figure 1.1. Mandatory payroll tax revenues paid by employees and/or employers finance both types of systems. Payroll tax rates range from 6 percent in Canada and Indonesia to 12.4 percent in the United States to just over 20 percent in Germany and Sweden to a high of 30 percent or more in Italy and several Central and East European states (Gillion et al. 2000, 141; Fultz 2004). In most developed countries, nearly 90 percent of employers comply with payroll tax requirements. In many developing countries, payroll tax compliance is much lower. Many countries have large "informal" sectors of the economy that operate outside the formal labor market and tax system. Some countries do not require all workers to contribute to pension systems, but only those in certain privileged sectors. Thus, the percentage of the work force covered by pension systems in many developing countries ranges from 10 to 30 percent (Gillion et al. 2000).

While both social security and privatized pension systems rely on payroll tax revenue, they differ in the use of these payroll taxes. In social security systems, current payroll tax contributions are used to pay current beneficiaries (though many social security systems also rely on general tax revenues and pre-funding to a limited degree). This type of financing is called "pay-as-you-go." Privatized pension reform systems are prefunded. Individuals deposit contributions in their private pension savings accounts during their working life and draw on these contributions, plus investment returns and minus management fees, in their retirement.

ADMINISTRATION

Social security pension systems normally are operated by a state agency, such as a "social security administration," that collects contributions, calculates and pays benefits, and makes actuarial calculations to ensure future fiscal balance. A social security administration is often a semi-autonomous state agency with professional management and a supervisory board that represents the interests of key stakeholders (Gillion et al. 2000, 426). In developed countries, this regulatory structure has worked well, with a highly trained cadre of social security experts involved in the management and administration of these systems (Reynaud 2000). In developing countries, social security administrations have been vulnerable to political manipulation of benefit formulas and awards (World Bank 1994; Gillion et al., 2000, 426). Technical supervision has been lacking and funds have been appropriated by governments during fiscal crises. Contribution evasion by large "informal" sectors of the economy has eroded the viability and poverty-reduction promises of these systems. Benefit levels and coverage have been erratic in some countries. This has provided one impetus for reform (World Bank 1994; James 1996).

Under pension privatization, governance and administration is partly privatized. Private investment companies undertake the tasks of investment management, collections, and administration. Private investment companies may be more competitive and provide better administration, investment management, and returns to investment, and therefore higher pensions (Iglesias and Palacios 2001). Some controversy surrounds this claim, because private pension funds also charge high fees to manage individual private accounts of a small size (Shah 1997; Gill et al. 2005). The state role is not eliminated, but it changes from one of direct administration to one of regulating the activity of private funds. The state needs to create a strong regulatory agency to ensure that regulations are being followed, that funds are solvent, and that they operate in the best interests of their many small investors. The pension fund management market also may be more or less competitive (Iglesias and Palacios 2001; Diamond and Orszag 2004).

REDISTRIBUTION

Social security systems combine aspects of pension savings, old-age insurance, and social redistribution in a single system. They require people to save for retirement, insure people against the risk of living to an exceptionally old age, and redistribute funds to those in relative need. Social security–type systems may redistribute funds in three ways: from those who die young to those who die old, from one generation to another, and from people in one part of the income distribution to those in another. As a social insurance system, social security provides higher overall benefits to those who live longer. Social security systems also redistribute between generations. A smaller generation may have to pay more to fund the retirement of a larger generation, for instance. And the first generation of social security retirees generally reaps enormous benefits, despite having never contributed into the system (Diamond and Orszag 2004). Finally, many social security systems tend to provide "progressive" benefits to poorer pensioners, through mechanisms such as a "minimum pension," a maximum pension, and benefit formulas that weight years worked in addition to earnings. Typically, men also subsidize women in social security systems, as men tend to contribute more and women tend to live longer in retirement.

Pension privatization dramatically reduces redistribution within pension systems, because they tie pension benefits firmly to individual contributions. This eliminates much inter-generational redistribution and rich-poor or male-female redistribution within pension systems. Advocates of pension privatization argue that aspects of savings, insurance, and redistribution within pension systems need to be separated out and that individual private pension funds are excellent tools for savings, while other government programs can achieve the goals of insurance and social redistribution (World Bank 1994). For instance, the government may choose to support a "minimum pension" benefit that achieves redistributive goals, while leaving savings to the mandatory private funds. Similarly, the annuities insurance market can be regulated to help equalize benefits between women and men (or other groups) in retirement, by requiring annuities to use a single age scale, rather than different ones for men and women. Because women live longer on average, separate benefit scales would result in women receiving lower benefits than men with the same pension accumulation at retirement.

RISKS AND RETURNS

Social security systems are vulnerable to a number of risks, and must be carefully managed and adjusted over time to deal with them (Gillion et al. 2000, 302). These risks include demographic risks, such as unexpected changes in birth and mortality rates from generation to generation that may compromise the ability of one generation to pay for another's retirement. Indeed, a central problem of social security–type systems today is broad-based demographic aging, due to increased standards of living, higher life expectancy, and reduced fertility rates in many countries (World Bank 1994; Feldstein 2002).

In addition, social security systems may face economic risks arising from unexpected changes in growth rates, wages, or prices that may reduce the ability of social security systems to obtain sufficient revenues through payroll taxes. There are political risks, such as the failure of the political system to respond to changes in the policy environment adequately or quickly enough to head off major challenges to the system. There are institutional risks that may arise from failures of the social security administration to predict system balance adequately or to administrate benefits properly. Finally, there are individual risks arising from uncertainties about the future of a work career and earnings.

Privatized pension systems face a different set of risks. Under pension privatization, demographic risks are substantially reduced, because pension benefits do not rely on the earnings of another generation. This is one of the major advantages of pension privatization at a time of demographic aging. On the other hand, individual economic risks are increased. Individual savings depends almost entirely on an individual's career trajectory and economic conditions during a working life. Those who live through poor economic times, such as a depression or hyperinflation, may suffer disproportionately. Institutional risks are also different, as pensions depend not on the health of a single government agency but on the health of a private pension fund and an annuity insurance company regulated by the state. While individual risk in these systems is generally higher (Hacker 2002), individuals may also receive higher potential individual returns to pension savings.

Is Pension Privatization Good for Growth?

One of the most controversial aspects of the debate over social security is the question of long-term economic impacts of alternative systems. From modest beginnings, social security pension systems have grown to encompass an ever-rising share of national expenditures in many developed countries. Indeed, public pension spending now accounts for between 5 and 15 percent of GDP in most of the wealthy OECD countries and Central and Eastern Europe (Gillion et al. 2000, 131; Holzmann et al. 2003b, 3), a sizable proportion of the overall economy. Therefore, concerns about the efficiency and economic effects of these programs are central macroeconomic issues (Auerbach and Lee 2001).

Critics of social security–type systems have argued that these systems have grown out of proportion and may no longer be affordable under conditions of global economic competition and demographic aging (World Bank 1994; James 1996; Kornai et al. 2001). They argue that social security payroll taxes add to labor costs, thus threatening the competitiveness of countries with expensive pension systems. Social security taxes add to the total tax burden, reduce employment levels, push employees out of the formal labor market, and cause companies to flee to lower-cost countries to do business. Moreover, they allocate benefits inefficiently, often serving higher-paid, more privileged workers at the expense of others.

Others argue, on the contrary, that more trade-exposed states use social security systems as a cushion against global economic competition and that large welfare states enable greater acceptance of international trade (Cameron 1978; Katzenstein 1985; Garrett 1998; Swank 2002; Glatzer and Rueschemeyer 2005). This debate has not been resolved, although it appears that the age of dramatic expansion of pension and other social welfare spending is over and that most developed countries have entered a period of sustained budgetary and macroeconomic pressure on pension spending (Pierson 1994; 2000). Governments feel inclined to keep welfare state spending under control, which is one reason why pension privatization appears attractive.

One of the primary arguments for pension privatization is that these systems are more pro-growth than traditional social security systems, and therefore better for the overall welfare of society, including pensioners (World Bank 1994; James 1996). The central argument is that rather than placing a drag on the economy, privatized pension systems create higher rates of savings, invest these savings in productive investments through financial markets, and thus provide an important source of finance for developing economies in particular. Returns on this investment accrue to individual pensioners, meaning that they benefit as the economy grows. Economists have debated many of these points, including whether private pensions truly raise the savings rate (Orszag and Stiglitz 2001, 21), whether they contribute to the development of financial markets, and whether they contribute to increased growth rates (Barr and Diamond 2006, 33). None of these points has been demonstrated beyond a reasonable doubt. However, neither are these claims completely implausible. Moreover, there is evidence from Latin America and Central and Eastern Europe that the expected benefits of pension privatization in increasing savings rates has made these reforms more attractive to policy makers (Chłoń-Domińczak and Mora 2003; Madrid 2003; Brooks 2004). This argument is consistent with the basic tenets of neoliberal economic policy that argue for relying on market mechanisms rather than the state and involving private sector managers, competition, and financial markets to produce higher economic growth. Pension privatization seeks to distribute the benefits of financial market returns to a broad cross-section of the population.

Another key argument for pension privatization is that such reforms reduce state budgetary expenditures on pensions over the long term. Over time, as people retire under the new system, a higher share of pension expenditures comes from individual savings and less from the state budget. This budgetary effect is appealing to policy makers in states facing large and growing pension liabilities.

Variations in Pension Privatization

The preceding sections have explored social security and privatized pension systems in a side-by-side comparison, as if policy makers must choose one or the other system. However, in many cases, pension privatization results in a system that combines a private and a social security system in either a "mixed" or a "parallel" reform. In mixed reforms, the private pension system partially replaces the older social security system, but both continue to operate side-by-side. In parallel reforms, participants continue to have a choice of whether to participate in the social security or private pension system. Reformers sometimes argue that a partial replacement of social security is the best option because it enables risk diversification (Hausner 2001). Retirees are completely dependent neither on the state pay-as-you-go system nor on investment returns and management of their private individual accounts. Both are important sources of retirement income. In the future, people will be able to compare their expected returns, and policy makers can choose whether to continue with a mixed system or to convert wholly to one or another system. Some argue that neoliberal reformers simply want to get a foot in the door, with the objective of totally eliminating social security sometime in the future. This may be true in some cases, as the above chapters show that along with the central pillar of mandatory savings in private, individual accounts, reformers have encouraged countries to adopt a variety of other reforms that represent steps on the way to privatization of social security.

Notional Defined Contribution Pension Plans

While the introduction of mandatory, private savings in individual pension savings accounts is the central element of pension privatization, there are other planks in the reformers' platform. These reforms share a general logic of increasing the linkage between individual contributions and pension benefits, increasing individual risk and returns, and reducing reliance on state redistribution (Williamson and Williams 2005).

Notional defined contribution plans are one of these new pension reforms (Feldstein 2002, 7). As mentioned, social security–type pension benefits are often only partially linked to a recipient's prior income. Notional defined contribution plans seek to strengthen the link between contributions and benefits in a pay-as-you-go system by creating "notional" individual accounts. In these notional accounts, there is no actual money. Instead, they are a type of passbook system, whereby contributions are recorded and credited with a notional interest rate each year, which represents the expected return on investment in the pay-as-you-go system. At the end of one's working career, the accumulation in the account forms the basis for pension benefit calculations. However, the system is still financed on a pay-as-you-go basis. In theory, these systems are supposed to make social security–type systems more transparent, providing information on the rate of return and providing incentives to link benefits more closely to contributions. They are also seen by reformers as a first step toward the introduction of private savings accounts, by changing the mentality of contributors and beneficiaries. Sweden has adopted such a system as part of its recent reform, for the income-linked benefit, as has Poland and a handful of other countries.

Voluntary Private Pension Insurance

In addition, privatizing pension reforms have sought to extend the scope of voluntary, private pension savings of various types. Indeed, some have argued that this represents a quiet revolution in pension systems in countries such as the United States and United Kingdom that have yet to implement mandatory private savings accounts (Hacker 2002). Governments may extend increasing tax breaks to individuals who choose to save, but these tax breaks tend to go to those in the upper income brackets, rather than those at the low end of the earnings distribution. In many countries with large state pay-as-you-go systems, introducing voluntary private savings can start the process of familiarizing people with the concept of individual private pension accounts, with an eye to eventual implementation of mandatory accounts.

Transition between Systems

One of the key issues for pension privatization is the process of "transition" between pension systems. For countries with traditional social security programs, all current payroll contributions are required to pay current beneficiaries. Where does the money to fund individual private accounts come from? Essentially, the current generation has to face the burden of saving for its own retirement, while also fulfilling promises to previous generations through the pay-as-you-go system. Therefore, the transition to a funded system must be financed, often by the state. The state must cover the full cost of any payroll tax contributions that are rerouted to individual private accounts. This payment can amount to a significant percentage of GDP and may come through a combination of additional taxation, borrowing, and spending reductions. For this reason, many countries choose to phase in a system of individual private accounts. Sweden, for instance, initially allocated only 2.5 percent of payroll to the private system, with the expectation that the program could be expanded in the future. Financing the transition is one reason that some international policy actors have expressed skepticism about pension privatization. Some IMF economists, for instance, have opposed the reform as bad for public finance, by increasing the indebtedness of states.

Other Pension Systems

This appendix has given a brief overview of the economics of pension systems, focusing on comparing social security and new pension reform systems. There are other types of pension systems, in theory and practice. In 1999, Nobel prize–winning economist Joseph Stiglitz wrote a paper with Peter Orszag that challenged pension privatization, by arguing that various elements of the system could be combined with social security systems, rather than constituting a wholly independent reform. For instance, state systems could be funded, even have individual accounts, and private systems could be pay-as-you-go. Advocates of pension privatization pointed out, probably rightly, that this was possible in theory, but not in practice, for reasons of tradition and political economy. A funded state pension system might own such a sizable proportion of the stock market, for instance, that it could cause a move toward state ownership of enterprises. Similarly, pay-as-you-go systems have never been operated by private actors, because these systems aim toward a level of redistribution that would not be countenanced by private companies.

There are different types of pension systems in existence, though. One common model in former British colonies in Asia is the "provident fund," a funded state system, in which the state uses pension system revenues to fund important development goals, such as housing construction, and uses the revenues from these projects to finance pension payments. Rates of return on these subsidized investments, though, are generally lower than in private markets, which is one argument advocates of pension privatization use to suggest that private, rather than state, managers should manage individual private accounts. In addition, there are no private accounts in the provident fund system, only a benefit level set by administrative statute. Therefore, the provident funds share elements of both the social security and private pension systems, and are different from both.

The original Bismarck system in Germany also differs from both dominant models today. That system was largely funded. Contributions were recorded and benefits linked to contributions, but without the use of individual accounts (Dawson 1912). Thus pension systems can come in more than two forms.

WITHIN-TYPE VARIATION

This appendix has shown that differences in the way pension systems are designed may have a substantial impact on contributors, beneficiaries, and the economy as a whole. However, there is also substantial variation within the two categories of social security systems and private, funded systems, and these differences can be as crucial as that between different forms. Social security–type systems have many parameters that can differ among countries or over time within one country. These include retirement age, differences between male and female re-

Table A1.1
Variation in Privatized Pension Systems

Country (year of reform)	First pillar [a]	Total payroll tax (%)	Contribution to individual account (%)	Fees and insurance premiums (%)	Participation in second pillar
Chile (1981)	Minimum	20	10	2.31	Mandatory for new workers; voluntary for self-employed
Peru (1993)	PAYG	20.5	8	3.73	Voluntary
Colombia (1994)	PAYG	33.8	10	3.49	Voluntary
Argentina (1994)	PAYG	46	7.72	3.28	Voluntary
Sweden (1994)	NDC				
Uruguay	PAYG	40	12.27	2.68	Mandatory, but voluntary for lower income workers
Mexico	Minimum	26	12.07	4.48	Mandatory
Bolivia	N/A	24	10	2.50	Mandatory
El Salvador	Minimum	13.5	10	3.00	Mandatory
Costa Rica	PAYG	26	4.25	N/A	Mandatory
Nicaragua (not yet implemented)	Minimum	21.5	7.5	2.50	Mandatory
Ecuador (not yet implemented)	PAYG	20	8.33	4.00	Mandatory
Dominican Rep. (2002)	Minimum	20	8	2	Mandatory
Hungary (1998)	PAYG	26	6		Mandatory
Kazakhstan (1998)	Minimum		10		Mandatory

TABLE A1.1 (cont'd)
Variation in Privatized Pension Systems

Country (year of reform)	First pillar [a]	Total payroll tax (%)	Contribution to individual account (%)	Fees and insurance premiums (%)	Participation in second pillar
Poland (1999)	NDC	32.52	7.2		Mandatory
Latvia (2001)	NDC	30.86	2 growing to 9		Mandatory
Croatia (2002)	PAYG		5		Mandatory
Bulgaria (2002)	PAYG	29	2 growing to 5		Mandatory
Estonia (2002)	PAYG	22	6		Voluntary
Slovakia (2003)	PAYG	28	9		Mandatory
Lithuania (2004)	PAYG	25	2.5		Voluntary
Romania (2004) (not yet implemented)	PAYG		8		Mandatory
Russia	NDC		2 to 6, depending on age		Mandatory for those under age fifty
Kosovo	Minimum		10		Mandatory
Macedonia	PAYG		7		Mandatory for new entrants
Ukraine	PAYG		2 growing to 7		Mandatory for new entrants
Nigeria (2004)	None		15		Mandatory
Taiwan (2004)					Mandatory for new entrants
China (1997)	PAYG		11		Mandatory for urban workers

Sources: Holzmann and Hinz 2005, 142–144 and 154–155; Fultz 2004, 11.
[a] PAYG = pay-as-you-go; NDC = notional defined contribution.

tirement age, cost of living increases, contribution periods required for eligibility, method of calculating prior contributions, and many others. Suffice it to say that one could design a social security retirement system that never paid any benefits (at the founding of the initial Bismarckian system, some complained that the retirement age was set higher than the average life span in Germany at the time) or one that was constantly in deficit (Argentina's retirement age was at one time fifty or fifty-five). Social security systems come in all shapes and sizes, with some systems functioning well over an extended period of time, and others in a situation of permanent weakness or collapse.

Sources of variation in privatized pension systems include contribution rates, principles for regulating pension investment fund companies, regulatory structure, management fees, and greater or lesser public confidence. Countries have designed in numerous features that suit local circumstances, and have sometimes substituted them for existing social security programs, run the two systems in parallel, or adopted a mixture of both. Sometimes, these differences are as important as the choice of model itself. Table A1.1 shows some of the diversity within pension privatization trend. Column one shows the country and year of reform. Column two shows whether the "first pillar" of pension provision is a social security–type system (PAYG), a notional defined contribution system (NDC), or a minimum guarantee. Column three shows the total payroll tax contribution to the pension system. Column four shows the proportion of total income directed to individual, private pension accounts. Column five provides an estimate of the total cost of all administrative fees in the private accounts. Column six shows whether participation in the funded system is mandatory or voluntary (as in a parallel system).

The Impact of Transnational Actors on System Parameters

One may ask how much influence transnational actors have had not only over the adoption of private pension systems, but over specific parameters of their design. The case studies presented in chapter 5 suggested that this influence has been quite substantial. While transnational actors had to compromise with powerful domestic interests, they often helped to decide whether a system would be "mixed" or "parallel," for instance, and to set the level of contributions to the new private system. In both Poland and Hungary, the final level of contributions to the new private system was somewhat lower than what the World Bank initially advised. However, both countries adopted the "mixed" model advocated by the World Bank and the contribution levels were within what the World Bank defined as an acceptable range. It is true that many aspects of reform were negotiated with domestic proposal and veto actors and reflect their preferences as well. Domestic actors were indeed important in co-determining the outcomes of reform; however, transnational actors have had a great influence over specific design parameters.

CONCLUSIONS

This appendix has explored in greater detail the nature of pension privatization systems and how they compare with social security pension systems that such reforms are designed to (sometimes partially) replace. It has also shown that there are substantial variations within types of pension privatization. These might make the difference between what one might label a "good" and a "bad" system. Furthermore, all pension systems are capable of being managed poorly and not producing sufficient benefits. In understanding pension systems, details of system design are a critical aspect of the debate.

Pension privatization represents a revolution in the post-war social contract that has underpinned the establishment of social security–type pension systems in most countries in the world. This book has analyzed the spread of pension privatization to more than thirty countries around the world. The impact of these reforms will continue to be debated in coming decades as their advantages and disadvantages become more apparent over time.

References

ARTICLES AND BOOKS CITED

Acosta, Csar R. 1944. Social Legislation in Paraguay. *International Labour Review* 50, no. 1 (July): 40–46.

Altmeyer, Arthur J. 1944. The Progress of Social Security in the Americas in 1944. *International Labour Review* 51, no. 6 (June): 699–721.

Anderson, Karen M., and Ellen Immergut. 2007. Sweden: After Social Democratic Hegemony. In Ellen M. Immergut, Karen M. Anderson, and Isabelle Schulze, eds., *The Handbook of West European Pension Politics*. Oxford: Oxford University Press, 349–395.

Andrews, Emily S., and Mansoora Rashid. 1996. The Financing of Pension Systems in Central and Eastern Europe: An Overview of Major Trends and their Determinants, 1990–1993. World Bank Technical Paper 339. Washington, D.C.: World Bank.

Auerbach, Alan J., and Ronald D. Lee, eds. 2001. *Demographic Change and Fiscal Policy*. Cambridge: Cambridge University Press.

Augusztinovics, Mária, Robert Gál, A. Matits, L. Mate, A. Simonovits, J. Stahl. 2002. The Hungarian Pension System Before and After the 1998 Reform. In Elaine Fultz, ed., *Pension Reform in Central and Eastern Europe*, vol. 1: *Restructuring with Privatization: Case Studies of Hungary and Poland*. Budapest: ILO, 25–93.

Barnett, Michael, and Martha Finnemore. 2004. *Rules for the World: International Organizations in Global Politics*. Ithaca, N.Y.: Cornell University Press.

Barr, Nicholas, ed. 2005. *Labor Markets and Social Policy in Central and Eastern Europe: The Accession and Beyond*. Washington, D.C.: World Bank.

Barr, Nicholas, and Peter Diamond. 2006. The Economics of Pensions. *Oxford Review of Economic Policy* 22, no. 1: 15–39.

Baumgartner, Frank, and Bryan Jones. 1993. *Agendas and Instability in American Politics*. Chicago: University of Chicago Press.

Beattie, R., and W. McGillivray. 1995. A Risky Strategy: Reflections on the World Bank Report *Averting the Old Age Crisis*. *International Social Security Review* 48: 3–4.

Becker, Charles M., Ai-Gul S. Seitenova, and Dina S. Urzhumova. 2005. Pension Reform in Central Asia: An Overview. PIE Discussion Paper Series. Hitotsubashi University.

Berry, Frances Stokes, and William D. Berry. 1999. Innovation and Diffusion Models in Policy Research. In Paul A. Sabatier, ed., *Theories of the Policy Process*. Boulder, Colo.: Westview Press.

Biersteker, Thomas J. 1990. Reducing the Role of the State in the Economy: A Conceptual Exploration of IMF and World Bank Prescriptions. *International Studies Quarterly* 34: 477–492.

Blyth, Mark. 2002. *Great Transformations: Economic Ideas and Institutional Change in the Twentieth Century.* Cambridge: Cambridge University Press.

Blyth, Mark, Rawi Abdelal, and Craig Parsons, eds. Forthcoming. *Constructivist Political Economy.*

Bockman, Johanna, and Gil Eyal. 2002. "Eastern Europe as a Laboratory for Economic Knowledge: The Transnational Roots of Neoliberalism." *American Journal of Sociology* 108, no. 2 (September): 310–352.

Bonoli, Giuliano. 2000. *The Politics of Pension Reform: Institutions and Policy Change in Western Europe.* Cambridge: Cambridge University Press.

Brooks, Sarah M. 2002. Social Protection and Economic Integration: the Politics of Pension Reform in an Era of Capital Mobility. *Comparative Political Studies* 35, no. 5: 491–525.

Brooks, Sarah M. 2004. International Financial Institutions and the Diffusion of Foreign Models for Social Security Reform in Latin America. In Kurt Weyland, ed., *Learning from Foreign Models in Latin American Policy Reform.* Washington, D.C., and Baltimore, Md.: Woodrow Wilson Center and Johns Hopkins University Press.

Brooks, Sarah M. 2005. Interdependent and Domestic Foundations of Policy Change: The Diffusion of Pension Privatization Around the World. *International Studies Quarterly* 49: 273–94.

Cain, Michael J. G., and Aleksander Surdej. 1999. Transnational Politics of Public Choice? Explaining Stalled Pension Reforms in Poland. In Linda J. Cook, Mitchell A. Orenstein, and Marilyn Rueschemeyer, eds., *Left Parties and Social Policy in Postcommunist Europe.* Boulder, Colo.: Westview Press.

Cameron, David. 1978. The Expansion of the Public Economy: A Comparative Analysis. *American Political Science Review* 72:4, 1243–61.

Campbell, John L., and Ove K. Pedersen, eds. 2001. *The Rise of Neoliberalism and Institutional Analysis.* Princeton: Princeton University Press.

Cangiano, Marco, Carlo Cottarelli, and Luis Cubeddu. 1998. Pension Developments and Reforms in Transition Economies. IMF Working Paper, October.

Cashu, Ilian. 2000. The Politics and Policy Trade-offs of Reforming the Public Pension System in Post-communist Moldova. *Europe-Asia Studies* 52, no. 4: 741–757.

Cashu, Ilian. 2005. The World Bank and Pension Reform in Romania. Mimeo. Syracuse University.

Castel, Paulette, and Louise Fox. N.d. Gender Dimensions of Pension Reform in the Former Soviet Union. Washington, D.C.: World Bank.

Charlton, Roger, and Roddy McKinnon. 2002. International Organizations, Pension System Reform and Alternative Agendas: Bringing Older People Back In? *Journal of International Development* 14: 1175–1186.

Checkel, Jeffrey T. 2001. Why Comply? Social Learning and European Identity Change. *International Organization* 55, no. 3: 553–588.

Checkel, Jeffrey T. 2005. International Institutions and Socialization in Europe. *International Organization* 59, no. 4: 801–826.

China Economic Research and Advisory Programme. 2005. Social Security Reform in China: Issues and Options. Unpublished report. January 27.

Chłoń-Domińczak, Agnieszka. 2002. The Polish Pension Reform of 1999. In *Pension Reform in Central and Eastern Europe, vol. 1: Restructuring with Privatization: Case Studies of Hungary and Poland*, ed. E. Fultz, 98–205. Budapest: ILO.

Chłoń-Domińczak, Agnieszka, and Marek Mora. 2003. Commitment and Consensus in Pension Reform. In Holzmann et al. 2003b.

Chłoń, Agnieszka, Marek Gora, and Michał Rutkowski. 1999. Shaping Pension Reform in Poland: Security through Diversity. *World Bank Pension Reform Primer.* Washington, D.C.: World Bank.

Chong-Bum, An. 2005. Implications of Efforts to Reform the National Pension System. *Korea Focus on Current Issues* 13, no. 6.

Chwieroth, Jeffrey. 2003. Neoliberal Norms and Capital Account Liberalization in Emerging Markets: The Role of Domestic-Level Knowledge-Based Experts. Paper presented at the annual meeting of the American Political Science Association, Philadelphia.

Clark, Gordon L., and Noel Whiteside. 2003. Introduction. In Gordon L. Clark and Noel Whiteside, eds., *Pension Security in the 21st Century: Redrawing the Public-Private Debate*. Oxford: Oxford University Press.

Cocozzelli, Fred. 2007. Kosovo. In Bob Deacon and Paul Stubbs, eds., *Social Policy and International Interventions in South East Europe*. Cheltenham, U.K.: Edward Elgar.

Collier, David, and Richard E. Messick. 1975. Prerequisites versus Diffusion: Testing Alternative Explanations of Social Security Adoption. *American Political Science Review* 69, no. 4 (December): 1299–1315.

Cook, Linda J. 2006. State Capacity and Pension Provision. In Timothy J. Colton and Stephen Holmes, eds., *The State after Communism: Governance in the New Russia*. Lanham, Md.: Rowman & Littlefield, 121–154.

Cook, Linda J. 2007. *Postcommunist Welfare States: Reform Politics in Russia and Eastern Europe*. Ithaca, N.Y.: Cornell University Press.

Craig, Isabel, and Igor Tomeš. 1969. Origins and Activities of the ILO Committee of Social Security Experts. *International Social Security Review* 22.

Dawson, William Harbutt. 1912. *Social Insurance in Germany 1883–1911*. London: T. Fisher Unwin.

De Oliveira, Francisco, ed. 1994. *Social Security Systems in Latin America*. Washington, D.C.: Inter-American Development Bank.

Deacon, Bob. 1997. *Global Social Policy: International Organizations and the Future of Welfare*. London: Sage Publications.

Demarco, Gustavo. 2004. The Argentine Pension System Reform and International Lessons. In Kurt Weyland, ed., *Learning from Foreign Models in Latin American Policy Reform*. Washington, D.C., and Baltimore, Md.: Woodrow Wilson Center and Johns Hopkins University Press.

Dethier, Jean-Jacques. 2005. Sustainable Growth and Equity in Developing Countries: An Overview of Research at the World Bank. Paper presented at the conference Research Bank on the World Bank, Center for Policy Studies, Central European University, Budapest, Hungary, April 1–2.

Diamond, Peter A., and Peter R. Orszag. 2004. *Saving Social Security: A Balanced Approach*. Washington, D.C.: Brookings Institution Press.

DiMaggio, Paul J., and Walter W. Powell. 1983. The Iron Cage Revisited: Institutional Isomorphism and Collective Rationality in Organizational Fields. *American Sociological Review* 48, no. 2: 147–160.

Dolowitz, David, and D. Marsh. 1996. Who Learns What from Whom? *Political Studies* 44, no. 2.

Dolowitz, David P., and David Marsh. 2000. Learning from Abroad: The Role of Policy Transfer in Contemporary Policy-Making. *Governance: An International Journal of Policy and Administration* 13, no. 1: 5–24.

Druckman, James N. 2004. Political Preference Formation: Competition, Deliberation, and the (Ir)relevance of Framing Effects. *American Political Science Review* 98, no. 4: 671–686.

Edwards, S. 1998. The Chilean Pension Reform: A Pioneering Program. In M. Feldstein, ed., *Privatizing Social Security*. Chicago: University of Chicago Press.

Ellerman, David. 2001. Sounding the Alarm on Neo-Chilean 'Pension Reforms': The Case of Kazakhstan. Mimeo. Washington, D.C.: World Bank.

Emmerson, Carl. 2003. Pension Reform in the United Kingdom: Increasing the Rold of Private Provision. In Gordon L. Clark and Noel Whiteside, eds., *Pension Security in the 21st Century: Redrawing the Public-Private Debate*. Oxford: Oxford University Press.

Epstein, Rachel. 2008. Transnational Actors and Bank Privatization. In Mitchell A. Orenstein, Stephen Bloom, and Nicole Lindstrom, eds., *Transnational Actors in Central and East European Transitions*. Pittsburgh: University of Pittsburgh Press.

Esping-Andersen, Gøsta. 1990. *The Three Worlds of Welfare Capitalism*. Cambridge, U.K.: Polity Press.

European Union. 1997. Commission Green Paper on Supplementary Pensions in the Single Market. COM(97) 283. Brussels: European Union.

Feldstein, Martin. 2002. Introduction: An American Perspective. In Martin Feldstein and Horst Siebert, eds., *Social Security Pension Reform in Europe*. Chicago and London: University of Chicago Press.

Ferge, Zsuzsa. 1997. The Actors of the Hungarian Pension Reform. Paper presented at the Fifth Central European Forum organized by the Institute of Human Studies, Vienna, October 24–25.

Finnemore, Martha. 1993. International Organizations as Teachers of Norms. *International Organization* 47, no. 4: 565–597.

Finnemore, Martha. 1996. *National Interests in International Society*. Ithaca, N.Y.: Cornell University Press.

Fischer, Frank. 2003. *Reframing Public Policy: Discursive Politics and Deliberative Practices*. Oxford: Oxford University Press.

Fourcade-Gourinchas, Marion, and Sarah L. Babb. 2002. The Rebirth of the Liberal Creed: Paths to Neoliberalism in Four Countries. *American Journal of Sociology* 108, no. 3: 533–79.

Frazier, Mark W. 2004. After Pension Reform: Navigating the "Third Rail" in China. *Studies in Comparative International Development* 39, no. 2: 45–70.

Fultz, Elaine. 2004. Pension Reform in the EU Accession Countries: Challenges, Achievements, and Pitfalls. *International Social Security Review* 57, no. 2: 3–24.

Fultz, Elaine. 2005. Individual Pension Accounts Earn Low Returns. *The ILO SRO Budapest Newsletter*, no. 1: 6–7.

Garrett, Geoffrey. 1998. *Partisan Politics in the Global Economy.* Cambridge: Cambridge University Press.

Garrett, Geoffrey, and David Nickerson. 2005. Globalization, Democratization, and Government Spending in Middle-Income Countries. In Miguel Glatzer and Dietrich Rueschemeyer, eds., *Globalization and the Future of the Welfare State.* Pittsburgh: University of Pittsburgh Press.

Gill, Indermit S., Truman Packard, and Juan Yermo. 2005. *Keeping the Promise of Social Security in Latin America.* Washington, D.C., and Stanford, Calif.: World Bank and Stanford University Press.

Gillion, Colin, John Turner, Clive Bailey, Denis Latulippe, eds. 2000. *Social Security Pensions: Development and Reform.* Geneva: International Labour Office.

Gilpin, Robert. 2001. *Global Political Economy: Understanding the International Economic Order.* Princeton and Oxford: Princeton University Press.

Glatzer, Miguel, and Dietrich Rueschemeyer. 2005. An Introduction to the Problem. In Miguel Glatzer and Dietrich Rueschemeyer, eds., *Globalization and the Future of the Welfare State.* Pittsburgh: University of Pittsburgh Press, 1–22.

Graham, Carol. 1998. *Private Markets for Public Goods: Raising the Stakes in Economic Reform.* Washington, D.C.: Brookings Institution.

Gray, Virginia. 1973. Innovation in the States: A Diffusion Study. *American Political Science Review* 67, no. 4: 1174–1185.

Haas, Ernest. 1990. *When Knowledge Is Power: Three Models of Change in International Organizations.* Berkeley: University of California Press.

Haas, Martine R. 2006. Acquiring and Applying Knowledge in Transnational Teams: The Roles of Cosmopolitans and Locals. *Organization Science* 17, no. 3: 367–384.

Haas, Peter M. 1992. Introduction: Epistemic Communities and International Policy Coordination. *International Organization* 46, no. 1: 1–35.

Haas, Peter M., and Ernst B. Haas. 1995. Learning to Learn: Improving International Governance. *Global Governance* 1: 255–285.

Hacker, Jacob. 2002. *The Divided Welfare State.* Cambridge: Cambridge University Press.

Haggard, Stephan, and Robert Kaufman. 2006. *Recrafting Social Contracts: Welfare Reform in Latin America, East Asia and Central Europe.* Manuscript.

Hall, Peter, ed. 1989. *The Political Power of Economic Ideas: Keynesianism across Nations.* Princeton: Princeton University Press.

Hasselman, Chris. 2006. *Policy Reform and the Development of Democracy in Eastern Europe.* London: Ashgate Publishing.

Hausner, Jerzy. 2001. Security through Diversity: Conditions for Successful Reform of the Pension System in Poland. In János Kornai, Stephan Haggard, and Robert Kaufman, eds., *Reforming the State: Fiscal and Welfare Reform in Post-Socialist Countries.* Cambridge: Cambridge University Press, 210–234.

Hays, Scott P. 1996. Influences on Reinvention during the Diffusion of Innovations. *Political Research Quarterly* 49, no. 3: 631–650.

Heclo, Hugh. 1974. *Modern Social Politics in Britain and Sweden*. New Haven: Yale University Press.

Henisz, Witold J., Bennet A. Zelner, and Mauro F. Guilln. 2005. Deinstitutionalization and Institutional Replacement: State-Centered and Neoliberal Models in the Global Electricity Supply Industry. *American Sociological Review* 70, no. 6: 871–897.

Hering, Martin. 2003. The Politics of Institutional Path-Departure: A Revised Analytical Framework for the Reform of Welfare States. University of Mannheim Center for European Social Research Working Paper 65.

Herrera, Yoshiko M. 2006. The Transformation of State Statistics. In Timothy J. Colton and Stephen Holmes, eds., *The State after Communism: Governance in the New Russia*. Lanham, Md.: Rowman & Littlefield, 53–86.

Héthy, Lajos. 1995. Anatomy of a Tripartite Experiment: Attempted Social and Economic Agreement in Hungary. *International Labour Review* 134, no. 3: 361–376.

Hewitt Global Report: Monthly Legislative Update: Latin America and the Caribbean, 2007 (April). http://www.hewittassociates.com/_MetaBasicCMAssetCache_ /Assets/Legislative%20Updates/hewitt_legupdate_latinamerica_April2007.pdf. Accessed April 2007.

Hewson, Martin, and Timothy J. Sinclair. 1999. The Emergence of Global Governance Theory. In Martin Hewson and Timothy J. Sinclar, eds., *Approaches to Global Governance Theory*. Albany: State University of New York Press, 3–22.

Holzmann, Robert. 1999. The World Bank Approach to Pension Reform. World Bank Pension Reform Primer. Washington, D.C.: World Bank (for publication in International Social Security Review).

Holzmann, Robert, and Richard Hinz. 2005. *Old Age Income Support in the 21st Century: An International Perspective on Pension Systems and Reform*. Washington, D.C.: World Bank.

Holzmann, Robert, and Edward Palmer, eds. 2006. *Pension Reform: Issues and Prospects for Non-Financial Defined Contribution (NDC) Schemes*. Washington, D.C.: World Bank.

Holzmann, Robert, and Joseph Stiglitz, eds. 2001. *New Ideas about Old Age Security*. Washington, D.C.: World Bank.

Holzmann, Robert, Landis MacKellar, and Michał Rutkowski. 2003a. Accelerating the European Pension Reform Agenda: Need, Progress, and Conceptual Underpinnings. In Holzmann et al. 2003b.

Holzmann, Robert, Mitchell A. Orenstein, and Michał Rutkowski, eds. 2003b. *Pension Reform in Europe: Process and Progress*. Washington, D.C.: World Bank.

Hooghe, Liesbet, and Gary Marks. 2001. *Multi-Level Governance and European Integration*. Boulder, Colo.: Rowman and Littlefield.

Huber, Evelyne, and John D. Stephens. 2001. *Development and Crisis of the Welfare State: Parties and Policies in Global Markets*. Chicago: University of Chicago Press.

Hunter, Wendy, and David S. Brown. 2000. World Bank Directives, Domestic Interests, and the Politics of Human Capital Development in Latin America. *Comparative Political Studies* 33, no. 1: 113–143.

Huntington, Samuel. 1968. *Political Order in Changing Societies.* New Haven, Conn.: Yale University Press.

Huntington, Samuel. 1991. *The Third Wave: Democratization in the Late Twentieth Century.* Norman: Oklahoma University Press.

Iglesias, Augusto, and Robert J. Palacios. 2001. Managing Public Pension Reserves: Evidence from the International Experience. In Robert Holzmann and Joseph E. Stiglitz, eds., *New Ideas about Old Age Security: Toward Sustainable Pension Systems in the 21st Century.* Washington, D.C.: World Bank.

Immergut, Ellen M. 1990. Institutions, Veto Points, and Policy Results: A Comparative Analysis of Health Care. *Journal of Public Policy* 10, no. 4: 391–416.

Immergut, Ellen M. 1992. The Rules of the Game: The Logic of Health Policy-Making in France, Switzerland and Sweden. In S. Steinmo, K. Thenlen, and F. Longstreth, eds., *Structuring Politics: Historical Institutionalism in Comparative Perspective.* Cambridge: Cambridge University Press, 57–89.

Immergut, Ellen M., and Karen M. Anderson. 2007. Editors' Introduction: The Dynamics of Pension Politics. In Ellen M. Immergut, Karen M. Anderson, and Isabelle Schulze, eds., *The Handbook of West European Pension Politics.* Oxford: Oxford University Press, 1–45.

International Labour Office (ILO). 1944. The Twenty-sixth Session of the International Labour Conference, Philadelphia, April–May 1944. *International Labour Review* 50, no. 1 (July): 1–39.

International Labour Office (ILO). 1945. Franklin Delano Roosevelt. *International Labour Review* 51, no. 5 (May): 559–563.

International Labour Office (ILO). 1948a. Preparatory Asian Regional Conference of the International Labour Organisation, New Delhi, 27 October–8 November 1947. *International Labour Review* 57, no. 5 (May): 425–437.

International Labour Office (ILO). 1948b. Regional Meeting for the Near and Middle East of the International Labour Organisation, Istanbul, November 1947. *International Labour Review* 58, no. 1 (July): 1–17.

Jacoby, Wade. 2004. *The Enlargement of the European Union and NATO: Ordering from the Menu in Central Europe.* Cambridge: Cambridge University Press.

Jacoby, Wade. 2008. Minority Traditions and Post-Communist Politics: How Do IGOs Matter? In Mitchell A. Orenstein, Stephen Bloom, and Nicole Lindstrom, eds., *Transnational Actors in Central and East European Transitions.* Pittsburgh: University of Pittsburgh Press.

James, Estelle. 1996. Providing Better Protection and Promoting Growth: A Defence of *Averting the Old Age Crisis. International Social Security Review* 49, no. 3.

James, Estelle. 1998. The Political Economy of Social Security Reform: A Cross-Country Review. *Annals of Public and Comparative Economics* 69, no. 4 (December): 451–482.

James, Estelle, and Sarah M. Brooks. 2001. The Political Economy of Structural Pension Reform. In Robert Holzmann and Joseph E. Stiglitz, eds., *New Ideas about Old Age Security: Toward Sustainable Pension Systems in the 21st Century.* Washington, D.C.: World Bank.

Johnson, Juliet. 2008. Two-Track Diffusion and Central Bank Embeddedness: The Politics of Euro Adoption in Hungary and the Czech Republic. In Mitchell A. Orenstein, Stephen Bloom, and Nicole Lindstrom, eds., *Transnational Actors in Central and East European Transitions.* Pittsburgh: University of Pittsburgh Press.

Kapur, Devesh, John P. Lewis, and Richard Webb. 1997. *The World Bank: Its First Half Century.* Washington, D.C.: Brookings Institution Press.

Katzenstein, Peter. 1985. *Small States in World Markets.* Ithaca, N.Y.: Cornell University Press.

Kaul, Inge, Isabelle Grunberg, and Marc A. Stern, eds. 1999. *Global Public Goods: International Cooperation in the 21st Century.* Oxford: Oxford University Press.

Kay, Stephen. 1998. Politics and Social Security Reform in the Southern Cone and Brazil. Ph.D. dissertaion, University of California at Los Angeles.

Keck, Margaret, and Kathryn Sikkink. 1998. *Activists beyond Borders: Advocacy Networks in International Politics.* Ithaca, N.Y.: Cornell University Press.

Kelley, Judith G. 2004. *Ethnic Politics in Europe: The Power of Norms and Incentives.* Princeton, N.J.: Princeton University Press.

Kingdon, John. 1997. Agendas, Alternatives, and Public Policies, 2nd ed. London: Pearson Education.

Kogut, Bruce, and J. Muir MacPherson. 2004. The Decision to Privatize as an Economic Policy Idea: Epistemic Communities and Diffusion. Unpublished mansucript.

Kogut, Bruce, and Andrew Spicer. 2003. Critical and Alternative Perspectives on International Assistance to Postcommunist Countries: A Review and Analysis. Washington, D.C.: World Bank.

Kornai, János, Stephan Haggard, and Robert Kaufman, eds. 2001. *Reforming the State: Fiscal and Welfare Reform in Post-Socialist Countries.* Cambridge: Cambridge University Press.

Kulu, Liina, and Janno Reiljan. 2004. *Old-Age Pension Reform in Estonia on the Basis of the World Bank's Multi-Pillar Approach.* Tartu: University of Tartu Faculty of Economics and Business Administration.

Kurtz, Marcus. 1999. Chile's Neo-Liberal Revolution: Incremental Decisions and Structural Transformation, 1973–1989. *Journal of Latin American Studies* 31, no. 2: 399–427.

Lindemann, D. C. 2004. Review of Recent Pension Reforms in the Baltic Region. In *Pension Reform in the Baltic Countries.* OECD Private Pensions Series 5. Paris: OECD, 7–24.

Lindstrom, Nicole. 2008. In Mitchell A. Orenstein, Stephen Bloom, and Nicole Lindstrom, eds., *Transnational Actors in Central and East European Transitions.* Pittsburgh: University of Pittsburgh Press.

Lukes, Steven. 2005. *Power: A Radical View,* 2nd ed. Basingstoke: Palgrave MacMillan.

Madrid, Raul L. 2003. *Retiring the State: The Politics of Pension Privatization in Latin America and Beyond.* Stanford, Calif.: Stanford University Press.

Mahoney, James, and Dietrich Rueschemeyer, eds. 2003. *Comparative Historical Analysis in the Social Sciences*. Cambridge: Cambridge University Press.

March, James, and Herbert Simon. 1993. From Organizations: Cognitive Limits on Rationality. Reprinted in Frank Dobbin, ed. *The New Economic Sociology: A Reader*. Princeton: Princeton University Press, 2004.

McCarty, Nolan. 2000. Proposal Rights, Veto Rights, and Political Bargaining. *American Journal of Political Science* 44, no. 3: 506–522.

Melo, Marcus André. 2004. Institutional Choice and the Diffusion of Policy Paradigms: Brazil and the Second Wave of Pension Reform. *International Political Science Review* 25, no. 3: 320–341.

Mesa-Lago, Carmelo. 1994. *Changing Social Security in Latin America*. Boulder, Colo.: Lynne Rienner.

Mesa-Lago, Carmelo. 1998. The Reform of Social Security Pensions in Latin America: Public, Private, Mixed and Parallel Systems. In Ruland F. Geburstag, ed., *Verfassung, Theorie und Praxis des Sozialstaats. Festschrift fur Hans F. Zacher zum 70*. Muller: Heidelberg, 609–633.

Mesa-Lago, Carmelo. 2002. Reassessing Pension Reform in Chile and Other Countries in Latin America. Washington, D.C.: Inter-American Development Bank. http://www.adb.org/Documents/Events/2002/SocialProtection/lago _paper.pdf. Accessed October 16, 2006.

Meyer, John W., John Boli, Goerge M. Thomas, and Francisco O. Ramirez. 1997. World Society and the Nation-State. *American Journal of Sociology* 103, no. 1: 144–181.

Ministry of Welfare and Ministry of Finance of the Republic of Hungary. 1996. Information prepared for the government session held on July 18, 1996, about the position of the elaboration of the mixed-financed pension system (version prepared according to the standpoint of thte Economic Cabinet of July 15, 1996), signed by György Szabó and Tibor Draskovics (July 16).

Minns, Richard. 2001. *The Cold War in Welfare: Stock Markets versus Pensions*. London: Verso.

Mintrom, Michael. 1997. Policy Entrepreneurs and the Diffusion of Innovation. *American Journal of Political Science* 41, no. 3 (July): 738–770.

Müller, Katharina. 1999. *The Political Economy of Pension Reform in Central-Eastern Europe*. Aldershot, U.K.: Edward Elgar.

Müller, Katharina. 2000. Pension Privatization in Latin America. *Journal of International Development* 12: 507–518.

Müller, Katharina. 2003. *Privatising Old-Age Security: Latin America and Eastern Europe Compared*. Aldershot, U.K.: Edward Elgar.

Myles, John, and Paul Pierson. 2001. The Comparative Political Economy of Pension Reform. In Paul Pierson, ed., *The New Politics of the Welfare State*. Oxford: Oxford University Press, 305–333.

Nelson, Joan M. 1990. Conclusions. In Joan M. Nelson, ed., *Economic Crisis and Policy Choice: The Politics of Adjustment in the Third World*. Princeton: Princeton University Press.

Nelson, Joan M. 1997. Social Costs, Social-Sector Reforms, and Politics in Post-Communist Transformations. In Joan M. Nelson, Charles Tilly, and Lee Walker, eds., *Transforming Post-Communist Political Economies*. Washington, D.C.: National Academy Press.

Nelson, Joan M. 2001. The Politics of Pension and Health Care Reforms in Hungary and Poland. In János Kornai, Stephan Haggard, and Robert Kaufman, eds., *Reforming the State: Fiscal and Welfare Reform in Post-Socialist Countries*. Cambridge: Cambridge University Press, 235–266.

Nelson, Joan M. 2004. External Models, International Influence, and the Politics of Social Sector Reforms. In Kurt Weyland, ed., *Learning from Foreign Models in Latin American Policy Reform*. Washington, D.C., and Baltimore, Md.: Woodrow Wilson Center and Johns Hopkins University Press.

Ney, Steven. 2003. The Rediscovery of Politics: Democracy and Structural Pension Reform in Continental Europe. In Holzmann et al. 2003b.

Novak, Mojca, and Katja Rihar Bajuk. 2007. Slovenia. In Bob Deacon and Paul Stubbs, eds., *Social Policy and International Interventions in South East Europe*. Cheltenham, U.K.: Edward Elgar.

O'Brien, Robert. 2002. Organizational Politics, Multilateral Economic Organizations and Social Policy. *Global Social Policy* 2, no. 2: 141–162.

Oravec, Ján. 2006. *The Story of the Creation of Personal Retirement Accounts in Slovakia*. Bratislava: Nadácia F. A. Hayeka.

Orenstein, Mitchell A. 2000. How Politics and Institutions Affect Pension Reform in Three Postcommunist Countries. World Bank Policy Research Working Paper 2310. Washington, D.C.: World Bank.

Orenstein, Mitchell A. 2001. *Out of the Red: Building Capitalism and Democracy in Postcommunist Europe*. Ann Arbor: University of Michigan Press.

Orenstein, Mitchell A., and Hans Peter Schmitz. 2006. The New Transnationalism and Comparative Politics. *Comparative Politics* 38, no. 4: 479–500.

Orifowomo, Odunola Akinwale. 2006. A Critical Appraisal of Pension System Reforms in Nigeria. *Gonzaga Journal of International Law* 10: 164–201.

Orszag, Peter R., and Joseph E. Stiglitz. 2001. Rethinking Pension Reform: Ten Myths about Social Security Systems. In Robert Holzmann and Joseph E. Stiglitz, eds., *New Ideas about Old Age Security: Toward Sustainable Pension Systems in the 21st Century*. Washington, D.C.: World Bank.

Palacios, Robert. 2003. Pension Reform in the Dominican Republic. Social Protection Discussion Paper 0326 (December). Washington, D.C.: World Bank.

Palacios, Robert, and Montserrat Pallarès-Miralles. 2000. International Patterns of Pension Provision. Social Protection Discussion Paper 0009. Washington, D.C.: World Bank.

Palacios, Robert, and Roberto Rocha. 1998. The Hungarian Pension System in Transition. Social Protection Discussion Paper 9805. Washington, D.C.: World Bank (March).

Palme, Joakim. 2003. Pension Reform in Sweden and the Changing Boundaries Between Public and Private. In Gordon L. Clark and Noel Whiteside, eds., *Pension Security in the 21st Century: Redrawing the Public-Private Debate*. Oxford: Oxford University Press.

Pierson, Paul. 1994. *Dismantling the Welfare State? Reagan, Thatcher, and the Politics of Retrenchment*. Cambridge: Cambridge University Press.

Pierson, Paul, ed. 2000. *The New Politics of the Welfare State*. Oxford: Oxford University Press.

Pierson, Paul. 2004. Ahead of Its Time: On Martha Derthick's Policymaking for Social Security. *PS: Political Science and Politics* 37, no. 3: 441–442.

Piggott, John, and Lu Bei. 2007. Pension Reform and the Development of Pension Systems: An Evaluation of World Bank Assistance. Washington, D.C., Independent Evaluation Group, World Bank.

Piñera, José. 1991. *El cascabel al gato: La batalla por la reforma previsional*. Santiago de Chile: Editoral Zig-Zag.

Pinheiro, Vinícius C. 2004. The Politics of Social Security Reform in Brazil. In Kurt Weyland, ed., *Learning from Foreign Models in Latin American Policy Reform*. Washington, D.C., and Baltimore, Md.: Woodrow Wilson Center and Johns Hopkins University Press.

Przeworski, Adam, Michael Alvarez, José Antonio Cheibub, and Fernando Limongi. 2000. *Democracy and Development: Political Institutions and Well-Being in the World, 1950–1990*. Cambridge: Cambridge University Press.

Queisser, Monika. 2000. Pension Reform and International Organizations: From Conflict to Convergence. *International Social Security Review* 53, no. 2.

Ramesh, Mitra. 2007. The World Bank and Pension Reforms. In Diane Stone and Christopher Wright, eds., *The World Bank and Governance: A Decade of Reform and Reaction*. Routledge/Warwick Studies in Globalisation. Abingdon, U.K. and New York: Routledge.

Reinecke, Wolfgang H. 1998. *Global Public Policy: Governing without Government?* Washington, D.C.: Brookings Institution Press.

Republic of Estonia. 2000. Memorandum of Economic Policies. Washington, D.C.: International Monetary Fund (February 14).

Reynaud, Emmanuel, ed. 2000. *Social Dialogue and Pension Reform*. Geneva: International Labour Office.

Risse-Kappen, Thomas. 1994. Ideas Do Not Float Freely: Transnational Coalitions, Domestic Structures, and the End of the Cold War. *International Organization* 48, no. 2 (Spring): 185–214.

Risse, Thomas, Stephen C. Ropp, and Kathryn Sikkink, eds. 1999. *The Power of Human Rights: International Norms and Domestic Change*. Cambridge: Cambridge University Press.

Rodgers, Daniel. 1998. *Atlantic Crossings: Social Politics in a Progressive Age*. Cambridge, Mass.: Harvard University Press.

Rodrik, Dani. 1998. Why Do More Open Economies Have Bigger Government? *Journal of Political Economy* 106: 997–1032.

Rogers, Everett M. 1995. *Diffusion of Innovations*, 4th ed. New York: Free Press.

Rosenau, James N. 2003. *Distant Proximities: Dynamics beyond Globalization*. Princeton: Princeton University Press.

Rutkowski, Michał. 1998. A New Generation of Pension Reforms Conquers the East—a Taxonomy in Transition Economies. *Transition* 9, no. 4 (August).

Sabatier, Paul A., and Hank C. Jenkins-Smith. 1999. The Advocacy Coalition Framework: An Assessment. In Paul A. Sabatier, ed., *Theories of the Policy Process*. Boulder, Colo.: Westview Press.

Schoenbaum, Emil. 1945. A Programme of Social Insurance Reform for Czechoslovakia. *International Labour Review* 51, no. 2 (February): 141–166.

Schulze, Isabelle, and Michael Moran. 2007. United Kingdom: Pension Politics in an Adversarial System. In Ellen M. Immergut, Karen M. Anderson, and Isabelle Schulze, eds., *The Handbook of West European Pension Politics*. Oxford: Oxford University Press, 49–96.

Scott, James C. 1985. *Weapons of the Weak: Everyday Forms of Peasant Resistance*. New Haven: Yale University Press.

Shah, Hemant. 1997. Towards Better Regulation of Private Pension Funds. Washington, D.C.: World Bank.

Simmons, Beth, and Zachary Elkins. 2004. The Globalization of Liberalization: Policy Diffusion in the International Political Economy. *American Political Science Review* 98, no. 1: 171–190.

Simonovits, András. 2000. Partial Privatization of a Pension System: Lessons from Hungary. *Journal of International Development* 12: 519–529.

Slaughter, Anne-Marie. 2004. *A New World Order*. Princeton: Princeton University Press.

Snelbecker, David. 2005. Pension Reform in Eastern Europe and Eurasia: Experiences and Lessons Learned. Prepared for USAID Workshop for Practitioners on Tax and Pension Reform, Washington, D.C. (June 27–29).

Soule, Sarah A., and Brayden G. King. 2006. The Stages of the Policy Process and the Equal Rights Amendment, 1972–1982. *American Journal of Sociology* 111: 1871–1909.

Stanovnik, Tine. 2002. The Political Economy of Pension Reform in Slovenia. In Elaine Fultz, ed., *Pension Reform in Central and Eastern Europe*, vol. 2. Budapest: International Labour Office, Central and Eastern European Team, 19–73.

Stone, Diane. 2003. Transnational Transfer Agents and Global Networks in the "Internationalisation" of Policy. Paper presented at the Workshop on Internationalisation and Policy Transfer, Murphy Institute, Tulane University, New Orleans, April 11–12.

Stone, Diane, and Christopher Wright. 2007. The Currency of Change: World Bank Lending and Learning in the Wolfensohn Era. In Diane Stone and Christopher Wright, eds., *The World Bank and Governance: A Decade of Reform and Reaction*. Routledge/Warwick Studies in Globalisation. Abingdon, U.K., and New York: Routledge.

Stone, Randall. 2002. *Lending Credibility: The International Monetary Fund and the Post-Communist Transition*. Princeton: Princeton University Press.

Strang, David, and Patricia Mei Yin Chang. 1993. The International Labor Organization and the Welfare State: Institutional Effects on National Welfare Spending, 1960–80. *International Organization* 47, no. 2 (Spring): 235–262.

Strang, David, and John W. Meyer. 1993. Institutional Conditions for Diffusion. *Theory and Society* 22, no. 4 (August): 487–511.

Strang, David, and Sarah A. Soule. 1998. Diffusion in Organizations and Social Movements: From Hybrid Corn to Poison Pills. *Annual Review of Sociology* 24: 265–290.

Swank, Duane. 2002. *Global Capital, Political Institutions, and Policy Change in Developed Welfare States*. New York: Cambridge University Press.

Tarrow, Sidney. 2005. *The New Transnational Activism*. Cambridge: Cambridge University Press.

Tavits, Margit. 2003. Policy Learning and Uncertainty: The Case of Pension Reform in Estonia and Latvia. *Policy Studies Journal* 31, no. 4: 643–660.

Thomas, M. A. 2004. Can the World Bank Enforce Its Own Conditions? *Development and Change* 35, no. 3: 485–497.

Tolbert, Pamela S., and Lynne G. Zucker. 1983. Institutional Sources of Change in the Federal Structure of Organizations: The Diffusion of Civil Service Reform, 1880–1935. *Administrative Science Quarterly* 28: 22–39.

Toots, Anu. 2002. International and National Actors in Estonian Pension Reform. Paper presented at the NISPA CEE Annual Conference, Krakow, Poland.

Topiński, Wojciech, and Marian Wiśniewski. 1991. Pensions in Poland: Proposals for Reform. Mimeo. Warsaw (May).

True, Jacqui, and Michael Mintrom. 2001. Transnational Networks and Policy Diffusion: The Case of Gender Mainstreaming. *International Studies Quarterly* 45: 27–57.

Tsebelis, George. 2002. *Veto Players: How Political Institutions Work*. New York and Princeton: Russell Sage Foundation and Princeton University Press.

Tuozzo, María Fernanda. 2004. World Bank, Governance Reforms and Democracy in Argentina. *Bulletin of Latin American Research* 23, no. 1: 100–118.

United Nations. 2002. *World Population Ageing: 1950–2050*. New York: United Nations.

USAID. 1997. Elaboration on the Kazkhstan Pension Reform Project Report: Recommendations for Future Pension Provision: A Macro Economic Paper. Mimeo.

USAID. 1998. Discussion of the Reinstatement of Special Retirement Conditions for Certain Classes of Workers. (April 23).

Vachudova, Milada A. 2005. *Europe Undivided*. Oxford: Oxford University Press.

Valdes, Juan Gabriel. 1995. *Pinochet's Economists: The Chicago School in Chile*. Cambridge: Cambridge University Press.

Wade, Robert Hunter. 2002. US Hegemony and the World Bank: The Fight Over People and Ideas. *Review of International Political Economy* 9, no. 2 (Summer): 215–243.

Wadensjö, Eskil. 2000. Sweden: Reform of the Public Pension System. In Emmanuel Reynaud, ed., *Social Dialogue and Pension Reform*. Geneva: International Labour Office, 67–80.

Walker, Jack L. 1969. The Diffusion of Innovations among the American States. *American Political Science Review* 63, no. 3 (September): 880–899.

Weaver, R. Kent. 2003. The Politics of Public Pension Reform. Center for Retirement Research Working Paper 2003–06. Chestnut Hill, Mass.: Center for Retirement Research at Boston College.

Weyland, Kurt. 2003. Theories of Policy Diffusion: An Assessment. Paper presented at the annual meeting of the American Political Science Association, Philadelphia, August 28–31.

Weyland, Kurt. 2004. Learning from Foreign Models in Latin American Policy Reform: An Introduction. In Kurt Weyland, ed., *Learning from Foreign Models in Latin American Policy Reform*. Washington, D.C., and Baltimore, Md.: Woodrow Wilson Center and Johns Hopkins University Press.

Weyland, Kurt. 2005. Theories of Policy Diffusion: Lessons from Latin American Pension Reform. *World Politics* 57: 262–295.

Weyland, Kurt. 2007. *Bounded Rationality and Policy Diffusion: Social Sector Reform in Latin America*. Princeton, N.J.: Princeton University Press.

Williamson, John B., and Matthew Williams. 2005. Notional Defined Contribution Accounts: Neoliberal Ideology and the Political Economy of Pension Reform. *American Journal of Economics and Sociology* 64, no. 2 (April): 485.

Woods, Ngaire. 2006. *The Globalizers: The IMF, the World Bank and Their Borrowers*. Ithaca, N.Y.: Cornell University Press.

World Bank. 1994. *Averting the Old Age Crisis: Policies to Protect the Old and Promote Growth*. Oxford: Oxford University Press.

World Bank. 1996. *From Plan to Market: World Development Report 1996*. New York: Oxford University Press.

World Bank. 2003. *World Bank Data and Statistics 2003*. Washington, D.C.: World Bank.

World Bank. 2005. *Economies in Transition: An OED Evaluation of World Bank Assistance*. Washington, D.C.: World Bank.

World Bank. 2006. *Pension Reform and the Development of Pension Systems: An Evaluation of World Bank Assistance*. Independent Evaluation Group Report. Washington, D.C.: World Bank.

Yang, Jae-jin. 2004. Democratic Governance and Bureaucratic Politics: A Case of Pension Reform in Korea. *Policy & Politics* 32, no. 2: 193–206.

Young, Oran R. 1999. *Governance in World Affairs*. Ithaca, N.Y.: Cornell University Press.

NEWSPAPERS AND JOURNALS CITED

Budapest Business Week (Hungary)
Express K (Kazakhstan)
Financial Times (United Kingdom)
Gospodarka I Przyszlosc (Poland)
Kazakhstanskaya Pravda (Kazakhstan)
Kovcheg (Kazakhstan)
Kustanaiskiye Novosti (Kazakhstan)
Magyar Hírlap (Hungary)
Napi Gazdaság (Hungary)
Népszabadság (Hungary)
Panorama (Kazakhstan)
Selskaya Novi (Kazakhstan)
Vilaggazdasag (Hungary)

INTERVIEWS

Emily Andrews, Social Protection Division, World Bank, Washington, D.C., multiple interviews.
Mária Augustinovics, Economics Institute, Hungarian Academy of Sciences, August 1998 and April 2, 2001.
William Baldridge, Mission to Kazakhstan, USAID, multiple interviews.
Nick Barr, London School of Economics and former World Bank official, February 5, 2007.
Charles Becker, Professor of Economics, Duke University, May 2005.
Andrea Bohm, Republic of Slovenia, May 14, 1998.
Carlos Boloña, Catholic University, Peru, 2000.
Lajos Bokros, Minister of Finance, Republic of Hungary, April 20, 1998.
Gábor Borbáth, SZEF trade union, Republic of Hungary, August 28, 1998.
Agnieszka Chłoń, Economist, Office of the Plenipotentiary for Penison Reform, Republic of Poland, multiple interviews.
Jean de Fougerolles, Institute for East West Studies, 1998.
Gustavo Demarco, reformer, Republic of Argentina, World Bank Institute, Washington, D.C., multiple interviews, 2005–2006.
Antal Deutsch, adviser to Ministry of Finance, Republic of Hungary, July 1998.
David Ellerman, former World Bank official, office of Chief Economist, 1999.
Elaine Fultz, ILO Central and Eastern Europe Team, Budapest, May 2005.
Gábor Futó, member of the Pension Insurance Fund presidium and Liga trade union, Republic of Hungary, August 25, 1998.
Robert Gál, Institute of Economics, Republic of Hungary, May 4, 1998.
Adam Gere, Head of Pension Reform Working Group, Ministry of Finance, Republic of Hungary, May 5, 1998.
Hermann von Gersdorff, Social Protection Division, World Bank, Washington, D.C., 2005.
Krzysztof Hagemejer, ILO Central and Eastern Europe Team, Budapest, July 1998.
Jerzy Hausner, Plenipotentiary for Pension Reform, Republic of Poland, multiple interviews.
Richard Hinz, World Bank Social Protection Division, Washington, D.C., 2005.
Robert Holzmann, Director, Social Protection Division, World Bank, Washington, D.C., multiple interviews.
Tom Hoopengardner, Social Protection Division, World Bank, Washington, D.C.
Estelle James, lead author, *Averting the Old Age Crisis*, former World Bank staffer and independent consultant, multiple interviews.
Tomáš Jelínek, pension adviser to Czech government, 1998.
Janko Kasar, Slovenia, May 13, 1998.
László Keller, Hungary, August 25, 1998.
James Kernan, Price Waterhouse, Warsaw, Poland, July 1998.
Dušan Kidrič, Deputy Chair, Socio-Economic Council, Slovenia, May 11, 1998.

Slavko Kinetic, Social Democratic Party, Slovenia, May 14, 1998.

Mihály Kökény, Minister of Welfare, Republic of Hungary, May 1998.

Skirma Kondratas, Adviser to the President, Republic of Lithuania, Member of Interministerial Working Group on Pension Reform, May 2005.

Denise Lamaute, Pension Specialist, USAID, multiple interviews, 1998–2005.

Ryszard Łepik, OPZZ trade union federation, Warsaw, Poland, July 1998.

Grigori Marchenko, Head, Pension Reform Working Group, Republic of Kazakhstan, July 1, 1998.

Marek Mazur, Adviser, Ministry of Finance, Republic of Poland, July 1998.

Péter Mihalyi, Undersecretary of Finance, Republic of Hungary, Budapest, April 3, 2001.

Krystyna Milewska, World Bank, Warsaw, Poland, July 1998.

Myrtill Nádai, HypoBank, Budapest, May 1998.

Sándor Nagy, Member of Parliament, Socialist Party, Republic of Hungary, May 6, 1998.

Joan M. Nelson, Overseas Development Council, 1998 and 2000.

Robert Palacios, Social Protection Division, World Bank, Washington, D.C., 1998.

Tibor Parniczky, Ministry of Finance working group on pension reforms, Republic of Hungary, May 7, 1998.

Miloš Pavlica, Vice-President, Social Democratic Party, Slovenia, May 12, 1998.

Vicki Peterson, USAID, Warsaw, Poland, July 1998.

José Piñera, Secretary of Labor and Social Security, Republic of Chile, January 2006, interview via email.

Gregor Repovž, Republic of Slovenia, May 13, 1998.

Szikszai Rezmovits, FIDESZ, Budapest, April 3, 2001.

Roberto Rocha, Social Protection Division, World Bank, Washington, D.C., May 6, 1998.

Melinda Roth, World Bank, Warsaw, Poland, 1998.

Michał Rutkowski, Social Protection Division, World Bank, Washington, D.C., and Head of Office, Office of the Plenipotentiary for Pension Reform, Republic of Poland, July 1998.

Andrzej Sadkowski, UNFE, Poland, July 1998.

Anita Schwarz, Social Protection Division, World Bank, Washington, D.C.

Alenka Selak, Ministry of Finance, Slovenia, May 12, 1998.

Dušan Semolic, union leader, Sdruzena Lista, Slovenia, May 13, 1998.

Marko Simoneti, Republic of Slovenia, May 14, 1998.

A. Simonovits, Institute of Economics, Hungarian Academy of Sciences, April 2, 2001.

Irina Sivriukova, Deputy Minister of Labor and Social Affairs, Republic of Kazakhstan, July 6, 1998.

David Snelbecker, Vice-President, Economic Policy, The Services Group, Arlington, Virginia, 2005.

Gene Spiro, Institute for East West Studies, Budapest, May 5, 1998.

Marko Straus, Ministry of Labor, Slovenia, May 12, 1998.

Sándor Szipos, Sector Manager, Social Protection Division, World Bank, Washington, D.C., 2005.

Rafał Szymczak, Profila public relations firm, USAID contractor, Warsaw, Poland, July 1998.

István Toth, TARKI public opinion research firm, Budapest, May 4, 1998, and April 4, 2001.

Klára Ungár, Member of Parliament, Alliance of Free Democrats, Republic of Hungary, May 6, 1998.

László Urbán, May 6, 1998.

János Vágó, President of the Pension Insurance Fund and Vice-President of the MSZOSZ trade union, Republic of Hungary, August 23, 1998.

Zoltan Vajda, Inter-Ministerial Working Group on Pension Reforms, Republic of Hungary, April 4, 2001.

Ian Vazquez, Director, Project on Global Economic Liberty, Cato Institute, Washington, D.C., 2005.

Index